The German Wedding

Pieter Waterdrinker was born in Haarlem, Holland. He studied Russian, French and Law at the University of Amsterdam. A novelist, journalist and broadcaster, he is the Moscow correspondent for the Dutch newspaper *De Telegraaf*. He lives in Moscow.

The German Wedding

Pieter Waterdrinker

Translated from the Dutch by Brian Doyle

Atlantic Books
LONDON

First published by Uitgeverij De Arbeiderspers, Amsterdam, Netherlands, in 2005.

First published in trade paperback in Great Britain in 2009 by Atlantic Books,
an imprint of Grove Atlantic Ltd.

1 3 5 7 9 10 8 6 4 2

A CIP catalogue record for this book is available from the British Library.

ISBN: 978 1 84354 638 2

Printed in Great Britain by J F Print Ltd., Sparkford, Somerset

Atlantic Books
An imprint of Grove Atlantic Ltd
Ormond House
26–27 Boswell Street
London WC1N 3JZ

www.atlantic-books.co.uk

Contents

Part One

Young and in Love

1.

On 11 May 1958, three days before the wedding, a wine-red Mercedes with German numberplates meandered its way along the road that unfurled like a sinuous grey ribbon towards the sea.

Sausage-maker Hans Matti Bender was at the wheel, his sandy-haired wife – who was not allowed to eat meat on account of a congenital stomach disorder – at his side. Their twenty-three-year-old daughter Liza had snuggled down into a mountain of cushions on the back seat. Bursting with curiosity, she gazed through the window and chewed on a chocolate filled with cloyingly sweet liqueur. Birds bolted skywards from the amber-yellow weed-choked verge: nightingales, crows, sparrows – she had no idea.

Liza had nausea for the entire journey and felt a hellish pain in her side. But once they had left the shadow of Amsterdam behind them, her physical malaise suddenly disappeared, though the blood-soaked tampon was still stuffed between her legs. She had completely forgotten to take the dreaded curse into account when they had set a date for the wedding. Now it was too late.

Hans Matti Bender turned his Mercedes – its steering-wheel sheathed in brushed salmon-pink calf leather – on to the broad coastal road. 'Look,' he cried enthusiastically. 'The sea!'

Kati peered over her butterfly-shaped sunglasses briefly, her pearl necklace with its white-gold clasp jangling about her freckled neck with every bump. She was indifferent to water, whatever form it took: a lake, a river or the vast ocean depths. She had been born and raised in an enchanting village in the Swabian Alps, and just as her husband frequently murmured under his breath about a pied-à-terre in Cannes or Ventimiglia on the Mediterranean, she had been dreaming for years of a sturdy house with a thatched roof in the mountains, the cheerful tinkle of cowbells, and a hazy dew shrouding the world each morning in a mystical veil.

The very idea that her daughter was about to put her future happiness to the test with a Dutchman was little short of a catastrophe. Kati Bender had struggled to the last to preserve her only child for the fatherland. Their domestic squabbles were now behind them, their throats no longer hoarse from screaming, the wallpaper in the back room, on which bespattered tea had left a ghostly stain for all of three weeks, had been replaced. The ball had spun and landed on an unspeakable number.

On a February morning, in a tiled hall where women were washing out pigs' intestines like fishnet stockings over steel basins, Liza had bluntly informed her mother that she was pregnant. And that was when it had all begun.

'So, no comments on the sea?'

'*Wunderbar, Vati!*' exclaimed Kati Bender, who had started to call her husband 'Vati' at some time or other. She glanced over her shoulder for a second but almost immediately reversed her hamster cheeks to face the front.

Two-faced bitch, thought Liza, staring outside with steely eyebrows. Her mother hadn't a clue about the tampon. Otherwise she would have grabbed the steering-wheel from her husband and screamed – as she had six months earlier – 'Turn around, goddammit! *Zurück!*'

2

The Bagman family had enjoyed much the same prosperity as the Benders had in the years after the war. In spite of budgetary restrictions, which meant that fewer than usual Dutch beefsteaks and Wiener schnitzels were being served on the white damask-covered tables in the restaurant, the business had expanded at lightning speed.

Their hotel was a legacy from the belle époque, which had managed by chance to survive the fury of the occupier. It served as one of the few premises where celebrations or parties of any substance could still be held. In winter, the main salon was a sizzling hive of club activity; the crème de la crème of metropolitan entertainers had performed there, and it was simply the best wedding location for miles around.

The board of the local trade association dined at the Bagmans' once a month. Jacob would often hire a pianist for the entire evening and purchase a couple of crates of extra special wine from Okhuysen's in Haarlem. As the women always remained at home, the evenings were occasionally rowdy.

One day, a baby-faced individual – a Limburger who had settled in the town a couple of years earlier and was now known to everyone as Mr Monjoux, manager of the clothing boutique The Colours of Mozart on the restored boulevard – had shouted: 'People, we're going to Paris!' He had climbed on a chair with a beer in his hand, his pale calves exposed above a pair of painfully boring socks, the pointed tail of his white shirt hanging out of his trousers.

But everything that happened within trade association circles remained secret. The trip to Paris took place six months later. A charcoal portrait of her husband sketched by Montmartre artist Maurice P., in which Jacob looked ten years younger, graced the wall above Maria Bagman's side of the bed, a souvenir of the occasion.

At the end of February, when Jacob Bagman was in Amsterdam on business, he had his palm read by a gypsy woman in a draughty tent at a travelling fair. The fortune-teller predicted an improvement in his digestive system and an excellent season's business, but neglected to mention that his oldest son Ludo would nonchalantly inform him three days later that he had decided to marry a German blonde named Liza Bender, the daughter of a sausage-maker from Cologne.

The hotel-keeper looked at his son with a mixture of astonishment and growing delight, then threw his arms around him and exclaimed, 'Maybe you don't deserve it, but I intend to give you the most beautiful wedding this town has ever seen!'

He drifted over to his wife who was sorting through a large pile of sheets and pillowcases in the linen cupboard, feeling as he had not felt since the birth of his first child, overcome with emotion and near-hysterical. Maria Bagman had uttered something incomprehensible and then started to sob gently. Jacob pressed her to his fifty-one-year-old chest.

In the meantime, the bridegroom-to-be was on the floor above, knotting his tie in front of the bathroom mirror with a lightning-shaped crack in it the colour of congealed blood. He splashed after-shave on his cheeks, headed outside, and jumped on a blue tram to Haarlem. A tenner rustled in his raincoat pocket, swiped in haste from petty cash. Look at how those rich bastards live, he thought as the tram trundled through Bentveld and Aerdenhout.

An hour later, he got off the tram at Spuistraat in Amsterdam, immediately opposite a café frequented by the office girls and the pigs from the sugar refinery and the stuck-up tarts from KLM, their filter cigarettes balanced between fingers manicured in Milan or New York, all propping up the bar like mannequins in a shop window. Few of them could resist Ludo's moist puppy eyes, his ample film-star face.

The hotel-keeper's son was aware of the effect he had on women and used it to his advantage, like someone desperately in need of a pee makes use of the first available toilet.

3

One week earlier, Jacob Bagman had gathered his family together for a simple meal at the round table beside the open hearth in the hotel restaurant. Off-season, Tuesday was the only day that Hotel New Deluxe was closed. He had asked a junior chef if he wanted to work overtime, and trusty Mr Zwaan – the hotel manager for donkey's years – had agreed to wait on them.

Maria had insisted on setting the table herself. The silver cande-labra and silver cutlery made it look like Christmas. A few days more, a couple of hundred hours more, and she was going to lose her Ludo. The imminent wedding of her oldest child felt like a loss, in spite of his plan to stay in the business and set up home with Liza in the old fisherman's cottage behind the hotel.

Jacob started the meal with a toast to life and what the future held. His wife echoed his sentiments to the sound of their sons' goblets clinking against theirs, but they all hesitated before drinking.

Engulfed in clouds of steam, Mr Zwaan brought in bowls of tomato soup on a tray with brass handles, and proceeded impassively to serve the first course.

'This may be the last time we meet as a family for dinner, do you realise that?' Jacob announced after a short silence.

The hotel-keeper looked around him, a compelling expression in his glistening eyes, like that of a notary reading a weighty document. The past was the past, water under the bridge, and, yes, they could laugh about it now it was behind them. But when he was no longer with them, at rest under the green grass, they would often remember their father's words.

Each of the three sons wore his linen napkin like a baby's bib. This likeness aside, the brothers couldn't have been more different. Out-side the town, Ludo was often taken for a Spaniard or a Frenchman, his caramel complexion contrasting sharply with Louis's dreadful freckles and Felix's smooth, geisha-like skin. Felix was the youngest and the only one to grin a moment earlier at his father's words.

'Maria, please don't cry,' Jacob continued, himself struggling to contain a sob. 'The birds are leaving the nest. That's the way it's always been. Besides, he's more than old enough.'

'I know, I know,' Maria replied with a soggy snivel.

Ludo had fixed his gaze on his fashionable red signet ring, a gift from his friend Edo Novak. The entire performance had irritated him from the word go. He had wanted to get out of the house that

7

evening. He stared for a moment at Louis, who dipped his gnawed left pinkie into his wineglass, closely examined its light red tip and then proceeded to stick it in his ear and wiggle it around with considerable pleasure. Louis grimaced apishly at his older brother who grinned, almost imperceptibly, back.

'Dad,' said Felix, who was dressed in a finely tailored jacket he had bought at a discount a couple of days before from Mr Monjoux's boutique. Was he allowed to say something?

'No more speeches for me, please!' Ludo cut the whole business short, flicking his glass with his middle finger as if it were a pellet of paper. He thanked everyone graciously for their fine words, but shouldn't they be getting on with it?

They clinked glasses a second time, and when everyone had finally sipped their wine, the paterfamilias realised that it was a tad musty – not off or sour but musty.

Ludo guzzled the contents of his glass like water, and proceeded to delve into the tomato soup. Mr Zwaan watched the spectacle from a discreet distance. He ran his tongue against the inside of his cheek, a grimace of pain on his face from a mouth ulcer.

A week later, a notice was posted in the window of the Hotel New Deluxe:

> *Due to a family wedding,*
> *Hotel New Deluxe will be closed*
> *from May 11–18*
>
> *The Management*

4

Twelve years earlier, with a loan from a bank whose head office was on the Herengracht in Amsterdam, Jacob had set about the purchase of the former Hotel Deluxe from its administrators, planning to reopen it with an adjoining restaurant. The dilapidation he had encountered, however, had been beyond his worst imaginings.

The bank-appointed surveyor, a polite young man who had driven up in a small French car, walked ahead of him, jangling a bunch of keys like a prison warden. Jacob had brought young Felix along to divert him, but now regretted it. A child should be protected from the filth and degradation of this world for as long as humanly possible.

'Try to see beyond the mess,' the man observed, as they made their way along an unlit corridor. The tiled floor appeared to have been bomb-damaged. Lengths of copper wire and cable had been wrenched from the ceiling. 'Who is responsible for all of this?' asked Jacob as images from the past merged with what he now saw.

'Vandals, thieves – who can say? The place has been empty for a couple of years.'

They entered a room where lead-grey daylight flooded through three oval windows. Bentwood chairs lay smashed to pieces on a sea of broken glass; a batten-plated wall had been rent open like a pig's belly; in an alcove the carcass of a grand piano was dimly discernible in an alcove, a couple of discarded condoms on the red velvet cushion of the stool in front of it.

Jacob tried to distract his young son by pointing to a half-deflated leather football in a corner, but the boy wasn't interested in sport. He raced over to the grand piano, pounding its keys with both hands and throwing back his golden curls with all the bravura of a young Mozart. Deep in the body of the instrument, a couple of strings rasped off-key. Felix looked over his shoulder, visibly disappointed but irresistibly impish.

'Haven't they left a mess, the dirty pigs?' said the surveyor, nodding archly at the wretched wafer-thin contraceptives. Scum, the lot of them, and the majority were still walking the streets. Should they proceed to the upper floor? There's a flight of stairs to the left.

9

'I know, I know,' muttered Jacob. He had been here often enough before the war. In those days, Hotel Deluxe had been renowned for its veal croquettes, lemon ice cream and warm apple pie with rum-soaked raisins, all served by waiters in white aprons. He grasped his son firmly by the hand and said, 'Don't touch another thing, OK? Don't touch anything. Well, well, what have we here?'

Maria, who had secretly followed her husband, marched towards them in the blue-grey gloom. A sort of stifled anger resounded with each step. Her doe-like face was drenched with rain.

'Jacob, what are you doing here?'

'Nothing, dearest,' gibbered her husband awkwardly. He had wanted to size up the property for himself first, and then tell his wife about it...

'Jacob Bagman,' his wife boomed, the vowels accentuated in schoolmistressy fashion, her face suddenly yielding to a gleaming pearl-white smile. What had he been up to? They had always made decisions together in the past.

She cast an apologetic glance at the unfamiliar gentleman, who looked back at her affably. Felix immediately hopped and skipped over to his mother, who stroked his stubborn curls as if he were a dog. Maria introduced herself to the surveyor and asked him to continue the viewing; she was expecting visitors at home in half an hour.

'Good, then let us resume our tour!' the man from the bank declaimed, a leather ring-binder pinned under his arm.

By way of a labyrinth of corridors and doors they arrived at the kitchen, in the centre of which stood a coal-fired oven the size of a lifeboat, a blue-black basting tray still on the hob. A begonia had even managed to squirm its way heroically through one of the grills. Maria peered up at the ceiling and noticed a damp patch the size of an umbrella, but said nothing.

'It's clearly in need of major renovation,' the surveyor noted equitably. He flipped open his leather ring-binder and rummaged busily through the papers. But, of course, that was all taken into account in the mortgage agreement.

The man closed the binder and was ready to move on when a triumphant peal of laughter resonated from the corner of the room. All three heads turned around. Felix had put on a mint-condition German army helmet, the strap of which dangled down to his chest. All that could be seen of his beaming face under the ridiculous headgear were his contorted lips. He was holding a rusty ladle in his left hand, similarly unearthed from the pile of rubbish behind him.

'Get rid of that bloody thing, this goddam minute!' Jacob roared, a horrified tone in his voice.

Maria hurried over to her petrified son, knelt down and kissed his cheeks. With two consecutive thuds, the helmet and the ladle were concealed within a velvet-lined iron chest. The boy started to sob gently, pretending to push his mother away with his little fists.

'There, there, hush now...' Jacob soothed, unable to bear seeing any of his children unhappy.

At that moment, a field mouse shot across the black-and-white speckled granite floor towards the stove. Maria shrieked and raced out of the kitchen, with her hands over her face like Popeye's Olive Oyl. It was so comical that her husband, the surveyor and finally Maria herself all had to laugh.

Felix sensed that his blunder had been erased, completely wiped from the slate.

'I hadn't expected it to be in such a state,' sighed Maria as they returned to the central corridor a moment later.

Renovation seemed pointless. No, they should forget the idea. There was a dreadful stench in the building, and she would always be reminded of what had happened there. Was Jacob aware that she had just seen a torn Nazi pennant near the entrance? She had thought it was a piece of carpet but when she turned it over, she realised. It was enough to make you sick!

The surveyor stared at his clients with an appraising, almost imploring expression, and then looked at his watch. What he did not know was that Jacob had already decided several weeks earlier to purchase the property at Boulevardweg 3.

Fine, perhaps it did stink, but he had a family to take care of. The Atlantic Wall was already a fact – the entire coastline had been dismantled, blown up brick by brick and brought 250 metres inland – but, in spite of it, the beach was still packed with tourists and day-trippers on a summer's day. He had faith in the building's potential, and in the future. But how could he convince his dear lady wife?

'Let's resume our tour!' the man from the bank repeated, and, a week later, Jacob bought the property for the sum of 26,000 guilders, at an interest rate of 3 per cent, payable in quarterly instalments.

When the deeds were finally signed at the notary's office, the surveyor, who was due a serious bonus, could not have been happier.

5

'*Mutti*, do please try to behave yourself later,' Liza impressed on her mother for the umpteenth time.

Hans Matti Bender turned his Mercedes into a tree-lined street flanked by imposing houses on both sides, their wooden porches giving them an air of Hollywood. Some of the properties had names painted in decorative letters on their façades: *Huize Juliana*, *Villa Elsbeth*, *Résidence Paula*, etc.

'What a dreadful town,' the butcher's wife complained, her head twisting right and left like a peacock. She gave a brief, deep sigh: you could feel the chill here, the lack of – actually, the lack of everything. Like the East.

Liza felt a sudden urge to smash the old dear's head in with the ivory handle of the umbrella behind the back seat. She whined in despair. Oh God, it was all going to go wrong, she knew it… Everything was about to go terribly wrong. She wanted—

'Kati, lambkin,' Hans Matti Bender interrupted good-naturedly, his Mercedes gliding past a chalk-white villa surrounded by a well-tended lawn trimmed to the very millimetre, with a statue of Jesus on a pedestal, his arms raised heavenwards, 'I think our daughter might have a point.'

On a shop-lined street, a group of townsfolk gazed, open-mouthed, at the luxury automobile. They passed a town hall with a fountain in front, water frothing and spouting from three brass herrings. A gentleman stood at the top of the stairs wearing what looked like an astrakhan hat. He had an ugly face, but Kati Bender wasn't quick enough to make out if the hat was made of real fur.

'Fine! If anyone asks me anything, I'll keep my mouth shut. And what about their German? My God, they do speak German, don't they?'

Kati adjusted her bra, in which her ample breasts were tethered like buoys in a drift-net, and pulled down the visor. She examined her face in the miniature mirror, pouting like a goldfish. Forty-eight years of age, she thought, and before you know it, you'll be fifty. But she still had her looks. God, he was an ungrateful dog; he just didn't see it, her voluptuousness, her uniqueness…

The sausage-maker had visited the Netherlands with Liza three months earlier to make the acquaintance of their future in-laws. Kati had stayed home with an insuperable migraine. When she estimated that the Mercedes had crossed the border, however, she jumped out of bed and treated herself to a long hot bath, a glass of wine within easy reach on the floor.

By way of apology, Kati had brought a cake with her today, a layered construction of cream and inlaid fruit that had survived the journey intact. With yelps of delight, Maria had sliced the treat and served the slices on porcelain plates when it was time for coffee. It was an excellent patisserie, the kind you couldn't find in Holland.

13

Hans Matti and Jacob had headed off to The Boulevard on that first afternoon like two old friends. They had wrapped up well against the cold, as if they were planning to hike to Murmansk. A biting, icy wind blew over the beach, which had turned into a snowy wilderness. Crusty layers of ice had formed on the surf; seagulls ranted insanely in the pitch-black sky above.

The German sausage-maker, who had worn a leather cap with earflaps, couldn't get enough of the Arctic spectacle. But when they returned to the living room and Maria had served up the pea soup, it was almost as if he had never seen The Boulevard, as if he had never—

'Is that it?' Kati asked.

Hans Matti directed the car into a broad street and tooted rhythmically at a well-built gentleman who was completely bald. A smile appeared on his Labrador face when he saw the sausage-maker from Cologne seated like a prince behind the wheel of his Mercedes.

Yes, this was their future, Hans Matti thought for a moment. What do you say to your daughter's father-in-law? Was there a word for it? Whatever... Liza's father-in-law-to-be...

He turned the car around in an elegant circle and came to a halt at the hotel entrance. Then Maria Bagman came running out, wearing a floral pinafore. Kati hadn't worn a pinafore for years, not even on the few occasions she had visited the factory on inspection. She had always dressed in the most elegant manner possible, in order to maintain her distance from the personnel.

'How was the journey, folks?' Jacob enquired in a mixture of Dutch and German, in which argot he would spin the longest yarns to seaside visitors during the summer, no single sentence ever grammatically correct.

'*Sehr gut!*' Hans Matti replied. He strutted energetically past the car's rattling grille and opened the passenger door for his wife. Liza glided from the back seat with graceful hips, looked around, and wondered where Ludo might be.

Hans Matti introduced his wife. He followed her name with 'my flower of the Swabian Alps'. Kati, who detested this epithet but didn't let it show, remained remarkably courteous and at ease. She had thought more than once in her life – and the same thought now occurred to her once again – that she had all it took to be an actress, famous and loved.

'Where is Ludo?' chirped Liza delicately, but her words were lost in a flurry of handshakes, exclamations, remarks and polite questions, back and forth, the behaviour of people who didn't yet know each other well, but already had a certain bond.

The sun was radiant, and the soapy smell of the sea mingled with the sweet scent of roses. But Kati Bender was impervious to it all. She kept thinking about the Dutch woman's hand that she had just shaken – as coarse as sandpaper. She surreptitiously scrutinised her absurd, delicate frame, the absence of any make-up. She watched with a bogus smile as Jacob Bagman – who seemed reasonably friendly – heartily embraced her daughter and jubilantly exclaimed, '*Meine liebe schöndochter!*'

Jacob, who had always secretly dreamed of a daughter – a younger version of Maria, who would make him laugh, tickle him, and pester him – had treated Liza as his own flesh and blood from the outset. She was a beauty, no question. The hotel-keeper inspected the mother for a moment and quickly calculated Liza's future prospects. He could see that she had inherited her mother's physical good fortune, but in the years to come – after children, his grandchildren! – she would probably turn out to be just as plump, something he personally considered quite agreeable.

'You've brought the good weather with you,' said Maria to the butcher's wife in remarkably good German. It was to be dry for the entire week. Yes, it looked as if Friday, too, would be fine.

Kati nodded and smiled as if she were being photographed, and mused once again on how Maria was dressed like a maid... unthinkable! The butcher's wife from Cologne remembered the words of her housekeeper, Gabi, the only woman in the world that she trusted, a woman who not only respected and admired her but also understood her. Gabi had remained her loyal ally in the failed endeavour to save Liza from this disastrous wedding. After learning that Liza was pregnant, the housekeeper had listened in horror, her tongue quivering, as Kati had informed her that her daughter was planning to marry the Dutchman responsible.

'The Dutch are an ice-cold race,' she stated in the same Swabian dialect as her mistress. 'That country is a graveyard for women.'

Kati lay on the divan smoking one cigarette after another, concealed from view by two house plants, listening restlessly in the hope that Gabi would provide her with ammunition to use against her monstrous daughter, somehow to cheat fate.

'No woman can ever survive in that swampland.' Of course, I was there during the war, her housekeeper had cautiously continued. A woman had to maintain her self-respect, know her own worth, especially during the war. That's the way it was in those days, surely?

'Exactly. Never give that up.'

According to the official version, Gabi had spent two years in Amsterdam working as a secretary for a senior military man, and hadn't met a single Dutch woman with class, finesse or refinement during the entire period. They were cows who preferred to cycle everywhere as long as they could. Incubators on wheels. The Belgian ladies she had later met in Antwerp and (magnificent) Brussels were very different. Compared to Dutch women they were fairies, full of spirit, fashionable refinement and passion.

Kati, her eyes red from cigarette smoke, had finally asked what she should do to save her daughter. But Gabi, who had, in fact, spent much of the war in a concealed corner of Vijzelstraat, where hundreds of tight-lipped officers had ejaculated between her pear-shaped breasts and pale thighs, responded only with a lengthy silence, like a doctor with an expert diagnosis but no cure.

Where the hell was Ludo? wondered Liza once again; she was the last of the procession to enter the hotel vestibule. Huge vases filled with tulips and daffodils scented the air, fresher and more enduring than the most expensive French perfume.

Kati pressed her nose into one of the bouquets, but pulled back quickly as a bumblebee emerged from the flowers, buzzing upwards like a helicopter and disappearing into the scintillating spring in a figure of eight.

6

Ludo Bagman had little in common with his parents. As a boy of seven, during an overnight stay at a friend's house in Leiden, he had stolen the rag doll belonging to the daughter of the house, and had caused the child unsparing distress when the doll was found the next day, half-cremated on top of a pile of charred twigs in the garden.

The girl's mother had asked him if he knew anything about it. Ludo had looked up at her with the most innocent eyes, and the woman, who was immediately charmed by the remarkably handsome boy, had believed him unquestioningly.

A week later, he turned up with a magnificent English toy truck that must have cost a fortune when new. The front and rear lights burned ruby red when the wheels turned. The tyres looked like liquorice, but tasted like turpentine. 'Bombay Company' was emblazoned on both sides in saffron yellow.

At supper, when his mother asked him where the truck had come from, he had answered, without batting an eyelid, 'Swapped it for my spinning top with a rich kid from Amsterdam.'

A born merchant, thought his father, looking on with satisfaction. Jacob, who had opened a business in antiques and curios not long before, asked his young son if he too would like to be a businessman when he grew up.

'A pirate!' Ludo had exclaimed, kicking wildly against the table leg, a spoon in his hand like a cutlass.

In reality, he had stolen the toy truck from a kid with wire-rimmed spectacles and limbs as limp as cushions in an alley behind the water tower, knocking the anxious child for six with a vicious judo tackle.

Louis had followed Ludo into the world three years later, a minor neurological defect the result of the breech birth after a sixteen-hour labour, according to the doctors. He had grown up in the ever-present shadow of his older brother. They slept in the same bed, went to the beach together in the summer and marched through the dunes with home-made spears.

One fine day, the brothers devised a way to lead the owner of the cigar shop on Kerkstraat up the garden path. The man's young daughter had perished under the wheels of the tram one year earlier. A brass-framed photo of her blurred smile gazed out at his clientele from the kingdom of the dead. While Ludo passed on his parents' invented best wishes and discussed what he might buy for half a cent, Louis enterprisingly filled his pockets with the sweets from the counter. It worked every time, and, as they left to the cheerful ring of the shop's bell, the man would always shout: 'Goodbye, dear boys! Be sure to send your parents my greetings! And take good care of yourselves.'

When Ludo was struggling with his technical school work and was forced to put up with newborn Felix bawling at the top of his voice from his cradle on the floor below, he toyed for a while with the idea of the perfect infanticide. By way of an experiment, he had once even covered the baby's face with an embroidered cushion, but was taken aback when the child started to turn blue after just a couple of minutes.

Felix's unplanned arrival was a source of joy and happiness for Maria, who was made to nurture, care and protect. When Jacob returned home of an evening from his travels around the province in search of merchandise, he would first climb the stairs to Felix's little room. The youngest soon began to recognise his father, and gazed at him like an angel with big, bright blue eyes.

Felix, Felix... Ludo detested the name and tried to work off his growing hatred for his youngest brother on the unfortunate Louis, who, in the meantime, had been set apart from the rest of the pupils in his class, and spent most of the time staring silently into space, interrupted now and then by a protracted dribbling yawn, or the image of an orang-utan.

Ludo's career at technical school came to an abrupt end just before his second year when the voices on the radio were expressing increasing concern about the inevitability of war. War! The first months, as soldiers sped through the town on olive-green motorcycles and the beachfront was decorated with cheerful Nazi flags, were a liberation to him. He noticed how people's faces fell to the ground like masks to be replaced by new masks. It was a period of confusion, during which his parents spent hours on end in silence, huddled around the paraffin heater in the kitchen, and Ludo came into his own.

He had observed that the access roads to Haarlem had been closed off with barbed-wire barricades; shortly thereafter, they started to demolish buildings along The Boulevard. The work was done by men from the town he knew by sight. A couple of German soldiers were always sauntering in the vicinity. When they caught sight of Ludo, he would call out to them excitedly.

In the meantime, his father's business had almost completely collapsed. While the supply of merchandise had increased dramatically, people were holding on to their money because of the uncertainty of the times. They sold virtually nothing, and, according to the laws of commerce, it therefore made no sense to buy anything.

7

Jacob Bagman had exchanged Amsterdam for the seaside resort in the early part of 1934, when it had still boasted a spa and a number of hotels with international appeal. From the outset, tourism had provided him with a welcome extra income. As soon as the season started, the first of the townsfolk moved to their summerhouses in order to rent out their homes to the seaside visitors, and the stock of perhaps one hundred and fifty mattresses kept in the barn behind the shop was quickly used up.

'So, Mr Bagman, doesn't time fly? Yes, back for another seven weeks, thank God. Do you have three respectable mattresses, please?'

In addition to beds and mattresses, the Bagmans also rented out beach wagons with bright white hoods, as well as crockery and cutlery, which was always in demand for use on the beach or in the multitude of bed and breakfasts. The rumour quickly spread that you could even pick up hair curlers made of gold that had formerly belonged to the family of the Tsar for just a couple of guilders at the Bagmans'.

When the weather was sunny and warm, the resort would be inundated with people from the city. You would then find Jacob standing in front of his shop at eight in the morning with a newspaper under his arm, ready to receive the flood of cyclists. The mattresses were all usually rented out by early May, and then the empty barn became an ideal bicycle shed.

Jacob had a rival on the other side of the street named Sam Stikker. In addition to his textile business, Sam owned a hangar that had once housed the local fire engine. They would tout for customers raucously like street vendors and the arriving cyclists would stand and watch in amusement as the two men engaged in a good-natured battle of wits before finally making their choice.

Jacob would sometimes wait until eleven o'clock on a chair in front of the barn, struggling to stay awake, a lone bicycle as yet unclaimed, more often than not by a customer who had had too much to drink. On one occasion, a young woman kept him waiting until shortly before midnight. She had sun-bleached hair and legs the colour of caramel. The latecomer was clearly under the influence. Inside the barn, where mosquitoes darted around a gas-fired lamp, she had pressed her gazelle-like hips against Jacob's trembling body, and made him an offer under her breath.

All of a sudden, Maria appeared in the doorway, her housecoat pulled tightly over her nightgown. With one eyebrow raised, she enquired in a thin voice if everything was all right.

A couple of months before he was evacuated to Haarlem with his family, Jacob lay wide awake one night beside his wife. She was sound asleep, anaesthetised by the sleeping pills she had taken without her husband's knowledge.

His friends and business acquaintances from Amsterdam no longer dared to visit. The resort's reputation was particularly bad and, in private, Jacob frequently rued the day he had decided to seek his fortune there. How long was this war going to last? Life didn't come with instructions. You had to do everything yourself when it came down to it. You were alone in the world, you were born alone, and you would die alone.

Fortunately, his parents had passed away, as had Maria's. His father would have been obliged to wear a yellow star under the laws of the occupier. It was insane, the terrible things people could do to one another; it was like a virus, a contagious disease that had even found its way into his own home.

Ludo was practically a boarder with the Prins family, fanatical collaborators who had enlisted both their sons in the Nationale Jeugdstorm. 'What is the matter with that boy?' Jacob had moaned to Maria earlier that night. 'Sometimes he's like a total stranger.'

Maria had remained on her back in silence, staring at the ceiling, watching patches of light cast by the passing cars turn into demons that almost drove her out of her mind. She was suddenly overcome with tears. When her sobs turned to shrieks, she buried her face in the pillow for fear of waking the children.

'Now, now, dearest, it's not as bad as all that,' Jacob tried to comfort her, caressing her trembling body with his hands. 'Maybe

21

it's just a phase, and before we know it he'll see sense. This bloody war has robbed them of their childhood.'

She lay in bed coiled up like a foetus, her blonde hair like a circle of light above her spotless pillow. He loved her so much. The instant he caught sight of her, an arrow pierced both their hearts, pinning them together for ever. She had Felix's nose and chin or, rather, his youngest boy had inherited these physical charms from his mother.

Jacob tucked his arm beneath his right cheek and tried to sleep. He then snuggled up to Maria on his back, rolling from his left side to his right, longing for a third side to turn to, lying on his belly for fifteen minutes breathing steadily, before returning to his original position out of increasing desperation.

After a while, he got out of bed and tiptoed to the toilet. The moon shone pale and full through the window, the only sound the clatter of urine in the bowl. All of a sudden, he heard the crash of breaking glass. Dripping all over the place, Jacob fastened his pyjamas, rushed towards the bedroom, changed his mind halfway, stormed down the stairs, and sped through the stockroom into the shop. The two boys were standing in front of him in their cotton nightshirts. Bleary-eyed yet excited, they told him what had happened.

'The whole window's been smashed to smithereens,' Ludo reported aloofly. He glanced furtively at Louis, whose eyes lit up like a cat's in the darkness.

'Right,' Louis responded hoarsely. 'What a din, eh?' They had run downstairs straight away.

'Get away from that window!' Jacob bellowed, as they edged to the front of the shop. Shards of glass the size of dinner plates had fallen on their one-hundred-year-old Scottish barometer with English markings – *strong wind, sun, rain,* etc. – shaped like the helm of a ship, but amazingly nothing had been damaged. 'Back to bed this minute. There's nothing to see here!'

The two brothers skulked upstairs, muttering in protest as if they had been denied some fun. Jacob put a pair of clogs on and shuffled towards the window. Between the fragments of glass on the floor, he found a brick wrapped up in paper and tied with string. He picked it up and read, 'Dirty Jew-lover, this'll teach you!'

The letters swam before his eyes, his heart skipped a couple of beats and suddenly 'Bagman's Antiques' seemed to morph into a cabin on the *Titanic*: wardrobes, sideboards, pitchers, dressing tables, standard lamps, rolled-up carpets standing like sentinels in the corner, candlesticks, bedpans, umbrellas and walking sticks all tumbled down upon him with an almighty crash.

With his tail between his legs, he finally scrambled upstairs on his hands and knees over the coarse carpet to weep in Maria's arms, and ask her what he should do, how he should react. But he had to wake her up first; she lay sound asleep.

8

The furnishings may be simple, Maria Bagman had said to Kati Bender, as they sat down opposite one another, Kati wearing a blue cotton dress with white polka dots, toying with the pearls around her neck, but she really hoped she would be pleased with the room. The hotel-keeper's wife poured tea from a pot of Japanese design – birds, butterflies, a honey-coloured woman with almond eyes in an emerald-green kimono. Sugar?

'Two, please.' After the dreadful car journey, all Kati had wanted was to relax in a warm bath, but she had had to make do with the lukewarm trickle of the shower. For every five rooms on each corridor, the hotel had a communal shower-room next door to the toilet. And this passed for luxury!

'I haven't taken sugar in years,' Maria remarked, as she placed the cup of tea on a side table next to the butcher's wife. 'I read somewhere that it's poison, pure and simple.'

Kati inspected the immaculate upstairs apartment. A typical Dutch interior, needlework adorning every chair, an excess of plants on the window sill and an imposing Friesian longcase clock against the wall. She thought: What's keeping that idiot? Hans Matti had left the hotel without saying a word.

'What a delightful place,' she observed, looking around approvingly for a second time. She was looking forward to seeing the rest of the hotel, and of course there was still so much to talk about before Friday. Did Maria happen to know where her husband had got to?

'He's gone with Jacob to fetch Ludo,' Maria replied. Her son had gone into Amsterdam briefly in preparation for Liza's visit, but his car had broken down outside Aalsmeer. Did she know Aalsmeer? It was where the flowers came from.

'Oh, yes, the flowers... I love flowers...' Kati sighed, lifting the teacup to her slightly pursed lips, leaving a grainy red impression on the mother-of-pearl rim.

In spite of the fine spring weather, she hadn't seen a single flower on the way from Cologne, only cows and the occasional sheep dotting the depressing landscape. Gabi had been right about that too – the country was little more than a swamp, kept from the sea by a couple of stupid dunes.

But the wheels of fate had turned; resistance was pointless; she had to push it from her mind.

Liza breezed into the room wearing a buttercup-yellow frock with a round, white collar, her long blonde hair tied in a ponytail with a berry-red ribbon.

'You look wonderful, my child!' Maria exclaimed, hurriedly pouring her a cup of tea.

'Thank you, Mrs Bagman,' said Liza with a smile, casting a glance of viscid loathing in her mother's direction as if to say, What did I tell you? 'Where is everyone?' she then enquired.

'Off to get Ludo, sweetie. His car's broken down.' Maria then slapped her forehead with flat of her hand, produced an envelope from her apron and said, 'Heavens! I completely forgot to give you this. It's from Ludo.'

Liza settled onto the sofa and crossed her legs, her long bronze eyelashes fluttering in the sunlight. She tore open the envelope with a fingernail and read the card inside:

My darling!

I've been unexpectedly called to Amsterdam. If I'm not back in time, you can kill me tonight. With a knife or a shotgun – the choice is yours. I'll be thinking of you every second of the day. Thousands of kisses!

Your little bunny rabbit.

'I'm so happy,' cried Liza, her voice penetrating her mother's tender soul like a jagged knife. 'Are you coming to the beach, *Mutti?* The deckchairs will be out by now, won't they, Mrs Bagman?'

The doors to the conservatory were wide open; in the street below, a large, high-spirited family was making its way up to The Boulevard, a barking dog running on ahead.

'We can sit outside if you like,' suggested Maria, gesturing towards the fluttering violets on the balcony.

But Kati, who was allergic to sunlight, and feared that her skin might become dehydrated, hastily announced that she was fine where she was. It would all be over in a couple of days. Then she would never have to see these people again. She had never seen her husband's parents, thank God, apart from in the rust-stained photo in his wallet.

'Aren't you nervous, Liza?' Maria broke the silence a little later. After all, you only get married once in your life. It must all be so new to her, like the birth of one's first child. Maria had wanted to tell her about her own marriage, but immediately realised she'd made a big mistake.

She saw how the powdered face of the woman sitting opposite had winced with barely disguised revulsion. Or was it shame? She apparently thought it a scandal that her daughter was pregnant. Bah, as if that made the slightest difference! In her village, in blessed and lake-rich Friesland, two out of three marriages were the result of just such a little accident. It had been that way for centuries and it would stay that way for centuries to come. But perhaps her view was too reasonable for this lady, who snootily inspected the room every five minutes, as if she were on some kind of state visit.

'My husband's been working on nothing but the wedding for weeks on end. It promises to be magnificent,' Maria continued. She stood up, smoothed out her apron, and said, 'Well, then, would you like a tour of the hotel while we wait for the others? They might be another hour or two. Oh, do be careful... No, no, not at all... It's nothing, really...'

With an ill-timed turn of her hips, Kati had knocked over the silver cow-shaped milk pitcher that Felix had tried to sketch hundreds of times as a child.

The hotel-keeper's wife fetched a cloth from the kitchen, and bent down to pat the pool of milk dry with a single swipe.

9

The sight of four young waiters immediately lifted Kati's spirits. They were dressed in green felt jackets and black trousers, their white collars set off by dark red bow-ties. One of them, a young man with jet-black curly hair, greeted her with unusual friendliness. He and his colleagues then continued to arrange the tables in diagonal lines across the enormous room.

Kati studied the good-looking lad, whose appearance released a warm feeling in her stomach, and nodded back as coolly as she could.

So, they had decent staff running the place, the butcher's wife observed, a hint of relief in her voice.

Maria pointed out the fireplace adorned with blue Delft tiles in the breakfast room, and Kati squealed with delight when she saw the collection of Chinese vases and decorative plates in ebony cabinets in the restaurant, but it was the main salon that impressed her most.

'What a magnificent stage!'

'In the winter we have all sorts of performances here,' Maria explained. Her husband did a lot of charity work with the elderly, which was its own reward – they gave so much love in return. As a matter of fact, there were no staff at all from September to May, excepting old Mr Zwaan, who just happened to be out at that moment. Off-season, they did everything themselves.

'And what do those poor souls do then?' Kati asked in an empathetic tone, as if she were talking about the starving in Africa.

Wait for the next season, Maria had wanted to say, but Kati had already walked on, her vigorous bust before her, casting a second glance at the curly-haired barman in his scrumptious pressed trousers.

They headed back towards the central corridor, where a boy was mopping the tiled floor. He had chubby cheeks and oyster-shaped eyes, his light blond hair hanging limply over his forehead. Oh, my God, thought Kati, taken aback, they have a Mongoloid in their service. What a tasteless display. The idea that had been doing the rounds not so long ago of sticking them all in a camp and sterilising them wasn't as wretched as it sounded.

Maria called him over in a special tone of voice. He looked shyly over his shoulder for a moment, biting his tongue, and continued to mop the floor.

'Louis, there is a lady here who would like to meet you,' the hotel-keeper's wife repeated, patiently. The boy approached reluctantly. Maria took hold of his hand, appended it to Kati's, and introduced her second child.

'Boy, she looks like a right Kraut, doesn't she, Mummy?' Louis grumbled, bubbles of spittle on his lips.

'What did he say?' asked Kati, almost breathless with disgust.

Her son thought she looked like a real German lady, Maria translated, the artery in her neck throbbing, glancing over at Liza, terrified she might have understood. But the bride-to-be seemed oblivious to it all.

'What a very special boy, what a wonderful child,' gasped Kati, quickly withdrawing her hand. She felt as if she had been toiling for hours on end, her hands in a vat of raw meat, as she had to in the early days, when the sausage factory had just opened.

At that moment, Jacob, Hans Matti and Ludo ambled along the corridor like carnival-goers gone astray. The bridegroom-to-be was carrying a bunch of flowers the size of a steering-wheel, not dissimilar to a wreath for graves and coffins. He walked up to Liza, draped the garland of tulips, daffodils and hyacinths around her neck, and kissed her on the cheeks, forehead and nose.

'Sweet darling, please forgive me! My petrol tank sprung a leak!'

'You mad silly billy... I'm going to enjoy killing you later with a shotgun!' Liza responded radiantly. She could already speak a few words of Dutch.

Kati stared over at her husband. The sausage-maker's angular face was radiant with the smile of a man soon to escort his only daughter up the aisle. He kept his eyes on Jacob, with the expression of a native delighted to have a white man as his friend, prepared to follow him in everything. Louis stood quietly in a corner, the mop like a lance against his chest.

Hotel New Deluxe was suddenly filled with an air of excitement and cheer in anticipation of the approaching wedding, which promised to be a major event. It had been the talk of the town for days.

10

The morning after the incident with the brick, Ludo stepped out onto the street and saw a Star of David chalked on the pavement in front of his father's shop. A shudder of disgust shot up his spine and seized his throat, as if he had been punched in the face.

'Bloody hell!' he cursed under his breath, and disappeared back inside like a weasel.

Jacob, who had already been pacing up and down between the antiques for several hours, was shocked by his son's horrified face and followed him outside. When he saw what had happened he gripped his overalls and started to groan from behind tightly closed lips.

Ludo was yet again disappointed in his father. He studied his profile: the old bugger was turning grey already. Not yet forty but what little hair he had had turned grey. At that moment he decided never to become a father, bald or grey. What kind of spineless attitude was this, standing there and blubbering? He should be clenching his hands into fists and yelling out that a terrible mistake had been made, that…

'They must have got the wrong address,' Ludo announced, spitting at the Star of David and rubbing it out furiously with the soles of his shoes. He would tell the Prins family what had happened. He could easily name a few of the right addresses…

The antiques dealer looked at his oldest son, his lips trembling. He had been trying to avoid him of late, a sense of powerlessness gnawing at him. He said: 'Come inside at once. And fetch little Louis from the barn. There's something I have to tell you all.'

'Boys, can any of you remember your Uncle Simon?' Jacob began, when they were all seated around the table shortly afterwards.

Maria had propped Felix on her lap, and was rocking him gently on her knees. The seven-month-old loved it. He beamed and looked around, his eyes like marbles.

'Who?' Ludo asked.

Suddenly, a flock of birds started squawking and shrieking outside in the chestnut tree. The boys raced to the open window in their short trousers and watched as the neighbour's cat, his mouth full of bloody feathers, slunk over the wall. Ludo traced the creature that was as old as the hills and sometimes slept in secret on his bed, with pride.

Jacob would have liked to call off the conversation. He turned to Louis, who was sitting beside Ludo and chewing his lip. His second son sometimes reacted unpredictably. The first time he had heard the word blackout, he had thought that men were going to attack the house and knock him unconscious. He had spent the rest of the day under his bed wrapped in a saddle blanket and looking like a sun-baked mummy. He had even refused to come down for dinner.

'Does anyone know who Uncle Simon is?' Jacob resumed, staring dejectedly at a sepia photograph on the mantelpiece. 'Come on, Ludo.'

But his oldest son was silent.

'That nice old man who took you to Artis Zoo in Amsterdam. You had pancakes afterwards on the Leidseplein.'

'Oh, him,' Ludo mumbled, picking at a pimple on his right cheek. But surely he had been dead for years?

Jacob looked back at the studio photo of his parents: a fragile blonde next to a jug-eared Buddha in a check suit, sitting on a wrought-iron bench edged by tastefully arranged ferns and indoor palms. Alkmaar, July 1921.

'Uncle Simon is your grandfather's brother. He was truly a very kind soul, your grandfather. He would have been so proud of his grandchildren, and very happy, that's for sure.'

Happiness doesn't buy you very much, drawled Ludo in a jaded adult tone. Jacob glanced at his wife in desperation. Where had he picked up that kind of language? Should he hold his peace, after all? But that was impossible, simply impossible...

Uncle Simon was still alive, Jacob continued cautiously. After he came back from South Africa he went to live in... It was a long story, but that wasn't the point. The point was... Damn, he shouldn't have to bother them with this. It was obscene, but, then, so were the times... For some time now, the occupier had forced Uncle Simon to wear a yellow star. He had paid them a secret visit the week before. Maybe that explains the stone...

'So Uncle Simon is a Jew?' Ludo's face had hardened, as if exposed to a gust of ice-cold air.

Jacob nodded.

'But what does that mean for us?' asked Ludo, panic taking hold of him.

Jacob tried to explain everything patiently: his mother's parents were both Dutch Reformed. His own dear mother – God rest her soul – was the same, of course. Only his father... Oh, it was all so sordid, so absurd... But now that they knew, from then on they would have to...

Ludo jumped up and exclaimed that he would explain everything to the Prins family as soon as he got the chance. It was all just some sort of...

'You're not going to explain anything to anyone, do you hear?' yelled his mother, who was standing by the table with Felix in her arms looking at her like a petrified seal cub.

Maria, who had seldom been so insistent, forbade her son from having anything to do with the Prins family from then on. They were a dubious bunch, and dangerous.

11

Stupid bitch, thought Ludo, going out later that day. He would hang around with whoever he liked. Why hadn't Uncle Simon just died sooner? Now he brought shame on the whole family. Might anyone have seen him when he was here?

The sound of the sea drifted over the town, rustling like paper. There was a lukewarm south-westerly breeze. An elderly man pushed a handcart bearing a bedside cabinet and a salmon-pink tub chair slowly along the Hogeweg. Two Germans appeared on motorbikes, their helmets dangling on their backs like coconut halves. They slowed down, a single boot dragging along the ground, and asked the old man for his papers.

The Prins family had moved into their modest villa a couple of months earlier. Scaffolding had been put up in the garden, and a painter was busily painting the front of the house. A splendid rose-bush in full bloom had been partially covered with newspaper. Sparrows hopped along the broken shell path that led to the front door, chattering away just as people would.

Arno and Paul were lying side by side on the lawn in cinnamon-coloured breeches. Their eleven-year-old sister Betsy watched in awe from a low wall as her brothers tried to set the cover of a book on fire with a magnifying glass. The girl already had gloriously pert breasts, which made her look at least fourteen.

When the boys caught sight of Ludo, they quickly hid their things in a tin, slammed it shut, and glared at him suspiciously. Arno jumped to his feet – 'Carpet bomb the Russkies!' – and rubbed the red streaks the grass had left on his thighs. What was he doing here?

'Hello, how are you?' Ludo asked in an ingratiating tone.

Paul looked him up and down and his eyes narrowed. Although he was two years younger than Arno, the brothers looked like identical twins. The same glossy raven's wing of hair dangled over both sculpted foreheads, giving them an aristocratic and unassailable air.

They had been conducting secret experiments, Arno announced, and he tapped the lid of his tin box with his knuckles. They had to be vigilant. The enemy was everywhere. Arno looked searchingly at his younger brother who was lying on the grass with his hand under his chin.

'But surely I'm your friend?' Ludo peered at Betsy momentarily. She had been following everything her brothers said and did with amusement, nibbling on a tress of her butter-yellow hair as if it were a pretzel.

'Of course you're our friend, Bagman. We just have one or two reservations, that's all. Do you believe in The Cause?'

'Yes,' said Ludo.

'Honestly?'

'I swear,' Ludo reaffirmed. He wanted nothing more than one of the magnificent blue Nationale Jeugdstorm uniforms. They knew he did, didn't they?

Arno cast a superior glance in the direction of his younger like-ness. Had Ludo heard the good news? No? Well, then, he should take a look at The Boulevard this afternoon; they had put up a couple of new signposts. Finally, the riffraff had been banned from the beach, and the rest would follow: the shops, the trams, the railway station. Their father was working on it; it was only a question of time. Did he want to come inside for a minute?

'Sure,' answered Ludo, deeply content that the two brothers still approved of him.

They entered the pleasantly cool house, which always seemed like a paradise to Ludo, the gateway to a world he himself hoped to access one day. The villa was tastefully furnished. A stuffed monkey with yellow eyes and a check cap stood in the hallway. The parquet floor was almost completely hidden beneath oriental carpets.

Apart from the housekeeper, a flabby woman whom everyone called Ankie, there was no one in. Their father was always at the town hall. Sometimes he would be summoned in the middle of the night to go to The Hague in his official car. Arno added that their mother had gone away with a friend a couple of weeks ago to a small hotel in the Eifel area, to recover from the grimy sea air.

33

A glass bowl full of apples and a bunch of tiny grapes beamed invitingly at Ludo from a table. Arno stuffed a handful of blue grapes into his mouth all in one go, grinding them wildly between his teeth until the juice dribbled down his chin.

'Help yourself.'

'Thanks,' said Ludo, and did the same.

Had he ever killed an Ivan, asked Paul, rotating a blushing Golden Delicious in his hand, examining it with a frown and then tossing it nonchalantly out of the window into the luxuriously verdant back garden.

'No,' Ludo confessed coyly.

Paul took a second apple and hurled it like a hand grenade after the first. 'We have,' he said; sixteen Ivans that very morning, with their brigade in the dunes. It was all a question of training. Next month they were to have their first rifle practice, with live cartridges. Eh, Arno?

Ankie blundered in like an elephant, and gestured that she was going out to buy groceries. When the Prins brothers started to brag once again about their adventures with the Nationale Jeugdstorm, Ludo could no longer contain himself. He felt he had to do something to demonstrate his commitment to The Cause, that he was daring and unafraid.

And he told them about the brick that had been thrown through the window of his father's shop the night before, about his old uncle's visit, about the terrible misunderstanding.

The brothers listened with bated breath. Suddenly, Arno jumped to his feet, his shoulders rigid, and, trying his best not to boom as his father did in the chambers of the town hall, shouted, 'But you do know what this means?'

Ludo shook his head in alarm.

'It means, Bagman, that you have Jewish blood. Hey, Paul—' Arno Prins glared at his younger brother with exaggeratedly terror-stricken eyes. 'Jesus Christ, we're standing here with a half-Jew!'

'No, it's not true!' Ludo groaned and almost doubled over in distress, like Louis did when he had one of his seizures.

'Yes, it is, you're lying!'

No, no, no... They had completely misunderstood. His grandmother and grandfather on his mother's side were Dutch Reformed, and his father's parents... And then Ludo had an idea, simple but brilliant. He stood up, walked calmly over to the window, turned abruptly and appealed conspiratorially, 'Can you keep a secret?'

'Of course,' the brothers responded in unison.

He was illegitimate, Ludo lied. His parents had adopted him as a baby. His real mother was dead, but his father was still alive. He was a high-ranking officer in Austria...

Arno and his brother exchanged fleeting glances; they were both evidently very confused.

'I knew it,' heaved Arno, his voice lowering in sympathy. He walked over to the fireplace and took a sword with a black wooden sheath from the wall. But the question was – he withdrew the sword from the sheath halfway, a wrinkle of curiosity furrowing his forehead – the question was whether he would be willing to offer a sacrifice. Eh?

'It would be a pleasure,' Ludo informed them, an incredible feeling suddenly coursing through his body.

Arno carefully returned the weapon, which his father had brought back from a boat trip to Sumatra, and resumed, 'Fine, but then we have to show you something first. Hey, Betsy!'

His little sister jumped up from the sofa and followed them upstairs via a spiral staircase flanked by open windows, the net curtains of which brushed against Ludo's face like a bridal veil. They climbed a second flight of stairs and followed a dark corridor into an oval room. A waterfall of ice-blue daylight cascaded through the frosted-glass pavilion roof, illuminating a four-poster bed in the centre under a fan-shaped canopy. Tiny white cushions were scattered all over the red cashmere bedspread.

Before Arno had even closed the door, Betsy had pulled her dress over her head, wriggled her knickers to the floor, punted them to the corner, and lain down on the bed, as cool as a cucumber, her arms above her head, her legs wide apart.

Ludo's mouth began to water; he thought he was dreaming. Paul crouched on a blanket chest in more or less the same position as the stuffed monkey in the hallway downstairs, and watched with a glassy grin on his bronzed face.

'Don't tell me that thing of yours isn't getting hard.' Arno then snapped his fingers and Betsy started to romp excitedly all over the mattress like a dog rooting around in the dirt. 'Don't tell me that, goddammit.'

'I'm not saying anything,' Ludo squeaked, not knowing what to do or where to look.

'Good, but before you get your grubby paws on Betsy, you have to take care of something for us. A patriotic deed.' Had he understood?

Ludo watched as Arno gave his little sister a peck on the forehead, his face as soft as velvet, like the faces of the men on the beach when there were still terraces on the beachfront instead of concrete blocks with iron tentacles that the seabirds crashed into at night.

12

In a cheerful flurry of voices, chuckles, huffs and puffs on account of the heat, the party had made its way upstairs behind a door marked 'Private'. Maria threw open the doors to the balcony once again and, with her husband's help, busied herself setting out wooden folding chairs on the decking.

Hans Matti offered to help too, but Maria politely parked him on the sofa beside his wife with a friendly smile. What did Kati think of the hotel? the sausage-maker enquired.

'I had thought it would be bigger,' Kati whispered, reminding herself of the curly-haired Adonis in the green felt jacket. Life is such a funny thing. Some people stand out immediately and others don't. It was just like taste and smell, probably something chemical.

'It's an outstanding enterprise,' Hans Matti muttered, watching attentively as an extendable table was opened out on the balcony and arrayed in a cornflower-blue tablecloth.

Kati looked on in silence as Maria darted back and forth between the sideboard and the balcony with plates and cutlery. Fifteen minutes later, the lady of the house emerged with a tureen of soup, which filled the room with a strong smell of beef. Who eats soup in this kind of weather? Kati thought, suddenly craving one of the six bars of white chocolate she had hidden in her suitcase beneath her underwear. She asked Maria whether the soup contained meat.

'Of course! Meat, meatballs, vermicelli. Genuine Dutch vegetable soup.' But why didn't she call her Maria? After all, they were now almost family.

'Thank you, but I don't eat meat,' stated Kati.

The hotel-keeper's wife was confounded.

'Kati is a vegetarian,' explained Hans Matti, hastening to his wife's assistance. Her digestive system has been unable to tolerate meat or meat products since she was a little girl. Yes, yes, he was quite aware that it was a bit strange for the wife of a sausage-maker. And she detests fish as well.

'But what do you eat, then?' Maria asked, panicking about Friday's five-course dinner. Apart from the veal, there was also duck pâté on the menu. She had talked it all over with the chef the day before in Ludo's presence, but he hadn't said anything. She had little experience with vegetarian dishes – an omelette, cauliflower cheese, that was about it.

'Oh, don't worry about me,' Kati replied cheerily. She didn't have much of an interest in food. She was of the firm opinion that food only made you fat. She then got to her feet, her bosoms bouncing, and accompanied her husband to the balcony where Jacob had already settled into a wicker chair next to Ludo and Liza under the filtered light of a blue-and-white striped awning.

'You would think it was the height of summer all of a sudden,' the hotel-keeper said with an elegant tone in his fantasy German, as if he had had a few drinks.

'Splendid, splendid, splendid' Hans Matti affirmed, rubbing his hands together contentedly, and quickly settled into a chair next to his host. Maria reappeared, handed her husband a basket filled with crispy rolls, and asked him to put them on the table next to the butter dish.

Kati fell into a chair, having peered fleetingly over the balustrade onto the street below. A pony in a harness with little bells on, its white mane dazzling, was pulling a herring cart towards the beach. When Maria started to serve, Kati asked if she ever allowed the servants to attend her.

'What do you mean?'

'You know...' Kati sighed, alluding to the waiters downstairs: they could surely alleviate some of life's everyday drudgeries. Why slave away and work oneself silly when the staff were available to take care of it all?

Maria shook her head indignantly. Such a thing was out of the question. She had always maintained a strict division between the hotel and her private life. In the summer, they might sell upwards of a hundred *coupes glacées* in one day, but she still considered a single scoop with a blob of whipped cream to be a luxury. She loved to wash and iron, didn't she, Jacob? And she held out a piping-hot dish to her husband who was squinting at a ray of yellow sunlight.

'Precisely, my dear, you're quite right. Oops, just a minute... Careful... my, my, there's no room for the spoon...'

'My mother hasn't washed a cup in years, have you, *Mutti*?' queried Liza, turning to face her with a false smile. But she suddenly stiffened when she felt Ludo's hand and then his wriggling middle finger on her lap under the table. She pushed the hand away, holding her breath and trying to avoid notice. The laughter lines around Ludo's eyes disappeared.

Kati clenched her teeth. She could scandalize them all right there and then if she wanted, and throw a bowl of red-hot soup in the little serpent's face. But she weighed up the consequences in an instant. Not long now and the nightmare would be over. Then she would head off with Gabi – for a month at least – to a former farmhouse in the Swabian Alps with its athletic masseurs in gladiator skirts, coarse towels and steaming eucalyptus baths; her husband was yet to be informed.

She took a bread roll from the basket and sank her teeth into the hard crust like a wild beast.

'Exceptionally delicious soup,' Hans Matti praised the lady of the house after the first spoonful, a string of vermicelli dangling from his moustache. 'Do you have salt and pepper?'

Maria apologised. She had used a fair amount of flavouring in the stock and people said salt was pure poison for the human body. She stood up, left the room and returned with condiments, two glass cylinders with silver screw tops shaped like lighthouses.

'My grandfather,' Hans Matti recounted, sprinkling his soup with one hand and calmly emptying his plate with the other. 'My grandfather ate a pound of pork every day, three Baltic herrings, and salted and peppered his potatoes and vegetables to his heart's content. He was never ill. But on his sixtieth he was gone in an instant: a burst blood vessel in the brain—'

'Awful!' exclaimed Jacob, resting his spoon for a moment, his chin swelling up like a balloon.

Lovebirds Ludo and Liza sipped dejectedly at their soup. Not because they didn't like it, Maria imagined, but rather because the young couple simply weren't hungry and were thinking of other things.

Having gulped down a second serving of soup at the same appreciative pace, it dawned on Hans Matti that it was the perfect moment to take a photo of all of them together on the balcony. Where had they put that magnificent garland of flowers? It had to be in the picture. Aha, there, inside, against the wall…

Jacob was about to stand up and fetch the thing, but the sausage-maker was already on his feet and gestured with a smile that he should remain seated. He had to go back to his room anyway, to get the camera from his suitcase. Hans Matti, who had maintained the physique of a schoolboy despite his fifty years, made his way inside, with the gait of a young footballer.

His wife, in the meantime, peered in disgust at her daughter from behind the carrot-coloured lenses of her sunglasses, at her smooth skin, her firm breasts, her glow of health and happiness.

And she wished for an atom bomb to fall and destroy the whole world, everything and everyone, including herself.

13

'You simply can't imagine the abominable state the hotel was in before we took over', volunteered Maria half an hour later, after a successful photo had finally been taken at the third attempt – the camera had been set to its self-timer next to the tureen of soup on the table. Her husband had opened a bottle of Moselle wine, a gift from the sausage-maker.

'I can well believe it,' said Hans Matti, who had removed his jacket to reveal a moss-green waistcoat in a sort of glittery material that Maria had never seen in the shops before. She rather doubted its quality.

It was a complete shambles, there was no other word for it; everything was dilapidated, neglected, ruined. They had spent a year and a half just trying to bring some order to the place. The curtains, the upholstery, Maria had done it all by herself.

'Really?' Kati remarked, the wine suddenly making her feel more relaxed. She took her time in drinking, so as not to give anything away.

Maria described how she had gone back to Amsterdam at least ten times for samples; the choice back then had not been so varied as it was now. Had she ever been to Amsterdam?

Kati shook her head; she detested big cities. Thank God they didn't live in Cologne, but rather in a small town nearby, although they were still part of Cologne when it came to local elections and taxes. It was just so terribly busy in big cities, swarming with people. And if you thought about it, every one of them had their own life, their own troubles and cares. The very thought of it almost drove her mad.

'I couldn't agree more!' proffered Maria, tittering in recognition. She tapped her on the knee with two fingers, pleased that they had finally found something in common, Kati apparently thawing slowly but surely.

Jacob had said no to the wine. Hundreds of things still had to be organised for the big day, on top of which he had a secret plan in mind, as Maria had sensed, though she kept this to herself, in part to avoid spoiling the fun, and because he would otherwise realise that he could keep nothing from her.

The plan consisted of surprising the young couple, both sides of the family, and an estimated two hundred guests during the evening festivities in the main hall after the meal with a major attraction: Mr Ivan Poestash, a mustachioed Hungarian, the kind you see on old-fashioned postcards. Jacob had seen him perform once at the Tuschinski Theatre in Amsterdam.

It was beyond the understanding of any normal person, but Ivan Poestash was able not only to conjure seven white pigeons from a top hat all at once, make them change colour in full flight and then rain like confetti on his head, shoulders and the palms of his hands, he could also do something Jacob had never seen in his life before: he could cut a person in two with a circular saw.

He invites a fragile young assistant to lie down inside a wooden chest with silver clasps, closes the shutters, and saws his circular blade through the middle until the chest is cut into two pieces, which are then wheeled apart. While the illusionist waves a tattooed arm majestically up and down in the space in between, the girl gazes blankly at the audience, her eyelids fluttering at one end, her toes wriggling at the other.

Jacob had phoned the Tuschinski a month earlier for information on the whereabouts of the mysterious Hungarian. To be on the safe side, he had informed them that he and the entire trade association attended the movie theatre's famous Saturday afternoon matinees at least once a year. A somewhat timid woman had passed on a telephone number in Alkmaar. He had dialled the number and someone with a heavy West Friesian accent had answered, calling himself Kees de Boer. Jacob had been momentarily confused, but the man turned out to be Ivan Poestash after all.

His impresario had demanded a small fortune for a performance. Jacob had later negotiated with Poestash directly, cutting out the middleman who had an office in Rotterdam. He had good reason to hope that he could secure his services for a reasonable price.

'Aren't you a quiet pair?' said Maria all of a sudden, turning her attention to the lovebirds.

'We're going for a walk,' said Ludo, standing up and jerking his fiancée out of her chair by the arm. Liza cooed in protest. Someone was apparently going to play Hawaiian guitar on the beachfront terrace at Bol's café.

'Enjoy yourselves, children, enjoy yourselves,' sighed Jacob, wondering if he still had time to finalise arrangements that day. A major attraction like Ivan Poestash would cost him a bob or two, Hungarian or otherwise. He would make him an offer. Art, after all, was also just a question of money.

14

Now that the young couple were finally out of the way, it was time for the parents to discuss a number of matters that they had been keeping to themselves. Maria Bagman was still in a quandary about

Kati Bender's vegetarianism. She decided to consult the chef that evening and work out a solution. There had to be something better than boring cauliflower cheese.

Hans Matti had told Jacob during his previous visit that he wanted to contribute towards the organisation of the wedding and the expenses. All of the organisational aspects had his blessing, but the sausage-maker could not possibly allow the Bagmans to pay for everything, especially given the considerable prosperity he had enjoyed in recent years.

By way of a compromise, they had finally settled on a sum that Hans Matti had discreetly handed over to the hotel-keeper in a salmon-pink envelope on arrival. Deutschmarks. Jacob decided he would not convert them into guilders for the time being, but lock them away in the safe in his office. There was time enough to convert them later, if he wanted to. And there was so much gossip doing the rounds these days about what people earned, received under the table, etc.

Jacob had learned after the publication of a sordid article in the local paper that an argument had started to gain momentum in the town, with a counter-argument as rebuff, the point of dispute being whether or not to accept the invitation to his son's wedding to the daughter of a German sausage-maker. He had no idea which side people were on, or who started the whole miserable affair in the first place, and he didn't want to know. But it was like a toothache – it could leave you in peace for hours at a time, and then the agony of red-hot needles jabbing at your gums became so intense that you wanted to scream.

Hans Matti had produced a lighter from his trouser pocket to light a thin cigar. It had the look of a classy fountain pen, the company name – *Benders Fleischwaren* – engraved in gold lettering on its side. Jacob, who had an extraordinary appreciation of fine workmanship, was intrigued.

'A handsome pen,' he said. Hans Matti laughed enigmatically and handed him the object.

The hotel-keeper ran a finger over the smooth barrel. Then he pressed a black button and a flame shot out like a lizard's tongue where he had expected the nib to be. Jacob grinned with childlike amazement. What a gadget!

'German,' Hans Matti stated. 'The things Germany has invented in recent years!'

Encouraged by his reaction, the sausage-maker conjured up further interesting gadgets from his pockets: a silver keyring with a tape measure; a foldout magnifying glass in a chamois leather case; a compass the size of a guilder; a miniature travel bag. When Hans Matti started to give instructions on the use of each item, Kati glared at her husband, her eyebrows raised, and coughed pointedly.

'Jacob, my dear fellow,' the sausage-maker continued after clearing his throat slightly, pronouncing the name of his near-relation as warmly as he could. He wanted to mention something else with respect to the day after next, a matter to which he and Kati attached considerable importance.

He told of how he had established a brass band a couple of years earlier together with the owner of a neighbouring meat concern who also produced for the wholesale market but in a different sector, and who was thus not a direct competitor. They called the band 'The Flesh Tones', and had financed it privately.

'What?' Jacob asked, having understood something like 'flesh stones', and glanced at Maria.

'The Flesh Tones,' Hans Matti repeated.

Maria said she thought it an original name, which made her rise considerably in Kati's esteem: she had devised the entire concept, the name included, one afternoon when she had had nothing else to do, and had guzzled half a bottle of bubbly.

He and Kati would be especially honoured – the sausage-maker cast a weary yet knowing glance towards his wife who was listening apprehensively – they thought it might be nice—

'If our daughter might proceed from the town hall to the church accompanied by our very own private orchestra,' Kati continued, swiping at a wasp that had landed on her left collarbone, her gold charm bracelet tinkling. After all, wasn't it also something of a German wedding?

Jacob thought it a magnificent idea. He planted both fists on his knees, got up, and announced that he would contact the mayor about the project that very afternoon, as they would certainly need permission from the local authority. Now he really needed a couple of hours to himself – there was still so much to be arranged.

'Dearest, isn't it time you showed our in-laws the love nest we've prepared for Ludo and Liza?'

A little while later Maria invited the sausage-maker and his wife to accompany her to the fisherman's cottage behind the hotel. A family of eleven children had once lived there, seven of them carried off by Spanish flu. A family tombstone covered with copperish moss in the cemetery on the edge of the dunes still testified to the fact.

But no one remembered them now, and the local archives had no account of the affair. People are inclined to forget, unless it suits them for some reason to cultivate the memory of an elephant, as with some of the townsfolk just then, who suddenly found it impossible even to mention the name Bagman without disgust or revulsion.

15

Hans Matti had really loved the sea when he was a boy, but in the crazy years after the war – almost as crazy as the war itself – he had rarely given the place of his birth a second thought.

Rauschen, the Pearl of the Baltic, what was left of it now? The place had been annexed by the Soviets, gobbled up as war booty, and now had an unpronounceable Russian name that he could never remember. It was probably a natural defence mechanism to protect him from the sheer sadness of it all.

Every now and then, however, when he detected a particular smell, heard a voice with a familiar tone on the radio in his study, or a passer-by on the street reminded him of one of his dead parents, Hans Matti would think back, for a brief kaleidoscopic moment, to his youth. But such moments always disappeared as quickly as they came.

A year after the opening of his first butcher's shop, he was already unable to satisfy the demand for meat. Germans always were and still remained incorrigible carnivores, even after the worst slaughter mankind had ever known. He opened a second shop and, six months later, a third, and then decided to focus instead on the provision of quality sausages for the wholesale market. Six years later, Kati would be shopping for shoes and dresses in Brussels, his first Mercedes parked in the drive.

His parents had never had the chance to share in his success in business, and that still bothered him. They had no marked grave, pre-sumably devoured by the hellish advance of the Soviet army that had consumed his Prussian homeland like wildfire. By then, Hans Matti had been living for three and a half years in the relative safety of Aachen, working as 'master butcher' in the household of a general, and in possession of a document that exempted him from active mil-itary service. Even then, he had heard no news of his twin brother Otto for years.

Immediately after the war, he had often walked the streets in fear. He was constantly plagued by the thought that his spitting image (the only difference between them was a minuscule mole above Otto's left eye) would emerge from a doorway somewhere. The young butcher had prepared his reaction and knew exactly what he would say, what he would ask.

But, as time passed, the likelihood of such an encounter became less and less, while the handful of attempts he had made to find out what had happened to Otto always came to a dead end. His past was a purple shadow that was to follow him for the rest of his life, perhaps even to the grave. The flesh that people entrust to the earth often nourishes the growth of trees and branches with abundant leaves that obscure the sun.

Completely in keeping with the spirit of the times, Otto had served as a soldier in an elite division. Hans Matti had received his last postcard from Riga: 'Dear Hans Matti, this is a terrible place. I am longing for the war to be over, like a drowning man longs for a beach of palms. Those rotten kidneys of yours are the best thing that ever happened to you.' Where did he go after that? To the Siberian inferno? Or to Hungary? France? Or perhaps to Africa?

Kati had once called Hans Matti 'insane', when he was reading the Friday papers one Sunday morning and started to mutter something about his brother, nervously jumping to his feet from his tub chair. In the column 'Various reports from beyond the fatherland', he had read a piece about three Germans who had been discovered in a village in the Urals, former prisoners of war spared by Stalin for one reason or another. Negotiations were under way at the highest level to secure their return. He read their names: Ulli Unterbauer, Franz Schönleben, Helmut Schröder. No, Otto Bender was not among them, but maybe...

'Idiot!' Kati snorted. His brother was dead, pure and simple, why couldn't he just accept it?

Dead, pure and simple, reflected Hans Matti, some time later. Well, there was nothing more normal than death, was there? In life, you can be all sorts of things: poor, rich, famous, a nobody, beautiful, hideous, athletic, fat, loved, hated, blessed with talents of every kind, or just the opposite. But in death we were all the same. Life was the time of opportunity, and if life couldn't make it happen, the opportunity was lost, lost for ever.

One day the sausage-maker had exchanged his old Mercedes for a new one, while Liza, whose eyes had begun to roll with boredom every time Kati spoke to her, was sent to the first of a long series of private schools. He was approached almost every week to invest in lucrative national projects; he was fit and successful, but, in spite of everything, he had been increasingly subject to bouts of melancholy, without actually being unhappy.

Hans Matti had once read that identical twins often had the same preferences and characters, even if they had grown up on the opposite sides of the world. They might have a shared loathing for cauliflower and fish, for example, or that both could be overcome at the same moment by severe cramps in the calves, or by feelings of joy or despair. If that were true, then it implied – logically speaking – that, on the death of one twin, the other must also die to some extent.

As a child, he had always been distinctly carefree. They lived in Rauschen in a house with a red-tiled roof, surrounded by a wildly overgrown garden with a swing at its heart that meant you could whiz past the leaves on the trees, grazing them with your cheeks. From the attic you could see the shimmering Baltic through the ranks of perpetually rain-soaked spruce trees that reached almost as far as the beach.

One summer morning, as Hans Matti and Otto sat beneath the water tower eating a juicy pear they had pinched from the old Jew who sold fruit at the railway station, a young woman with sunglasses in her hair came up and spoke to them, squealing with delight. Shortly afterwards they were sitting beside her in her landau cabriolet and heading for Cranz, a much more fashionable spot twenty kilometres further up the coast. For the first time in their lives, they were whistling through the sun-drenched Prussian landscape, lime trees to the left and right with white painted rings around their trunks, storks clattering through the foliage above. The woman was constantly stroking their fluttering hair with her free hand.

Under the awning of a beachfront hotel, the mysterious woman bought the two brothers a bowl of vanilla ice cream. A corpulent gentleman in a black bathing costume approached them on the terrace, dripping like an elephant seal. He suddenly let fly at her in angry language full of puffing and hissing sounds. She covered her face with her pale hands, and he then walked away, a freshly lit cigar in his mouth, his towel over his shoulders like a wrestler, muttering under his breath. After he left, the blonde woman, who was clearly upset, gazed at the boys for a long time with red eyes.

Later that afternoon, she sent them home in a baking-hot taxi. As they were leaving, she gave them both a soft leather purse filled with toy soldiers made of amber, which they held as tightly as gold in their sweaty fists. The driver was Polish and said nothing for the entire journey. What year was it? Who was that woman? What happened to her? And the amber soldiers?

Such were the thoughts of Hans Matti as he stood on The Boulevard beside Jacob a couple of months earlier, peering over his glasses at the laboured waltz of the North Sea waves.

He had other things on his mind too, of course, as he was still getting used to the idea of the imminent wedding of his only child.

16

'You must avoid any form of sexual contact for a while,' said Dr Bodisco, washing his hands at a water fountain with a piece of soap that lathered like whipped cream. His loose white coat hung open to reveal a check three-piece suit.

Ludo was climbing the walls with pain. The gunge that had been injected into his pecker with a chrome syringe had set the entire lower half of his body on fire. It must have been that blonde slut he had screwed in her father's car – he was some bigwig at Fokker – a couple of days earlier.

He was getting married in a week. The party, the wedding night... God almighty, how was he going to get himself out of this mess? He could pretend he was totally drunk... Sorry, honey... Go on, then, kisses only... No, please, not tonight... But then there was the honeymoon in Paris too...

The doctor returned to his desk, which was lined with green felt, and started to write a prescription with elegant strokes of his fountain pen, his reading glasses teetering on the tip of his shiny nose.

'How long, Doctor?' Ludo asked in a gravelly voice. 'I mean, is it a question of days or weeks?'

'Weeks, weeks,' the doctor replied calmly. He knew about the wedding, of course. As a matter of fact, that article about his father in the paper not so long ago, that was a nasty piece of work, he continued, changing the subject abruptly. He had known him for years, an excellent man. He had once treated his father for an inflamed hammer toe, did he remember that?

Ludo shook his head, as another demonic jab darted through his groin and tortured member.

As he had understood the article, the doctor resumed, groping at an imaginary tuft of hair on his bald and freckled head, certain parties objected to the wedding. Ha! What a joke! And in this dump of all places! Ludo would be well aware of the scum that used to live round here, he growled, and started to write out a second prescription.

'I'm not really into politics, Doctor,' the hotel-keeper's son babbled, silently imploring him to shut up and get on with the prescriptions. His bride-to-be's parents were perfectly respectable; they had done nobody any—

That wasn't the point, of course, the doctor interrupted without raising his voice even slightly. He had German friends himself. But did he think the Americans or the French were any better? Or the Russians?

The doctor stared at his patient for a moment, expressionlessly.

'Oh, well, the world is full of hypocrites,' the doctor resumed in his hammy tenor, which won him the starring role every year as the darling officer in the local operetta. We were all part of the conspiracy from the day we were born, every generation managing to produce bands of so-called innocent adherents of those who divided the world into 'for' and 'against'. That was the obscenity of it all.

His eyes drifted over to the wall, which was covered in French watercolours – little girls dancing on a rocky beach, slightly risqué. 'And then there's love.'

His own hobby was history. There was a theory, apparently, that saw history as a succession of favours performed for the love of women. Books, paintings, music, even entire countries had been created in response to the erotic charms of the opposite sex. According to the same hypothesis, kingdoms had fallen because of man's longing for sex. Nonsense, of course: women were no better than men; the desire for sex was mutual. Forgive his slightly untoward language, but showing up at the doctor's with syphilis a week before his wedding, he should be able to deal with it.

'Here, I've written the prescriptions out to a chemist in Haarlem. There are too many gossips in this town.'

Ludo had listened timidly to his diatribe, like a condemned man in a courtroom. The doctor handed over two scripts and thanked him for the invitation. He would certainly attend the wedding reception, although he himself had been a bachelor for all of fifty years – by principle and preference. It promised to be something of an occasion, if he had understood correctly.

That guy is completely nuts, Ludo thought, heading towards the town centre under the chestnut trees on Kostverlorenstraat. Who invited him? Could only have been his father.

'I'm not really into politics.' Right, that was by far the wisest strategy for the time being. After the silence of the cocoon, a butterfly must first crawl around as a caterpillar before it can take wing and flutter away, leaving behind the filthy mess that once held it captive.

A truck loaded with yellow wicker chairs and white tables juddered past; the cafés along the beach were officially open but due to

51

the cold weather many had remained closed, and some had yet to be set up.

Ludo looked at his watch: half past twelve. He had arranged to meet his father and a builder in fifteen minutes at the door of the fisherman's cottage that he and Liza would be using as a temporary home. The shower unit, which had arrived from Cologne a week earlier in a stylish white box two metres tall and wrapped in red ribbon, was ready for installation. Although his future mother-in-law had tried to insist on a bath, there was simply not enough room.

Let the old bugger sort it out himself for once; I've got to get to the chemist's first, and then to Edo, the hotel-keeper's son thought, jumping on a blue tram a moment later on Tramstraat. He sat on the back seat and lit a cigarette, and before long the trees adorning the privileged back gardens of Aerdenhout were hurtling past to the rattle of the wheels, all bathed in an abundance of sunlight.

A huddle of blondes in cocktail dresses had assembled under yellow parasols on the lawn in front of a wooden villa. They looked no more than eighteen, but gave the impression that they already had the world in their pockets. First-year students or perhaps even grammar-school kids who had just completed their exams. A good fuck on the kitchen table is what they all need, thought Ludo. Jesus, who did those bitches think they were? Another party was on the go a couple of gardens further along; men only this time, in grey slacks and unbuttoned jackets, just like the ones Felix had taken to wearing.

He hadn't seen his youngest brother since the family supper. Felix spent most of his time in a rented attic in Leiden, studying hard, attending classes. God almighty, 'classes', the miserable word always made him choke. Only retards and pansies studied biology, Edo Novak said. They were the laughing stock of universities the world over. And he should know...

'Tickets, please.' A conductor with the face of a guinea pig was standing in front of him, sweating in a tight uniform jacket, ticket punch in hand.

'Sorry, I just jumped on. I had an urgent appointment at the hospital,' Ludo apologised, a painful wince on his charming face, and showed him Dr Bodisco's violet scribbles, which even a Latin teacher would have had trouble deciphering.

'Fine, OK, I believe you,' the conductor mumbled, as they juddered over the first of Haarlem's canals. He would forget the fine this time... To the Tempelier? That would be thirty cents.

Ludo bought two packets of Lexingtons from a cigarette machine on the corner near the tram stop. Later, walking along Gierstraat, he felt as if he had just recovered from a fever, and realised the full drama of his situation. Jesus, I'm getting married with a fucking ulcer on my dick.

A shaven-headed young man in a spinach-green jacket stood on a chest under the shadow cast by Brinkmann's restaurant on the main square, holding forth at the top of his voice. A handful of people had gathered in a semicircle before him. As Ludo turned away in disgust at the sight of the bloke's degenerate skull, he overheard a few lines of the poem that he was reciting:

And who of us still thinks back to then?
The sledge that glides through dark streets of blue snow,
where once I saw your saddened face slip by
so fleeting and so swift – and where I wept
for love that never was, that had departed.

'Arrest him and shunt him off to a labour camp,' Ludo babbled to himself, disappearing down a dark alley, digging work all the way along it, as if it had just been hit by a comet. Jesus, an ugly bastard, that bloke. A face like seven shades of shit.

Ludo acknowledged for the umpteenth time that he had a serious loathing for anything to do with art. Felix, of course, was the exact opposite. It was like night and day between them. Felix would eat stale bread for a month to be able to buy tickets for some play or

53

other, or, even worse, a concert, where he would listen to the cater-wauling screeches of an orchestra that might have drawn an audi-ence of women but certainly not real men.

Most artists were closet queers, filthy perfumed shitpackers. He had seen enough of them out on the town in Amsterdam. Maybe Felix was… No, he didn't even want to think about it.

'Comrade, come in!' Edo Novak greeted the hotel-keeper's son.

Ludo followed his friend along a dingy corridor, with statues of Our Lady in chalk-white niches on both sides, to the back of the town house that he rented.

'How are you?' the former student asked, turning towards him in a red silk dressing gown in front of a sideboard overwhelmed with clothes.

'Miserable,' the bridegroom-to-be responded. He asked for a whisky and collapsed into a leather armchair, its cushions receiving him gently with a rasp of escaping air.

17

Kati had managed, with a bit of effort, to spend a penny in the shared toilet on the corridor, and was now looking at herself in the wardrobe mirror of her hotel room, the ochre yellow sunlight filtered by Maria Bagman's handstitched curtains, stark naked except for a pair of fluffy white slippers.

Constipation was a scourge that had made her life a misery for the last three years. She had tried spoonfuls of olive oil, yoghurt, bran, all three together, but nothing helped. As she flattened the folds of skin round her navel with her incredibly slender hands – mani-cured by Gabi before she left – she could hear Liza getting into a tizzy about all sorts of things in the room next door.

The walls were ridiculously thin. Kati carefully trimmed a wiry curl or two from her abundant pubic hair with a pair of nail scissors. Her pubic region was pitch black, like a hedgehog in white sand between her thighs, something few would suspect, given her otherwise red tresses. She wondered how many men had taken communion in her humid chapel – she hated dirty talk – and concluded that she could still have any man that she desired.

She put away the scissors and lit a filter cigarette; she then turned on the spot a couple of times and – confronted by the mirror once more – was simply delighted that her nipples were still so manifestly firm, like the buttons on French berets. That whole morning, she'd been unable to get the hideous face of that halfwit child with his mop out of her head, his ugly fish-eyes, and drooling mouth.

'Why didn't you warn me?' Kati snapped at her daughter as she waltzed into the room unannounced a moment later in a yellow dressing gown to ask her mother for some soap. She was determined to wash away the filth between her legs and perfume her entire body in Palmolive. The bride-to-be was terrified that someone might get a whiff of something.

'What do you mean?' Liza responded, eyebrows raised, ignoring her mother's distasteful nakedness.

'Ludo's feeble-minded brother. Did you know that imbecility can run in the family? I don't want a moron for a grandchild, do you understand? Your father and I have built an entire company. We have a right to healthy successors.'

God almighty! Listen to her – she's hysterical. 'Healthy successors' – what was she on about?

Liza herself had come forth from that monstrous body; it had given birth to her, no matter how much she tried to suppress the idea. Moreover, she was the only heir to *Benders Fleischwaren*, and realised she would have to oblige her mother to some extent, or else all hell would break loose at the wedding banquet.

If only she knew I was having my period, Liza thought. So far Ludo had made no physical advances, which she thought at once strange and fortunate. But she wasn't going to be able to fake a headache on their wedding night. Perhaps she could tell him that the doctor had prohibited intimate relations for a while in order to avoid damaging the foetus…

'Well?' Kati asked.

'What do you mean?' Liza repeated. She was on first-name terms with her mother, something Maria had found strange at first until Ludo had explained that it was quite normal in Germany.

'We've granted our permission for this wedding,' Kati stated, still bitterly regretful, if her voice was anything to go by. She had reconciled herself. But Liza should have rid herself of that bastard in her belly. She knew a woman in Cologne. How many months was it? And then she should get pregnant again as quickly as possible by another man. Men never notice that kind of thing. Well?

'I'll think about it,' said Liza, who had nothing to lose one way or the other, but where was *Vati*?

'He's gone to the beach again,' said the sausage-maker's wife. 'He thinks you can see England from The Boulevard. Here, the soap. But be careful. The garbage they use here is like tar. And I don't trust the shops in this godforsaken hole. If you ask me, the whole country gets by on cheap substitutes.'

18

Dressed in blue linen trousers, a casual white shirt and leather sandals, Hans Matti climbed the gently sloping street of restaurants, bistros and souvenir shops towards the beach, binoculars dangling over his belly.

A fragile girl in a yellow silk dressing gown with ornamental stitching was at work in the window of a Chinese shop as he passed by. The sight of her exotic beauty struck him like a punch in the face. Hans Matti suddenly remembered something Ludo had said about women that could be seen in Amsterdam behind purple-lit windows, like dogs in a pet shop.

The sausage-maker lumbered cheerfully over the cobblestones, his face in the sun, murmuring about what he would do with his life if he were still young, knew then what he knew now, and had the same amount of money at his disposal. He had never believed in the romantic dreams of the destitute.

Jacob was such a decent bloke; he earnestly hoped that Ludo had inherited some of his character. The last time Ludo had been in Cologne, Hans Matti had taken him to a bowling club, where his future son-in-law won two games in a row. The members quickly took to the friendly Dutchman. He worked in the family business and was the oldest son – that was at least something. Further, he was the father of his future grandchild. But the economy in Holland still creaked like an arthritic old man, while in Germany it was thundering ahead like a well-oiled machine.

Perhaps Ludo would be interested some time in the future, when he and Kati had retired to a pleasant villa by the sea, somewhere in the south... Oh well, there was time enough for that... He was only fifty after all, still had at least fifteen productive years ahead of him, perhaps even more. As long as Liza made sure her children could also speak decent German, the language of thinkers and poets. That was something this country didn't have, in spite of the charming Dutch temperament and the friendly people, who had exceeded his expectations.

'Yes, a fine figure of a man,' Hans Matti said to himself, walking under the archway of a brick-built hotel to face a stiff breeze on The Boulevard.

Maybe he and Jacob would become real friends. After Otto's death, or rather his disappearance, Hans Matti had never really been able to share his thoughts and feelings with anyone else. With Kati it was out of the question. His wife believed a man should be hard – like her father, a champion wrestler from Dresden whom she had worshipped until the day he died – and that feelings and sentiment only got in the way of doing business and building up the company. In the early years, Kati had defended the company like a mother hen protecting her chicks, until suddenly she had become fed up with it.

Their conversation was usually about business matters; money, staff, unmanageable Liza. The one time they had talked about politics, Kati proceeded to divide the world into two camps: the capitalists and the Communists. When she read in the paper one day that a number of Communists had been arrested in America for treason, she cut out the substantial article, with its photos of the suspects, and spirited it into the factory the following morning.

The two men that happened to bear a slight resemblance to the poor buggers who had been dragged in front of the courts for espionage 10,000 kilometres away both worked in cold storage. In spite of Hans Matti's objections, they finally had to pay the price. After all, revolt and terror always started in private companies, just as it had in Russia. And did Hans Matti imagine those bastards would spare their daughter? It didn't bear thinking about.

Hans Matti loved the sea! Yet the coastline here seemed just as desolate as it had the first time he had seen it, not because of erosion but because of the lack of trees.

No, he preferred the paradise of his youth, where the water was turquoise and the broad sandy beaches meandered into fragrant pinewood forests. Hans Matti saw a boy, a shrimp net over his shoulder, stepping down onto the beach. A melancholy smile appeared under his bristly moustache. He had done exactly the same thing when he was little.

Standing on The Boulevard, the sausage-maker peered through his binoculars and started to scan the horizon, turning the lenses excitedly in the hope of catching a glimpse of England. But all he could make out were the silver scales of the sea, which made him think of a hefty carp, and a single cloud drifting eastwards against a pink-streaked background. It was just like a painting.

He then focused his binoculars, which he had purchased not long before in a first-rate photographer's shop in Aachen, on the solid sand where the waves lapped the shore. A quirky old gentleman, with curly white hair and a walking stick, hobbled along next to his much younger wife, a grey poodle on the leash. The dog managed to break free and scampered, its tail wagging furiously, towards a horse-drawn fish cart. The couple shouted and whistled in desperation.

Hans Matti, who shared his wife's dislike of fish, automatically turned away, and then heard a man asking in reasonable German, 'So, just checking if the sea is still there?'

The sausage-maker turned, let his binoculars fall to his belly, and looked at the face of the young man staring back at him with a grin.

'I beg your pardon?'

'I asked if you were checking if the sea was still there,' the Dutchman repeated with a hint of scorn, sizing him up with appraising eyelids.

Hans Matti noticed that the young man's left ear had been completely ripped off. All that remained was a lumpy mass of flesh, like those growths on the udders of ailing cows that would be brought into his factory from time to time, and could easily be blended into his spicy sausages alongside the healthy meat.

The earless part of the man's skull was covered with a patch of jet-black hair, which flapped in the wind and made him appear even more frightening.

'I beg your pardon?' the sausage-maker said again, suddenly wishing he were somewhere else.

'Austrian, Swiss?' The man before him grinned; the absence of both his upper and lower front teeth had left a gap like a keyhole. Before the war, the place had been crawling with Germans and only Germans, but now it was just the Austrians and the Swiss. Strange, eh?

'Er, yes… Of course, I see what you mean,' Hans Matti murmured sympathetically, and pretended he urgently had to get back to his binoculars. The man asked him where he was from.

'From the city of Cologne,' Hans Matti solemnly informed the unfamiliar passer-by. But he was originally from Rauschen, a little town in the middle of nowhere, near Königsberg. Nobody had heard of it, but…

'Königsberg?' An ominous rattle issued from the one-eared Dutchman's gullet, like bubbles from a newly opened bottle. Königsberg? My God, he had been there! They had had dumplings filled with pork. 'Meat is the best vegetable,' they used to say. He had stuffed himself silly. 'And we had plenty of Polish skirt. Have you ever had a bit of Polish skirt?'

'Excuse me?'

'Have you ever had a bit of Polish skirt?' the man repeated, his sinister eyeballs glaring impudently in Hans Matti's direction. Why was he acting like an idiot? They had both served in the forces of the Führer, hadn't they? He had been open about it – cost him four years of his life… Jesus Christ… Had he also done time?

'I lived in Aachen in those days. I was…'

Hans Matti was saved by a Neptune lookalike in white clogs who shouted at his tormentor from a distance, 'Hey, Prins! What are you up to now? We still have to get the fish cart loaded up. Get over here. You're not paid to natter with strangers!'

The man's rasping roar, broken by the western wind, could have been Icelandic. The sausage-maker hurried past the shops and bistros back to the hotel in a fevered frenzy, his binoculars beating painfully against his breastbone with every step.

How was it possible? Someone was running around this godforsaken place who had been to Königsberg. Was he dreaming? He felt naked, as if the depths of his soul had been exposed, as if a shell that had protected him until now had fallen away.

And he started to look differently at the coastal town, which hadn't troubled him before. What kind of people lived here? His daughter's behaviour had been an endless source of concern since nursery school. What kind of trouble had Liza got him into now?

19

The ice tongs had disappeared into the globe somewhere near Alaska. Edo Novak gulped down his whisky and produced a hoarse blast of air from the bottom of his lungs as if he had burned his mouth.

'Bloody Dutch bitches!' he declared, after Ludo had informed him of his visit to the doctor. He was still in his red silk dressing gown; the nail of his big toe stuck out through a hole in one of his slippers. 'But you have to keep thinking systematically. Rome wasn't built in a day and Carthage wasn't destroyed in a week. Get my drift?'

Ludo puffed on a cigarette with a cardboard filter-tip from a box with Cyrillic lettering that Edo had offered him. The taste of the tobacco was almost intolerable, but he made nothing of it.

Streams of burgundy, blue and ochre daylight filtered into the room through a stained-glass fanlight. Ludo was suddenly faced with the stifling realisation that he would not only be paying a visit to the town hall in the next couple of days but also to the local Catholic church. He had only ever visited the building once. The musty smell and damp walls left him thinking of a crypt. The Bagmans had never practised any sort of religion. Liza, on the other hand, had been tutored in all of the subtleties of the Roman tradition, and Kati had insisted on a blessing at the altar of God. A compromise had been hastily agreed upon.

'How are the arrangements for the banquet going?' Edo Novak stared with a frown at a slightly bedraggled dress suit, which was draped over a coat hanger in a shadowy corner and looking as if someone were still wearing it.

'Excellent,' Ludo scoffed. His father had been running around like a circus director for the best part of a week.

The hotel-keeper's son was struggling to hide the nauseating effects of the Russian cigarette. Or was it the crap the doctor had pumped into his loins? After taking a course of penicillin for shingles, his mother had never been able to drink another drop of milk, although she had been raised on buckets of the stuff in Friesland.

'Now, now, now...' Edo scolded him, pretending to pout his lips in reprimand. Honour your father and your mother. It was a biblical commandment. Was Ludo actually familiar with that outstanding book of fairy tales? Without waiting for an answer, Edo proceeded to inform Ludo that it was high time he read something. He had faith in his dedication. The tide was turning, but without theoretical foundations he would get nowhere. Had he finished the book he lent him last week?

He had started it but found it a little boring, to be honest, Ludo confessed. *Das Kapital*, which he first thought had to do with accountancy and business, took him all of nine months to finish, and he hadn't understood a word of it.

'Jesus Christ... Boring? Do you know what's boring?' Edo stood up, fluttered over to the bookcase and pulled a leather-bound book from the shelf, his splayed nostrils quivering. 'Look, this is boring, words, lines, grammar.' His knuckles came down on the cover with a hollow angry thump. But not the immortal masterpieces of Maxim Gorky, he added, although he actually considered the famous Russian with his drooping moustache to be a miserable author and a conceited fraud.

Edo continued his performance. He had read Marx three times in German, cover to cover, and once in Russian! Did Ludo think it was easy? It was unremitting torment. But there was no pleasure without pain. Remind me who said that. The historian headed back to the globe, flipped open the northern hemisphere, and the Scotch reappeared. 'Did you finally manage to get a look at that will?' he asked in a subdued tone.

'Honestly, everything is just fine. And Liza is like putty in my hands. Why do you keep asking?'

Edo rubbed his unshaven chin and stared at the hotel-keeper's son, for whom he felt both a pragmatic sympathy and an instinctive contempt, with a twinkle in his eye. 'Did I ever tell you about the night I was entertained by an Uzbek belly dancer in Moscow?' he enquired, falling back into his easy chair, glass in hand.

'No,' replied Ludo. He glimpsed at his watch, thought about the chemist, but didn't want to miss a story from his friend who was intimately acquainted with the ways of the world.

'I was with a bunch of Chilean comrades in a Volga driving to Red Square. The snow was terrible and then... Yeah, that was really funny... God almighty, what's the matter with you? Your face looks like a pumpkin all of a sudden... Wait, I'll fetch you some vodka... Vodka can drive out the devil...'

20

Jacob walked into the town hall reception room dressed in a handsome blue suit from 'The Colours of Mozart', which he was also planning to wear on the big day. He presented himself at the desk, only to hear that the mayor had been forced to cancel their appointment at the last minute.

'That's strange.'

'Nothing of the sort,' was the brusque response.

'That's extremely strange,' the hotel-keeper persisted, gripped by an unpleasantly apprehensive feeling. He had spoken to him on the phone only half an hour ago.

The receptionist lifted a receiver, bleated, 'Mr Bagman is here to see you,' and returned the receiver to its cradle. Councillor Nederleven was willing to see him. He would be there in a couple of minutes. Would he like to take a seat?

Jacob walked over to a bench, about to sit down, but changed his mind, his attention drawn to a series of black-and-white photographs of the seaside resort before the war. Hotel d'Orange, the mustard-coloured houses along The Boulevard, the old water tower, the historical buildings surrounding it. They were all gone, had either been blown up or knocked down, reduced to ashes. And what were they putting up in their place?

He examined the colour prints on the wall next to him, depicting projects that had been recently completed, brick and concrete monsters in the worst possible taste. But protest made no difference, because the people had to be housed as quickly as possible as part of the National Reconstruction Programme, in glorified chicken sheds if need be. Hideous housing complexes for private-sector workers had also appeared where the synagogue and the circus theatre used to be. Not even a quarter of them had sold.

'Good afternoon, Jacob!' Herman Nederleven, the youthful socialist councillor, strode towards him across the marble floor in a pair of highly polished shoes. 'Sorry to have kept you, but I just had The Hague on the line. The ministry wants final plans for the race-track development by next week. Come along, this way... Shall I order us some coffee?

'Please don't go to any trouble, Herman,' Jacob mumbled good-naturedly. His unpleasant sense of apprehension had completely disappeared.

He followed the councillor through the sunlit but agreeably cool corridors to his office. They passed the council chambers with its prominent paintings and cherry-wood panelling, where Ludo and Liza would pledge their vows on Friday under the local coat of arms. 'Till death do us part' resounded in Jacob's head, as he slowed down for a second and recalled his own wedding day, then the cheapest option available in Amsterdam. It now seemed a century ago.

Councillor Nederleven invited the hotel-keeper to sit down, took his place behind an enormous desk piled high with paperwork, and asked what had brought Jacob to the town hall.

'Didn't the mayor tell you?'

Jacob and the councillor were on first-name terms. They had both been members of the same party for years, the only political movement that concerned itself with the man in the street. Although Jacob had recently started to collect Chinese porcelain, he would never forget that he'd begun picking potatoes on a farm as far north as you could get. The gentleman farmer for whom he had worked had a penchant for silver and antiques and the man's collection had awakened something in Jacob that no one would ever have suspected: a receptiveness to beauty; the desire to beautify life as much as he could.

'It's been insanely busy all morning. I heard something about a German brass band. But I'm sure you understand that such a thing would be out of the question. The wound is yet to heal, Jacob... I don't have to explain that to you of all people. Are you sure you don't want some coffee?'

'Is it still fresh?' Jacob sniffed. The penny dropped and he understood everything: the mayor had delegated the dirty work to the councillor.

'You know what I mean,' Nederleven specified dryly.

The beach will soon be full of German tourists, Jacob countered with a healthy dose of reality. It was true, he made his living from the Krauts, and if Nederleven was aware of the amount of local tax and other dues he had to pay each year as the owner of a business, he would also be aware that the local authority survived indirectly on much the same income and that it ultimately paid his salary as councillor.

'My salary is paid by the government,' Nederleven subtly corrected his fellow party member. His face broke into a nondescript smile, neither good-natured nor ill, neither cynical nor comic, and as such completely incomprehensible. It was the same inscrutable smile he had once seen, sitting next to Nederleven in the burgundy velvet of the Moulin Rouge.

In those days the councillor had been a geography teacher at the vocational school. One day Mr Monjoux had approached him on behalf of the local trade association and asked him to organise a trip to Paris. He had chosen to study French at college and was one of the few people in the town who understood the language and could even speak it with a bit of effort.

The rooms in the hotel in the Rue de Coulaincourt, where the trade association had reserved lodgings for three nights at full board, were simple and clean. But for Herman Nederleven – thirty years of age and smouldering with ambition – nothing was good enough. When he detected a couple of residual hairs in his washbasin on the second day after lunch, he took it out on the girl at Reception in a most inappropriate manner.

They breakfasted every morning amid the aroma of *café au lait* served in sturdy white cups. The future councillor had a comment to make with every sip, however, muttering that the service had been much better when he had visited Provence with his parents. When Jacob passed around a hat for the hotel staff on their last evening, Herman Nederleven had refused to contribute; the service had been poor for one thing, and, secondly, as a matter of principle: as a socialist he believed that a good wage was the responsibility of the employer and not the paying customer.

'What I mean,' councillor Nederleven resumed in a conciliatory tone, avoiding the hotel-keeper's eyes, 'is that I fully understand your request but I'm afraid we really can't give permission.'

'May I ask on what grounds?' Jacob enquired, his temples reddening, his hands on his lap, his veins pulsing.

'Public order. And, on top of that, the recent notice about you in the paper...' Herman Nederleven hesitated and looked up at the portrait of the Queen on the wall, his eyelids fluttering. He knew, of course, that it was all nonsense, gossip, but that was the way the world thought nowadays: there's no smoke without fire. Or was he mistaken? People tended to react in the most simple and primitive ways. And the more conservative they are... Bah, surely he didn't need to explain any further?

Jacob, who had initially pushed the newspaper that Maria had given him back to her side of the table unread – as if it contained the obituary of a loved one that he preferred not to acknowledge – was overcome with rage. Not sadness but rage.

'Jesus Christ, Nederleven, what are you saying?' The hotel-keeper's right fist crashed to the desk with a quivering thud. They had known each other for years, had shared the same concern for their fellow human beings, and had been in Paris together, as good friends...

'Now, now, now, Mr Bagman, what *are* you saying?' The councillor's face hardened, his voice suddenly anxious and formal. 'You realise you are speaking to me in my capacity as councillor? I hold public office. Surely you're not attempting to blackmail me?'

'Blackmail? What do you mean?' Jacob genuinely had no idea what his political cohort was implying. But when he looked up and caught a glimpse of an answer in the councillor's deep-set eyes, everything suddenly became clear. He was appalled. Why in God's name does he hold such a low opinion of me? Blackmail?

He had only been alluding to Nederleven's address, delivered six months before, under a white banner with a red rose in the main hall of Hotel New Deluxe, a lecture on the importance of national unity, and the further expansion of the idea of Europe. The banner had read: TOGETHER AS ONE!

That was all Jacob had wanted to recall, rather than the time he had seen him climb a narrow staircase to his room with a gangly French girl at one-thirty in the morning, the entire trade association already long in their beds, heads buzzing from champagne, Jacob having left his room for a moment to go to the communal toilet down the corridor. The teacher had 'caught in the act' written all over him, but Jacob had simply lifted a finger to his smiling lips and closed his eyes benevolently. It was the same girl the future councillor had lambasted at the reception desk the previous afternoon.

Some things in this world, in which life was short and only the eternity of death was certain, were simply beyond understanding.

21

The world was an upturned inkpot peppered with the silver glitter of the traffic and golden stars when Liza arrived in Amsterdam on a cold and rainy September evening.

She had hurtled down the stairs six hours earlier with nothing but a pair of black pumps and some lipstick in her linen bag, her mother screaming after her. After sprinting 600 metres up the road, she had stuck out her hand at the first set of headlights to emerge from the mist.

Before she knew it she was seated inside the warm cabin of a truck. The driver had frizzy hair and a reddish horseshoe moustache that dangled under his nose and around his mouth. He had a strong Berlin accent, although he said he came from Düsseldorf where he had a wife and two boys.

'The oldest is the best in the team. I used to be a good footballer myself, but what with the war and everything... I'm hoping Ulli will turn professional. They earn decent wages abroad these days. Where are you heading?'

'Aachen, please,' requested Liza, no idea what she should do. But as if there was some being hovering about her that had whispered advice in her ear, she added, 'I want to go to the Netherlands, to Amsterdam.'

'That's lucky, so do I...' A cigarette fell from the trucker's grinning lips in a rain of ash; he groped around for the burning butt, cursing under his breath, causing the truck to slalom wildly all over the road. 'Excuse me, do you smoke?'

'No,' Liza lied, observing an unpleasant glint in the driver's eyes. His black irises seemed to leer at one another, and he stank. She would have preferred to get out there and then, but it was too late. The man had already driven onto the main road. Shortly afterwards they crossed the border, and the truck had to drive through curtains of rain and spray that made a terrible racket inside the cabin.

'Rain,' the trucker growled. 'I hate this country. It rains here all the time. Do you come here often? You don't mind me asking?'

'I have an uncle in Amsterdam,' Liza lied again, trembling like a bird in the passenger seat. He lived in a windmill by the canal. He expected her around eleven that evening. When were they going to get there?

'In a windmill by the canal? Never seen anything like that before in Amsterdam. *Scheisse!*'

A navy Fiat suddenly emerged from behind the wall of rain and into the hazy glare of the headlights. The truck driver slammed on the brakes, yanked at the gear stick and twisted the steering-wheel like a madman, braking a second time to avoid a crash.

Liza, who always preferred to sit in the back of her father's car, stifled a couple of squeals; they drove past the Dutch idiot amid the bluster of his expletives and aggressive honking. Once they were back on the unlit roads of Limburg, the driver switched on the radio.

The sausage-maker's daughter closed her ears to the disgusting sentimental drivel. She had the impression that nothing was real, even though she knew that it was.

Liza had only just turned twenty-two, but was often paralysed by the idea that her entire life had passed her by. A couple of hours earlier, she had threatened to stab her mother with a kitchen knife, and not for the first time either, although her father – away on yet another of his business trips to Hamburg – never believed his wife's reports. Liza was the apple of his eye – as far as he was concerned, she could do no wrong.

It was thus in silent resignation that Hans Matti Bender had collected his daughter from the school in Karlsruhe where girls were prepared for a career in tourism or fashion, this choice determined in the second year. She was easily the oldest in her class, but because of her enchanting appearance – the baby fat had not yet completely disappeared from her round face – her age had never posed a problem. The difficulty was that she had brought the prestigious institution, where even Swiss parents sent their children, into disrepute.

His name was Heinrich, and he was a former athlete employed at the school to teach PE, one of the establishment's core subjects alongside French and English. By the end of the first week, Liza had already heard the whispers along the long monastic corridors that this half-Italian jock, who combined an angular Teutonic physique with a cascade of dark shiny curls and was straight out of a Titian painting, organised trips to 'paradise' for certain favoured students.

Paradise consisted of a musty, windowless shed that housed the sports equipment, where Heinrich would take one of his students every Friday afternoon without fail, after the school had emptied out at three. He mostly settled his prey on the leather seat of the vaulting horse, and before long they would either be underneath him or on top of him thrashing about with pleasure. Heinrich was expert in every sexual technique, an erotic gymnast.

The heavenly contractions of his biceps, his washboard stomach and agile tongue all provided his pupils with something they could reflect upon for the rest of their lives, once they had married one of the local men, perhaps twenty years their senior, bald and flabby and with a tongue that was only designed to curse the stock-market figures and swear at waiters when they brought the wrong wine, sending them back for another bottle.

Heinrich confined himself to the best-looking girls, which meant that he was playing with fire, as he of course well knew, but couldn't help himself. From time to time he would take one of the less attractive girls – for fun, and to give a little hope to the ugly.

The PE teacher preferred Liza to lean forward over the lowest of the parallel bars, her wrists clutched in his vice-like hands, her thighs pushed further and further apart by his knees, while he took her from behind in a tender frenzy, she looking back at him every now and then through her wild hair, ecstasy and complete submission all over her face.

Maybe it was because Liza had matured earlier than the other students, maybe it was something else, but by the fourth time he had lured her into his den the muscular idol had actually fallen in love with the sausage-maker's daughter, and she with him.

One day he stuffed a message in her coat, suggesting that she go with him to Baden-Baden. They spent two nights in a hotel behind the Lichtentaler Allee, looking out on white acacias and trees whose branches meandered whimsically, as in a foreign land, distant and exotic. They made love relentlessly in the swimming pool on the third floor, which Heinrich locked from the inside with his brass key. They even did it once on the springboard, which bounced up and down like a quivering oar.

They had barely arrived back in Karlsruhe when the German-Italian was summoned to see the rector who fired him on the spot, triumphantly brandishing a crumpled ball of paper with the words '*Meine kleine verrückte Katze…*' Liza was next to appear before the one-man tribunal. Bald as a billiard ball, Herr Doktor Posendorff – who taught Religious Education once a week and had written a hefty tome on the eating habits of the ancient Romans, obligatory reading for every pupil – had insisted that Liza describe her sexual escapades with his former employee in full. 'Do you hear me, Miss? Every last detail…'

The rector shook his head in dismay at Liza's account, gasping in shock on occasion. Then he suddenly appeared to have had enough. He sprang to his feet with a military posture, informed Liza that she was a disgrace to the entire school, and that she had three days to get her things together and leave.

A colourful parade of images marched through Liza's fevered mind. She had dozed off, but the sudden silence of the engine and the absence of rain on the windscreen brought her back with a jolt to the cabin of the truck. The trucker yanked angrily on his handbrake. Liza looked on as he straightened himself, unzipped his trousers and pulled out his hideous thing.

'Please, I still have a two-hour drive ahead of me,' the panting trucker begged, his moustache quivering beneath his working-class nose. 'And the relief every time... it's just what a man...'

Liza had had to fight and the trucker had fought back, his ridiculous member still hanging out of his trousers. He grabbed at the damp clothes covering her body, snarling that she was no more than a dirty whore. Liza bit his wrist like a dog and wrestled her way out of the cabin, wrenching her linen bag from his grimy clutches with both arms.

For the second time that evening, Liza ran through the cold rain in the hope of finding something better. Her fretful sobbing sounded just like her mother's had the night the air-raid siren had sounded over Aachen and she had cursed everything English and American to hell and back, not realising that happiness and the end of the war were just around the corner.

22

Someone was indeed playing Hawaiian guitar on the terrace at Bol's café, but that wasn't the real reason why Ludo and Liza had gone to the beach. They now had only thirty-six hours before the wedding and there were still so many things to discuss that other young lovers would have found a week too short.

A pleasure boat bobbed up and down on the waves, immediately beyond the first sandbank. Two men with landing nets stood in the tidal channel, gracefully loading shells on to a cart being edged along the beach by a horse. Seagulls, the white rats of the skies, flocked and squawked around it.

'What are those guys doing?' Liza peered at the panorama beyond the rim of her sunglasses, slowly slurping on her bottle of chocolate milk through a straw.

'Collecting shells,' said Ludo mutedly.

'What for?' asked Liza, who had never been interested in the physical exertions of labourers, but sensed that something was bothering Ludo. She wondered anxiously what it might be, and tried to keep the conversation going.

'They make glass with them, I believe, and use them for garden paths. A meagre living for the poorest of the poor.'

The Nivea parasol flapped rhythmically in the wind over their heads; the terrace's wooden decking felt fantastically coarse beneath Liza's bare feet, smelling of sorbet. A ship drifted on the horizon, smoke trailing from its funnel, as in a child's drawing.

'It's cruelty to animals,' Liza suddenly declared. Did the poor horse have to stand there the whole time? Did Ludo actually know what kept a huge ship like that afloat? No? Their parents seemed to be getting on well together, didn't he think?

Ludo gestured at a waiter and ordered another beer. He was thinking about Edo's advice: make sure she does exactly what you say; be a little hard and insensitive now and then; the harder you are, the readier she'll be to eat out of your hand. As if he didn't know!

'I tried on my wedding dress again this morning,' Liza whispered, dreamily. She was curious about his outfit, though. Any chance of a quick peek?

The way she spoke German mixed with a word or two of Dutch excited Ludo. She had a truly sexy voice. It needled him that he had to take those bloody pills, that he was still infectious, that he couldn't just take her... in the fucking toilet... He still had to manufacture some kind of excuse for the next couple of days.

'What did you say?'

'Why are you screwing with me, Liza?' Ludo interrogated, his sombre face turning in fabricated anger to his fiancée.

'W-what do you mean?' Liza stammered. She took off her sunglasses, her fingers trembling, her nose lifting as she glared, wide-eyed, at her future husband.

Ludo watched in silence as the Hawaiian guitar player – a midget with a cheerful face who had rolled his trousers halfway up his aspirin-white calves – trudged through the sand towards the next beach café.

He then directed a whole series of calculatedly cold accusations at Liza. She wasn't to be trusted; she hadn't fulfilled her promises; surely, if she loved him, she would have given him the papers that he'd requested about her father's business by now. Did he have to ask her again? He wanted an idea of the company's assets, its worth, its turnover and profit.

Liza begged him to forgive her. She had already asked the accountant three times, but he always gave her the same answer: 'Fräulein Bender, what are you so worried about? One day you will be a millionaire. May both your parents live to be a hundred!'

'Did he say millionaire?' Ludo asked, his eyebrows raised, musing on the idea. Then suddenly his expression changed to one of sheer joy as he saw his fair-haired drinking buddy Elias Bol making his way towards them.

The two thirty-year-olds shared the same fate – their families were both in the catering business and they were both oldest sons. They routinely bumped into each other in bars in Haarlem and Amsterdam. There was no escaping the catering business. A closed economic circuit, whatever they earned in it they spent in it.

'Hey, big man. May I introduce my very dearest future wife?' Ludo greeted him with a bar-room drawl.

Elias Bol smiled, his teeth as white as snow, and looked down at the blonde beside Ludo, in the shade of his mighty torso. She reminded him of something sweet he'd tried in its manifold different flavours.

'Liza Bender,' said the slightly blushing girl from Cologne to the beach playboy. Was he a friend of Ludo's?

Absolutely, they'd known each other for years, he responded in rusty German. They had always talked a lot about politics. The planet was going to rack and ruin and the politicians were to blame. A shower of thieves and profiteers, didn't she think?

'My father,' said Liza, delighted that Elias's arrival had cut short her painful conversation with Ludo, 'my father says it's the first time ever we've had decent people running our country. I'm not so sure, it doesn't really interest me that much. Hey, are you coming to the wedding the day after tomorrow?'

Let me show you something, Elias responded with a cheerful grin, and, as if it had all been planned, withdrew the card of invitation from the back pocket of his khaki trousers and flipped it open.

It was a classy invitation – black letters on marbled white paper. At Maria's suggestion, a green-stemmed poppy had been printed in the upper right-hand corner, otherwise it might have appeared a little stuffy.

The text read:

Mr and Mrs Jacob Bagman
request the honour of your presence
at a wedding banquet
to celebrate the marriage of
Miss Liza Bender
to their son
Mr Ludo Jacques Bagman
in the Main Hall of Hotel New Deluxe
at eight o'clock in the evening

Live music and a celebrity attraction

'The weather's supposed to stay like this for the next few days,' Elias observed. He wouldn't mind such weather for his own wedding, but sadly none of the girls wanted him. The luck of the draw, no female flesh for him, eh...?

'You're kidding!' Liza declared, her eyes wide open in complete surprise. The sausage-maker's daughter took the Viking before her at his word, didn't know he was a born joker, poking fun whenever he got the chance. It was a gift. Even his best friends would fall for his pranks, every time.

'Ludo beat me to it, otherwise I'd have chosen you,' Elias responded, stoking the fire a little more. Oh, well...

'You can have her,' Ludo offered, without batting an eyelid. 'Half a million, and she's all yours.'

'For so little?'

'OK. A million, but take her now, if you don't mind.'

'It's a deal!'

'Good,' said Ludo. As far as he was concerned, they could sign the paperwork before the day was out.

Liza tickled the instep of one foot with the painted red toes of the other, glanced back and forth like a little kitten between two chirping birds, put on her most charming smile, but in actual fact couldn't understand a word of what was going on.

23

The report in *The Boulevard*, which had set tongues wagging in the town in recent days, and left others conscience-stricken, insinuated that Jacob Bagman had paid for the Hotel New Deluxe with money derived from illegal wartime transactions.

'Did our fellow townsman, whose son – nota bene – is about to marry a German, enrich himself in secret c/o his Jewish contacts? We have evidence that he did.' The two-column piece ended with the statement: *'The investigation continues.'*

It was a perfect example of gutter-press gossipmongering that no one could refute. Strangest of all was that *The Boulevard*, in which the disappearance of a cat tended to make headline news, had never previously attempted to publish reports of such social consequence. Perhaps it was all due to the new editor-in-chief, a certain Joris Pakhoed, who had earlier replaced Herman Nederleven as geography teacher at the vocational school when the latter had become a councillor. The presence of the 'nota bene' led some to suspect that Pakhoed himself was behind this piece of journalistic ingenuity.

When Jacob did finally get acquainted with the article's content, he lapsed into a silence that Maria found almost unbearable. This was followed by a constant low groan, similar to the sound he had made the day the Star of David was daubed on the pavement in front of his antique shop. What proof did they have?

Fiscal measures introduced by the government after the war, making old money more or less worthless, had resolved a number of problems in the last few years. But gold and diamonds were harder than hard cash. And Jacob had indeed received a bag of gold coins, two kilos' worth, all told.

Three weeks after a terrible incident with Felix, Jacob had accompanied his only surviving relative to a safe house north of Drenthe.

He had only seen his uncle four times in his youth. His father's younger brother by seven years, Simon was always on the move, up to all sorts, until one day he took off for the East Indies where he amassed a small fortune before moving to South Africa. In the spring of 1937 he was arrested in Cape Town and deported on a Dutch merchant ship to Rotterdam, where his debtors encircled him on the quay like flies round a rotten cadaver. His life thereafter was dominated by one thing: escape from the country he so totally hated. But, in spite of all his efforts, he never managed to escape.

Uncle Simon had failed to show up when Jacob and Maria got married, and he never sent a card. For Jacob, it was more or less like sitting next to a stranger that hot August day as they lurched along in the back of a covered lorry, thrown together like sacks of potatoes at every bend in the road.

'I've been a bastard all my life,' Uncle Simon had confessed as they rumbled through what appeared to be a forest, branches lashing the steel cabin like circus whips. 'I've only ever thought of myself, never wanted children, but I always had a good time, let me tell you!' He didn't believe in God or the bible; that was just haggling with the hereafter. Besides, only an idiot would think he could work his way into the black after a life in the red. Or the other way round. He was doomed; he knew it. He was grateful to his nephew for his help, but it wouldn't make any difference...

'Don't say that, Uncle,' Jacob implored, his voice hoarse from the strain of it all. The thought of being held up at a control post, of the tarpaulin being pulled back, of staring into the barrel of a gun, nearly drove him crazy. Maria had no idea about any of it. Jacob had told her that he was on a two-day business trip, but he was no hero, and it suddenly dawned on him that he didn't want to die.

'But I have no regrets,' Uncle Simon continued his own epitaph. That was probably the worst part: he would do it all over again, his whole ludicrous life. He had been unfair to people, cheated God knows how many of them, men and women alike. But he had always slept soundly, all the same. He was driven by a sinister force, a terrible undercurrent, a black energy he was aware of but could not defeat. Was he, perhaps, a degenerate? Thank God he had no children; his bloodline had come to an end. Now he was doomed. His intuition had never failed him. Maybe he should just get out of the truck and hand himself over. Maybe that was the...

'No!' Jacob shouted, having reached the end of his tether.

Three angry thumps followed from the cabin in front. Just before they reached a village somewhere south of Assen, Uncle Simon had abruptly got to his feet, started to rummage around in the antelope-leather suitcase he had personally heaved into the back of the truck before they had set off, cursing its weight and his miserable plight.

Jacob suddenly felt something heavy in his hands.

'Here, take it. All my gold coins! Make sure you and your family survive this nightmare. This is all I can do for you. You're lucky, you don't have my twisted mind. It could have been different, though – nephews are often like their uncles... Hey, what's all that about? There's no need to cry... Jacob Abraham Bagman, stop crying this minute... Jesus, I beg you... if there's one thing I can't bear—'

24

'Why are we doing this, Ludo?'

They had crept down the stairs, slipped outside and were now standing in the dank alley next to the house, ready for the next hurdle: how to open the gate without its making any noise. 'Hey, why don't you answer me?'

'Shut up! Here, hold him!'

Ludo handed the baby to his brother, his mouth taped shut like a parcel for the post.

The gate opened without its dreaded creak. Ludo peered right and left into the street, where a milky-white sun had just appeared over the horizon. He had decided it was safer to carry out his plan now rather than a couple of hours earlier. Darkness might have been better, but there would still have been a lot of cars and motorbikes on the road.

'Are we really going through with this?' whined Louis, handing Felix, who, amazingly enough, was still sound asleep, back to his brother.

Ludo simply repeated the instructions: they had to get to the post office, where Louis was to stand watch behind the advertising pillar and keep an eye out for any traffic on Haltestraat. Two bars stayed open there until the early hours of the morning, their roller blinds down.

It's a sin, thought Louis. Ludo had told him that the Devil had taken possession of Felix, and that he had to be abandoned on the street by the light of the full moon. It was the only way to save their family. Did he know who the Devil was?

'The enemy of God,' said Louis.

In a flurry of excitement, Ludo considered the splendid promises that the Prins brothers had made to him: membership in the Nationale Jeugdstorm (our father can organise everything), Betsy with her delicious marzipan breasts, and...

'Now, idiot!' Ludo snarled, raising his hand. They set off at full speed, racing past the shadows cast by a couple of parked trams to reach the chestnut trees by the post office, where a cluster of dozing pigeons cooed and fluttered into the air, suddenly disturbed by their arrival. They froze in the doorway of the post office, puffing and panting. A second setback followed a few moments later: a black Mercedes turned out of Haarlemstraat and drove towards them, its loose bumper clattering along the road like a tin can. The car circled the square in front of the town hall a couple of times and then came to a halt. The engine stopped. An abrupt, almost tangible silence descended over the town.

A handsome man with Brylcreemed hair and a dress suit – Ludo immediately recognised Mr Prins – stepped out of the car, walked around it in his black patent leather shoes, pulled open the passenger door and grunted something at the passenger.

'No!' an alto voice blared from the interior.

Mr Prins wormed halfway into the car and yanked a blonde girl in a silver dress by the arm with a single mighty heave onto the street, roaring, 'Get out, filthy whore!'

Her head seemed detached from her shoulders, like those felt-covered dogs they used to sell by the hundred as souvenirs on The Boulevard. Mr Prins angrily slammed the passenger door, hurried back to the driver's seat, and raced off at high speed.

The girl wasn't much more than sixteen. Ludo found the sight of her decadently painted face extremely attractive. She looked around drunkenly, lurched forward on her high heels, and twisted her ankle, her skinny arms and legs crashing to the ground.

The two brothers watched the incident with bated breath. Felix was awake by this time. He stared at Ludo fearfully but didn't put up the least resistance, as if he were possessed by an angel instead of the Devil, an angel whispering that he had nothing to be afraid of.

The girl sat on the street, her pale starfish hands with red varnished nails in her lap. She suddenly burst into tears, scrambled to her feet, and slunk across the square under the knaggy chestnut trees, her party shoes dangling like pistols in her hands.

Once she had disappeared from sight, Ludo rushed out of the doorway, deposited the mummified Felix on the granite tiles in front of the town hall fountain, and planted a crown of brambles on his tiny head.

'Let's get out of here!' he barked at Louis, and both of them took to their heels.

When Maria Bagman realised a couple of hours later that Felix had disappeared from his cradle, she was momentarily paralysed. 'Jacob!' she screamed, followed by an agonising shriek.

The words 'THIS IS WHAT THE DIRTY JEWS DID TO JESUS!' were scribbled in capital letters on a piece of cardboard found that morning by a street sweeper next to the abandoned baby. The town council immediately notified the local press. A few days later, a photo of Felix trussed up in a blanket was spread across three font-page columns of *The Boulevard*.

Grunting with every comma, a policeman grudgingly typed up the report on an ailing typewriter in a sweltering room, exposing his mouthful of fillings every now and then and gaping at a calendar on the wall that depicted a violet mountain landscape. There were no suspects and no witnesses. Jacob and Maria had both read the document twice, their lips moving, their fingers tracing every line, and then signed it timidly. They then had to wait an hour before they could collect their child. The infant's lips appeared a little tender but he was otherwise in perfect health.

'Another signature here, please,' grumbled an official. Jacob knew the man, who was a decent enough chap, a hard worker with a large family who had often rented mattresses from him in the past. Now he was deeply embarrassed, and tried to conceal it by putting on an air of haughtiness. 'Try taking better care of your kids next time, Bagman.'

Felix was fourteen before his parents dared to tell him about the dreadful escapade, but as he had already heard all about it by then on the grapevine, he just shrugged his shoulders. 'I remember seeing Ludo's teeth glinting. Suddenly, I was lying on the ground. I must have dreamt it all. How old was I, then? Barely seven months! I must have imagined it.'

Of course, of course... He must have imagined it.

25

The evening before the Benders were expected, Jacob phoned his son at university in Leiden and told him that he'd truly appreciate it if he could be present for the occasion.

Leafing through a book about species of South American butterfly that he'd borrowed from the library that afternoon, Felix told his father that it was simply impossible. He had two classes the next day and an important experiment; the professors would be absolutely opposed to any absence.

'Professors,' Jacob mumbled a couple of times. His son mixed with professors. 'OK, that's fine, son. And how about the day after?' persisted the hotel-keeper. He had a plan. In addition to the performance by the pseudo-Hungarian, he had something else up his sleeve.

Fine, he promised to be there. Felix hung up and peered out the attic window at the canal. A couple of ducks were playing on the water amid the pale pink leaves of Japanese cherry blossom. Poor creatures, snared and shipped from China to France, slaughtered, seasoned, sautéd and scoffed. Wasn't it time he became a vegetarian? How can you study God's creations and enjoy eating them at the same time?

But the dreadful and dull fact remained that Felix was always hungry. The portions in the refectory were never big enough. During a feast in honour of the royal family, a limitless supply of meatballs in tomato sauce was on offer, and he had gone back for both seconds and thirds. He stuffed his face with chocolate bars and almond slices in the cafeteria, and couldn't resist when the herring cart went by. It amazed him that he remained so thin, so athletic, without the slightest trace of fat.

The hotel-keeper's son appeared at the university every day without fail wearing his faded green jacket; he never missed a class. He avoided student life, which made him seem boring and tiresome to others. Mr Monjoux's tailoring didn't quite meet Leiden's usual standards. His raincoat, which his father had worn when he worked for the occupier during the war, looked like it belonged to a Russian deserter from the cinema newsreels.

Early on, the odd student union member had commented on his appearance, but Felix simply stared at them in silence with his icy, Siberian gaze until the arsehole in question shut up. He wasn't only intellectually superior to the majority of his fellow male students but also sexually superior. They could smell it, somehow. It was the inescapable law of the kennel. With hair the colour of sun-bleached corn and fine facial features, which even in primary school had seemed to guard a secret, he was an object of desire among the girls, though the first-year student didn't pay any of them the least attention. On one occasion, three different girls had invited him to a party at a castle outside Utrecht. Felix had managed to fob them all off with excuses, feigned illnesses, problems with his exams, physically and mentally in peak condition all the while; he occasionally pondered taking two or three degree courses instead of just one.

Arabic, perhaps? Did that world of minarets, donkeys, sugar-sweet dates and swaying palms sited on the horizon of a searing desert plain really exist? A fellow student, an ornithologist and collector of fossils, had spent six years in Morocco as a child. Felix would have given anything to have lived in that magical place for a couple of years. Casablanca! He had never been beyond Maastricht, where he and his father had once collected an antique silverware cabinet that was now propped up against the restaurant's panelled wall.

'You're off your rocker, Bagman,' scorned the vicar's son that partnered him on an experiment (who was always bragging about his own sexual successes with women) after he'd rejected the third invitation with a shrug of the shoulders.

'What do you mean?' Felix mumbled in response, a pipette full of violet liquid between his slender fingers.

Amalia Swellengrebel was without question the first prize in this tired little town: her dad was rich, a big cheese at Credit Lyonnaise in Amsterdam, and she was as horny as Cleopatra. 'I'm telling you, she could suck the sheet off the bed through your arsehole (here he held his right fist in front of his half-open mouth excitedly), honestly. Hey, surely you're not…?' The vicar's son's mouth widened and thinned.

'Shit, my pipette's leaking,' Felix anxiously interrupted, and indeed there was liquid dripping over his books and on to the marbled folder that held his detailed notes.

Felix had devised a plan to specialise in tropical agriculture and botany after his degree. There was a possibility he'd have to transfer to Wageningen, but he wasn't sure yet.

Now that the country had unfortunately been obliged to give up the

East Indies and the faculty had removed Colonial Law from the curriculum for good, Felix figured that the study of biology was his best gateway to exotic distant shores. As a child, he was always playing in the dunes; he knew every shrub and thistle. But the serenity of the Dutch landscape paled into insignificance alongside the romance of a Brazilian fern or a date palm. Felix visited the botanical gardens nearly every day. As he walked around in the warm womb of the hothouse, he could hear the screech of rainforest monkeys, smell the aroma of fresh coconut and lime juice in the compost, and he dreamt of sunrises over distant bays, where flamingo-pink coral reefs flourished.

Studying came easily to him and left him ample time to read or spend whole afternoons playing his downstairs neighbour's battered old piano. Bokma was from Groningen, a long-haul helmsman who was generous with his house keys. Felix's life would thus have been one of extraordinary balance and happiness, notwithstanding his feelings of guilt towards his family, but for one thing.

While Louis washed plates in the damp and steamy side kitchen stinking of scraps and leftovers, and Ludo was forced to serve in the restaurant until late at night, he was free to laze around and do what he pleased. He was permanently conscious of his parents' hard work. He felt as if he had committed a crime, and that the world hadn't yet noticed, but that he would have to pay the price one day and there was no way round it. Hey, surely he wasn't...?

What had he meant by that?

Felix had been plagued for weeks by a pain in his chest; his usually attractive pallor had become sickly and consumptive. He suffered from delusions. Nothing helped, not even his visit one afternoon – his first ever and entirely unplanned – to a whore in The Hague. The waiflike blonde cooed beneath him with seeming pleasure, but couldn't exorcise the ghost of the goddess he really loved; not for a moment could she displace the divine creature whose image he had defiled a hundred times, panting her name out loud or biting his pillow, not knowing what to do.

A month earlier, he had run to the ruins of Leiden castle early in the morning and slowly climbed the mossy steps like a man condemned to the gallows. His eyes parched from a string of sleepless nights, he watched as a silver parrot with violet wings flew over the lake towards the sea against the green sky. The student took it as a sign.

Before this omen, he had spent a long time on the ramparts staring at the skyline of the slowly stirring city. When an ice-cold squall hit him out of nowhere, he wanted to hop, skip or jump his way down into the depths. What could be simpler? But he didn't jump, he lived on, just like everyone else.

Of the one and a half billion women populating the planet – Eskimo women who smooched with their noses, and were given to strangers as gifts; ebony beauties rollicking like panthers under palm trees; almond-eyed visions with hairless vulvas from the Kingdom of Siam – he had fallen in love with a German girl, his older brother's fiancée to boot, the daughter of a sausage-maker from Cologne, idiot that he was.

He loved Ludo and wished him all the happiness in the world. But his forthcoming marriage to Liza Bender seemed to Felix personally no less than a journey into hell, as in Dante's famous tale, which he had just bought from an old bookshop in an English translation that he'd not yet read.

26

The weather was perfect the following day, as predicted. Kati had slept like a log, soothed by the pure oxygen that blew in from the sea. She had been visited by blissful dreams throughout the night. Hans Matti lay twenty centimetres from her, tossing and turning, trying to organise things in his mind; the encounter with the disfigured young man beside the sea had seriously upset him.

The sausage-maker had difficulty conceiving that someone from the town had visited the place of his birth. He could only have passed through on his way to Smolensk or Moscow. Although the idea was insane and absurd, of course, in theory it wasn't impossible that the man had seen his twin brother Otto, perhaps even met him. A one in a million chance, but Hans Matti was furious that he hadn't asked the Dutchman about him. On the other hand, if he had really known his brother, he would surely have shown some sign of recognition. Hans Matti's physical features had barely changed over the years.

'Another magnificent day, dear friends!' Jacob saluted the sausage-maker's family as they descended the stairs into the central corridor of Hotel New Deluxe at the stroke of nine. How had they slept?

'Fabulously,' Hans Matti responded heartily, a tiny blob of shaving cream gleaming in the moist fuzz of his moustache. Kati noticed the soapy residue and removed it from his bewildered face with a quick swipe of the claw.

The hotel-keeper accompanied his guests to the restaurant, where a long table had been set for breakfast. What appeared to be two knitted tea-cosies, clearly Maria's handiwork, immediately caught Kati's eye, an embroidered label on the left reading *Four-Minute Egg Warmer* and another on the right reading *Six-Minute Egg Warmer*. There were serving dishes laden with all sorts of cold meats, a mosaic of young and mature cheeses on another plate, and a basket full of fresh croissants and crisp rolls. The big day was approaching, and the Bagmans wanted everyone to see them at their heartiest and most hospitable.

Jacob was the first to sit. He tucked a lightly starched napkin under his chin and made a start. Maria's sister, uncle and five nephews and nieces would be arriving the following morning by train from Friesland. All of them had requested private rooms and, the in-laws included, the hotel would be completely full. Sadly Jacob's side of the family had all passed away. Hans Matti should watch out for those Friesian chaps, they were a bunch of beggars and…

'Ahem… what's that you're saying?' Maria interrupted, standing in the doorway with a pot of home-made blackberry jam. She stopped for a moment, glared at her husband, adopting an angry face, and then took her place beside him at the corner of the table with a broad smile.

Dressed in his black suit, his white collar as spotless as ever, Mr Zwaan served hot steaming coffee from a silver coffee pot. When Kati asked for tea, the manager nodded without a word, disappeared, and returned within thirty seconds, teapot in hand.

Jacob, in the meantime, began to hold forth about the people of Friesland, who had their own unique culture and language, which was perhaps even older than German, and—

'Older than German? I hardly think so!' Kati interrupted indignantly. Surely everything spoken by Germany's neighbours was nothing more than a corrupt German dialect?

'Oh, yes?' smirked Liza. She watched in disgust as her mother hastily removed an egg from the *Six-Minute Egg Warmer*, peeled it to reveal its sickly blue hue, and stuffed it whole between her ruby lips.

Liza had just peeled herself off Ludo's chest. Her future husband hadn't made any attempt the previous night to strip off her black panties, jam his stiff member inside her, and grunt like a Neanderthal, as he had done on their first night of passion. She had fantasised on previous occasions that he was a famous criminal, feared and desired by one and all. Yes, physically at least, they were made for each other.

Ludo, of course, was still under the impression that she was three months pregnant with his child, and didn't know any better. Plenty of men liked pregnant women; the idea got them excited. What, then, had saved her till now? His self-control was a stroke of luck, but it also worried her. Did she smell unpleasant, perhaps?

'I also wanted to—' Jacob had then begun, turning to Hans Matti. 'I also wanted to mention…' But, suddenly becoming aware of the presence of the bride-to-be, he quickly swallowed his words. He would have to save the news of the town hall's refusal to grant permission for the brass band until they were alone. Now he split open a croissant with his thumbs, buttered it thinly, sprinkled it generously with sugar and ate it, a shower of flakes and granules falling onto his chest and his lap. After spreading a couple of slices of brown bread with Maria's blackberry jam and washing them down with a deluge of cold milk, Jacob took a different tack. Were they really expecting no one for the wedding? One of his fellow hotel-keepers would surely have empty rooms, and if not…

A sadness fell over the sausage-maker's face. He pushed his glasses up his angular nose with a trembling little finger and replied that he and Kati had both lost their families. He had business acquaintances, of course, but as a family they had always preferred the warmth of their own company. Exceptionally tasty saveloy, incidentally… Might he ask where it came from?

Jacob named its maker, a butcher from Haarlem who had provided him with meats and sausages for over ten years. He reared his own animals and slaughtered them with a rare devotion to his trade, hence the quality.

'It's juicy, but still has a firm texture,' Hans Matti analysed, having placed a wafer-thin slice of liverwurst on his tongue like a cough sweet. 'Liverwurst is very difficulty to make. It's the measure of a master. Yes, this fellow knows his stuff. Aha, the full committee is here!'

All eyes turned to a sliding door that suddenly opened to reveal Ludo, Louis and Felix. The brothers were dressed up to the nines, as if they were on their way to church or the notary's office. The bridegroom stepped forward, smacked a kiss on radiant Liza's forehead, and then turned to his father. 'When are we off?'

'Shortly, boy, shortly,' the hotel-keeper responded, thrown, before looking around with an intriguing smile. 'Come and have breakfast first. You don't want an empty stomach to ruin the rest of your day.'

Maria sensed that she was being kept in the dark again. Leaving? What was going on? Even Hans Matti wasn't sure what they were up to. Kati, in the meantime, was eyeing the youngest of the three brothers, her plucked eyebrows raised; a fine figure of a lad, she thought. Blond curls, almost Germanic-looking. For a moment, his pleasant features banished thoughts of the dark-haired waiter who had visited her dreams the previous night (he was at school and she was his very severe schoolmistress), whose arrival she had been looking forward to all morning with hidden longing. Why was that decrepit horse-faced old stick in his ghastly black suit serving breakfast and not the delightful young waiter?

'Jacob, what are you up to?' Maria asked for a second time, her husband's mysterious smile lingering, unabated.

He had a little surprise, Jacob announced in his fantasy German. The wedding preparations were all going according to plan; the main hall was ready; the champagne was on ice; the waiters and the army of chefs in the kitchen had everything organised to a T. Everyone was therefore invited to accompany him on a mini-tour of the surrounding countryside.

'*Wunderbar!*' proclaimed Hans Matti, who thought that everything his future in-law did was simply excellent.

What was going on? In panic, Kati turned to her daughter, sitting beside her. Mini-tour? The last thing in the world she felt like doing. She was still recovering from the dreadful journey from Cologne. She was about to offer some excuse when Felix's athletic frame suddenly appeared before her.

'Felix Bagman,' he introduced himself, extending his hand charmingly. He then welcomed Hans Matti like an old friend, and walked over to kiss his mother on both cheeks. He hadn't seen her for all of two weeks.

'Our youngest is studying at university,' the hotel-keeper announced, as proud as punch, tenderly turning to his wife. Maria thought Felix looked pale and thin.

'Is that right?' Kati remarked. She had always had a profound, perhaps Germanic respect for university titles. Was he a future chancellor in the making?

Felix muttered something in reply, and sat down as far from the sausage-maker's daughter as he could. But just as he was about to tuck into a slice of ham, a voice said: 'Felix, my dear, are you short-sighted, or have you forgotten me already?'

Liza looked at him, her face both delighted and chastising.

It was all Felix could do to cheep inanely. He turned his eyes in confusion to Louis, who had met him at the station. The unfortunate boy was still standing between the sliding doors, beaming; he was clearly delighted to see his younger brother again.

27

What the hell am I going to do? thought Liza, after the man who had picked her up on the road near Eindhoven had dropped her off on the bank of some murky canal. His car had followed the blue signs above the road, and they had arrived in Amsterdam two and a half hours later.

A black Alsatian had lain on the back seat. The creature hadn't moved a muscle, but every so often had made a hissing sound and filled the car with a noxious smell. The man had rolled down his window slightly each time, apologetically. 'Boris is sick. They think it's bowel cancer. I'm taking him to the vet. Do you like animals? I prefer them to people. But that's what happens when you get to my age.'

The bastard with the red moustache was now firmly out of mind. Even the crazy argument with her mother had dissolved in the hazy mist of her thoughts. She longed for fun, but most of all for freedom. Her mother refused her both.

'You're no better than a common whore!' Kati had screamed, standing before her daughter in a silk dressing gown, a glass of sparkling wine in hand, like a down-and-out actress. The bitch had been harping on again about the letter from the headmaster at Karlsruhe that had arrived that morning, in which he demanded some degree of financial compensation for the institution's loss of prestige. She had humiliated her family. What could they do with her now? Nothing! The story had spread like wildfire…

'I loved him,' Liza interrupted.

The sausage-maker's daughter then briefly enjoyed a blissful sense of her own power and complete detachment as she stared at her mother in silence, as if she had fallen into a trance in her chair, or even died. She saw the pockmarks on her mother's face hopelessly camouflaged with creams and powders, her double chin, flabby breasts and the rings beneath her eyes from too much drink. She could easily have pitied her if she hadn't hated her so much.

Her father was in Hamburg. She had only twenty marks in her pocket, and no one to turn to. But a prison sentence for her mother's murder would have been better than than spending another night with her under the same roof. Either that or commit suicide. It no longer made any difference.

'Slut!' her mother continued, brandishing the half-empty wine bottle. She then suddenly doubled over, as if she had been kicked in the stomach, but straightened herself up and re-filled her glass, spilling wine all over the place. How many times had she done it with that bastard? How many?

'Hundreds,' Liza answered calmly, her eyes thinning. That certainly got her going, eh? He had also tied her up with American stockings, forced her to go down on her knees, and…

'I'll kill you!'

Kati only indulged her latent alcoholism when her husband was away. Hans Matti always brushed aside his daughter's stories about it. He repressed it, pure and simple, as if it didn't exist, like wars and strange diseases in foreign countries.

'Go ahead,' challenged Liza, with a harsh splutter. 'Go on, then, do it!'

The sausage-maker's wife snorted with contempt and emptied her glass in a single gulp, her fingers trembling. She then stormed into the kitchen amid a tirade of Swabian curses, the parquet groaning under her weight. Liza heard her rummaging around in the cutlery drawer. Jesus Christ, had the old hippo lost it completely?

Quicker than her mother, Liza darted along the corridor and yanked a Prussian dagger from the wall. When Kati returned to the living room in a flurry of dressing-gown silk, Liza started to circle around her, blade in hand, her legs arched, dancing like a native around an open fire. But Kati had only gone to get a new bottle of wine, which she was now trying to open with a steel corkscrew.

'He tied you up?' she snorted for a second time, ignoring the dagger her daughter held, as if everything going on around her was a dream. 'Is that right? Tell *Mutti* all about it… Tell your mother…'

The film of these shards of reality suddenly starts to flicker, a cat claws at the screen, the reel snaps.

A second or two later Liza left the house, pressing the bag she had snatched from the coat hook close to her body, as if it were a baby. Her mother's voice pursued her. 'Get back here! We'll cut you off! You'll go to your grave without a penny! D'you hear? Not a single penny! Come back, goddammit!'

Her words were like bullets in search of a target.

'Good evening, young lady!' Someone in a tailored overcoat with a white leather collar was standing beside her, a hat flapping dramatically over his head, Goethe-style. 'Lost your way in this magnificent global village? Not to worry, all roads lead to Rome…'

'*Wie bitte?*' Liza muttered bashfully.

'You must be kidding? It's not possible!' The man responded in such perfect and elated German that anyone would wonder where he had picked it up. Could he be of any help at all? He had just come from the Concertgebouw. Shostakovich. Had she heard of him?

Might he introduce himself? Theodor Blok, poet and journalist, the classic combination.

'Liza Bender,' said the sausage-maker's daughter, alone for the first time in a foreign land and feeling completely liberated all of a sudden. Even the air seemed lighter here and the tiredness that had overcome her in the car earlier had now completely disappeared.

'I'm on my way to my favourite bar,' the man continued, his face a light brown and pleasant oval. Would she like to join him? He was a gentleman, an exception in Holland, but, then, he had East Indian blood and even a drop or two of French. 'May I carry your bag?'

Liza followed him along the banks of a canal spanned by little bridges, some of which were illuminated. The light reflected in the black water seemed to Liza like a shoal of trembling goldfish. As they turned into a street, a tram departing it in the opposite direction, its bells ringing like a fairground attraction, the man suddenly said, 'The place will be full of stockbrokers today. Do you mind if I say you're my girlfriend?'

Liza followed the Dutchman through swing doors into a room full of men and women in a cloud of smoke, shuffling sand underfoot like animals in a stall. There was no music. The tinkle of glasses and plates at the bar could barely be heard over all the hustle and bustle.

'What would you like to drink?' her benefactor enquired.

'Water, please. Just some water.'

The man made his way to the bar with all the pomp of a cardinal, graciously greeting acquaintances on the way. Liza suddenly felt exposed, dizzy, and tried not to look at the people around her, to avoid their stares. What came next? What did they expect of her?

Just as she was about to take cover behind an overloaded coat stand beside a cigarette machine, she suddenly felt a hand on her shoulder. She turned around. Was she hallucinating? Was life trying to make fun of her? Her eyes radiant, Liza found herself face to face with a handsome Hollywood hunk. The young man looking smilingly back at her was the spitting image of Heinrich.

'My name's Ludo. Isn't this place a bore? Where are you from, if you don't mind me asking?'

'*Wie bitte?*' said Liza for the second time that evening, quickly glancing over her shoulder. Her first admirer was on his way back with a glass in each hand. He caught sight of the apologetic look in her eyes, the laughing face of the oik next to her, realised that the battle was lost, and turned on his heel, trying to hide the humiliation from his bar-room friends.

The hotel-keeper's son had hit the jackpot yet again. Just before closing was always best. A runaway, it was written all over her. Alone in the world, what a shame; where should they go from here?

He took a quick look at his watch and thought he'd best get a move on with this chick. The last tram to Haarlem left in half an hour. What a pair of knockers! A titty ride with a Boche bitch, what would Edo have to say about that? He'd probably find it amusing.

'You remind me of a woman I used to know,' Ludo confessed sympathetically, embellishing his German with a sonorous bass tone. 'A very interesting woman. She had your eyes. But there's something about you, I can't put my finger… Dear girl, has someone upset you?'

'Yes, yes!' Liza exclaimed. She thought she had met a god, a saviour who'd come down to earth at that moment especially for her. How otherwise could he have known the extent of her misfortune and sadness?

28

By a quarter past ten, everyone was aboard the minibus hired for the occasion from a local firm. Jacob sat next to the driver, the microphone in his hand, ostentatiously.

With everyone on board, there was theoretically still room for four more people, but the unoccupied space was filled with all sorts of bric-a-brac: neat little sandwiches, which Maria had hastily put together from what was left over from breakfast; a Thermos of fresh coffee wrapped in a linen cloth; a bag filled with apples and peeled walnuts; napkins for lips and fingers; finally two woollen jackets and a couple of umbrellas, which Maria had advised Kati to bring along just to be on the safe side. The Dutch weather wasn't to be trusted; sometimes it would just start raining out of the blue.

'Testing, testing… one, two, three…' Jacob experimented with the microphone, fiddling with a black cable that curled its way into the dashboard. A nerve-racking electronic shriek followed. The hotel-keeper frowned and twiddled with a dial, hoping for the best. The volume finally returned to normal and Jacob resumed, 'Good morning once again, ladies and gentlemen. Can everybody hear me?'

Amplification was absolutely unnecessary, of course, but the microphone was hanging there anyway, and didn't cost a penny more. The last time Jacob had used one had been during a pensioners' outing to the 'Pyramid of Austerlitz'. After the trip, the entire group had been treated to a surprise feast of drinks and sandwiches, a Flemish singer and flautist on hand to provide extra cheer. Jacob considered the organisation of such excursions to be his duty. In his opinion, the state did far too little for the previous generation.

'Loud and clear, Dad, loud and clear,' shouted Louis, beaming next to his mother, a hat made from card and silver glitter atop his ample head. Were they going to sing a song?

'Of course, dear boy, of course…' his father replied, with a conspiratorial wink at his second son. 'Is everyone sitting comfortably? Our first port of call is the Bollenstreek, or, for our German guests, the place where bulbs are cultivated, between Haarlem and Katwijk.'

Nature had graced the minibus driver with boorish bristly hair, wide nostrils and the flat face of a sow. Jacob knew him from way back. As a schoolboy, the driver had worked every summer in Sam Stikker's bike shed. He went by the distinguished-sounding name of Adriaan Pruis Cannegieter, but everyone called him Aadje Pruis.

Rumour had it that one of his forefathers had won a naval battle against the Russians off the coast of Arkhangelsk. In any event, Sam Stikker and his entire family were rounded up, deported, and murdered during the war, and his fabric shop now sold lamps and light fittings. By an ironic twist of fate, the new proprietor's name was Schuilburgh, which means 'hideaway'.

The broken German with which Aadje had introduced himself to Jacob's guests from Cologne had made Kati cringe. If only she had stayed at home, never given birth to a daughter, done something else with her life. Better to be dead than endure this.

Hans Matti, who had positioned himself with all due formality behind Jacob, feasted his eyes, peering through his binoculars at every opportunity. Villas with turrets and tennis courts; castles made entirely of brick; white country houses hidden behind crooked trees. You don't see the half of it when you're sitting behind the wheel. Wasn't it time he employed a chauffeur? Some of his colleagues had had drivers for years. It created a job for someone, and he could then relax in the back and take in the view. Advantages all round.

Beyond the pale green dunes and woods surrounding Aerdenhout and Vogelenzang the landscape became more panoramic. When they crossed a wooden canal bridge and drove through the gravel soil of Hillegom, Jacob realised to his disappointment that most of the flowers had already been harvested and taken to market. It was a bit of a setback but he didn't let on.

Five minutes later and his luck changed for the better. They passed a field full of tulips flanked by poplars and a windmill, its sails circling gently in the wind, a carpet of yellow and velvet-red flowers as far as the eye could see. This was Holland at its prettiest.

The Benders, Liza included, had never seen such a display before, and gasped and crooned in amazement, although nothing could match the euphoria that possessed Jacob Bagman. The hotel-keeper uncoiled the microphone from its rest and held forth once again: a unique sight, dear friends. Nowhere else in the world was the soil so good and fertile, *so gut und fruchtbar*, for tulips and daffodils as here in this ancient landscape beyond the dunes. Wasn't it beautiful?

'*Wunderbar*, Jacob!' Hans Matti exclaimed, fiddling with the lenses of his binoculars and cursing himself for forgetting his camera.

Ludo and Liza sat hand in hand at the back. Felix had watched the tulip fields drift past a couple of hours earlier on the train from Leiden to Haarlem. Why hadn't he told his father he had lectures to attend, or made up some other weighty excuse? The wedding was bad enough, but this was torture beyond words. The curved mirror above the driver's seat provided the student with a perfect view of Liza's delectable face, bathed in rays of orange sunlight. She was wearing a sky-blue hairband that lent her an Egyptian look. Yet another lightning dart of sheer desperation seared his soul.

At the beginning of March, when Hans Matti had visited Holland with his daughter to make the acquaintance of his future in-laws, Felix had travelled home at full speed to meet Liza for a second time. He had been hoping for a miracle, full of unrealistic expectations, just like most people when head over heels in love. Over dinner, Liza had snuggled up to Ludo, resting her right cheek on his shoulder, and lisped that she was only attracted to dark-haired men. Blond hair reminded her too much of German men. She wasn't really attracted to her own people.

It was a couple of days later that Felix had headed off in the early morning, the collar of his raincoat raised against the wind, ran to the castle ruins, nearly throwing himself from the ramparts. Was this scourge a punishment for his privileged intellectual position? Was he fated to suffer in love?

He envied Ludo but felt some sympathy for him at the same time. His brother had only had two years at secondary school, and was condemned to work behind the hotel bar, and serve tables for the rest of his life, while *he* was doubtless destined to board a ship one day, no more than a single suitcase in hand, or disappear into the clouds on a plane.

98

Ludo would never know the joy derived from casually opening a volume by Maupassant or Chekhov; he would never be enveloped by a feeling of intense happiness induced by a Beethoven sonata. All he knew was jukebox music, the weekly football results and politics – the usual topics of (sometimes passionate, sometimes irate) conversation with the guests at the hotel bar until closing time.

Love was a biological process, a commonplace matter of hormones and anatomical sensations. Yet Felix knew how unpredictable the fire of love could be: a lock of hair disappearing behind an ear; the silent music of a collarbone, the provocation of someone's gait.

At least he looked all right. Louis stared at the world with a hazy smile as if he was seeing it for the first time. The elastic holding his party hat in place cut deep into the folds of his chubby chin, where a lattice of red streaks was forming from the constant shifting of the pinching plastic.

According to the doctors, his brother had a mental age of twelve. Aadje Pruis had planted the magician's hat on Louis's head as a joke just before they had set off, and had looked around, grinning, for approval. Felix could barely contain his anger. He wondered all the same what went on in Louis's head, what he dreamed of, what desires he possessed, whether he even masturbated. In the end, it was better not to think about it. It was always too painful, too sad.

Life had supplied Ludo with endless girls and women, but now he'd won the lottery: a German Marilyn Monroe with electric-blue eyes that promised limitless pleasure, but also hid a hint of sorrow, Felix felt. Perhaps he was the one she secretly…? Now, hang on, idiot… But who knows…? Anything was possible…

Felix was startled by a rattling sound. The minibus bumped and jerked to a standstill at the side of a field. 'Jesus Christ, a flat tyre!' Aadje Pruis cursed in his unpleasant falsetto. Why now of all moments?

'Don't worry, it always has to happen at some point,' Jacob re-assured him affably, turning his Labrador face to his eldest son with an expression that said, Shall we perhaps sort this out together?

Setbacks were par for the course, after all. If everything in life ran according to plan, it would probably be very boring.

29

At the entrance, a girl dressed in traditional costume pinned a daf-fodil to Jacob's lapel for twenty-five cents. He looked down at it, smiling shyly, as if he'd just received a medal.

Shortly afterwards, the visitors were strolling through the wooded domain of the Keukenhof, the country's best-known attraction.

Ludo had cut his hand when changing the wheel. Maria exam-ined the wound closely with an expert eye, as if it were a stain on a pair of trousers, and assured him it would heal by the day after next. Liza had wanted to lick the cut clean but Ludo had started to roar at this, and pulled his arm back in panic. His mother had instead covered the wound with a plaster she found in her handbag.

Louis headed directly towards a barrel organ, his party hat sticking up in the air like the horn on a rhinoceros. A man in a traditional Volendam outfit shook his collection box to the rhythm of a waltz. Louis fished a guilder out of his pocket and popped it into the copper slot. The organ grinder was lost for words, took the slow-witted boy by the arms and danced in a circle, stamping his clogs in a per-formance usually reserved for young women and girls. Louis looked around in delight, enjoying the attention for once.

'What a delightful boy!' Kati exclaimed hypocritically, waving her butterfly sunglasses at her husband. 'Come, Hans Matti! Give that wretched clogdancer a penny or two!'

A few moments later they arrived at a little artificial waterfall, water clattering over imitation rocks on to an arrangement of white and pelican-pink tulips. Maria decided to return to the question of Kati's vegetarianism. She had consulted her head chef the evening before. He was a man of some experience, who had travelled a great deal, and frequently to the Far East. He had suggested a tofu dish. There was a shop in Haarlem that sold the stuff and he knew a couple of excellent recipes.

'Tofu?'

It was a sort of vegetarian meat, Maria explained. She herself had never heard of it before, but it was apparently very tasty, easy to digest, and good for one's health.

'Thank you, but I really don't eat meat of any kind,' Kati retorted, suddenly sensing the intense sunlight on her hyper-sensitive skin.

'It's pointless, dear Maria. You can't talk her into it,' Hans Matti intervened, peering through a hole in a privet hedge with his binoculars. 'Kati simply can't tolerate meat. It's something she was born with.' He focused the lenses, and caught sight of a breathtakingly slender young girl rising up from a field of pale blue hyacinths like a bare-breasted mermaid emerging from the waves, a lad with dishevelled hair following her, unhurriedly pulling up his trousers, as if in the privacy of his own bathroom. 'Dear God!' the butcher exclaimed.

'I'm sorry?' Maria enquired, but when he didn't answer right away, she reiterated that tofu was a sort of meat for vegetarians.

'Either it is meat or it isn't,' Hans Matti told the hotel-keeper's wife in an unexpectedly grave tone, letting the binoculars slip from his sweaty hands. 'Take it from an expert. Meat is what mammals, birds and reptiles are made of, or at least so I learned as an apprentice butcher. If it's not meat, then it's fish or some kind of vegetable material.'

'But it looks like meat.' What was she going to do? It was really bothering her.

'It'll be fine,' Kati capitulated, not wanting to inconvenience her future in-laws. I can stuff the garbage in my handbag under the table, if need be, she thought, no one will notice. Her willingness to oblige was partly motivated by her urgent need to have Maria answer a question. 'What, may I ask, is the name of that smart waiter, the one with the dark hair who works in your hotel?'

'Ah, you mean Mr Zwaan,' Maria answered with a smile. He had been there from the very beginning, a real gentleman. The summer guests are always very taken with him.

Kati suddenly felt her body tingle and glow amid the scent of the flowers, a sensation she hadn't experienced in an eternity. She meant someone else, of course, not Mr Zwaan but the young fellow with the black curly hair. The chap with the green felt jacket.

Oh, that was Guillaume, an old friend of Ludo's. He had waitered the previous winter in an establishment in Haarlem, but had had a difference of opinion with the management, and was now working his first season at the hotel. They still weren't sure what to do with him. Why? They had...

But Maria didn't get the chance to finish her story. Her husband had appeared from the wings with a necklace of daffodils. He walked up to her and draped the flowers around her neck, as if she were being welcomed to Hawaii.

'Jacob, Jacob... Such foolishness...' the hotel-keeper's wife spluttered, blushing like a schoolgirl.

The former antique dealer took his wife by the little finger and led her to the shadow of a rosebush, kissed her neck and whispered, 'You thought I'd forgotten you yesterday, I bet, when we got back from Aalsmeer?' But he hadn't forgotten her, because he loved her with all his heart, as he had for over thirty years. She did believe him, surely?

'Jacob, silly Jacob...' she whispered back.

What a lucky life they led, the hotel-keeper resumed in the tone of one who had come far in life and was deeply content with his lot. Wasn't it wonderful that they could enjoy all this together, that all their sons were doing so well and that Ludo was about to get married?

Cheek to cheek like two young lovebirds, they gazed at the pond. Two swans floated over the water with serene and regal elegance.

Jacob and Maria could see Ludo and Liza over on the other side, talking and gesticulating wildly. They probably needed to be alone, away from everyone else. Understandable, really. Perhaps they were discussing the baby's name. Did Maria still remember that?

Kati removed her sunglasses and shivered as she watched the episode from a distance, her eyes red. Her contorted mouth looked like a dried prune. All at once, she started to rummage in her handbag as if her life depended on it. Hell, where was it? She was sure she had hidden some chocolate in there. Aha... She ripped the bar from its wrapper and stuffed a huge chunk of it in her mouth. When was the last time Hans Matti had hugged her unprompted? Ten years ago? Twelve? God, she just had to have that Guillaume, even if only for half a minute... even if it cost her half a million. She had to have him, before the grave engulfed her for ever.

Where was that man of hers? Ah, there he is, the impotent wreck, binoculars on his chest. Jesus, he looks just like a frog.

30

After a glass of sweet white wine, which made her feel terribly dizzy, as if she'd spent an hour on a merry-go-round, Liza followed Ludo out of the bar and into the Amsterdam rain. She was prepared to follow this godsend of a man to the moon and back. His broad chest and considerate company had put her at her ease immediately, and she told him everything that had happened in the hours before they had met.

'The filthy pig!' Ludo had exclaimed, wisely making no comment about the trucker's dick. Without averting his dark eyes for a second, he continued to gaze at her, nodding understandingly or conjuring up an expression of pained empathy on his lips. And what was she going to do now?

'I don't know,' Liza sighed, her dress still agreeably fashionable and sexy in spite of its now slightly grubby appearance. Her parents were rich, swimming in money. But she had only a measly twenty marks to her name and no passport. Was she breaking the law?

'What exactly do your parents do?' Ludo then asked, as nonchalantly as he could, breathing deeply, his eyelashes fluttering charmingly. Nicotine always focused his mind.

'My father owns a sausage factory. He employs more than a hundred and fifty people. Where are the windmills around here, by the way? There wasn't a single windmill on the canal...'

Hmm, this chick was a goldmine! But where in God's name could he take her? He looked at his watch: the last tram to that stinking seaside resort had left a minute ago. If they ran, they might just make the train to Haarlem. But what kind of impression would that give?

There was only one option: Edo Novak's place. Edo was his friend and comrade. He had supported him through thick and thin (and vice versa) for a year and a half. It wouldn't be the first time he'd made use of his attic room, which was stuffed to the gunnels with Javanese masks and smelled for all the world like a spice shop. But after that? He had to work the next day. They had a group of 120 coming, all expecting afternoon tea and a cold buffet. His father expected him at eight o'clock sharp and...

'Is it a long walk, where we're going?' Liza asked as Ludo stopped and wavered. She shivered under her thin jacket.

Walk? Surely she didn't think he would allow his princess to walk in weather like this? That was for labourers, for working folk... He hailed a taxi that was heading their way from the Spui. 'Haarlem!' he commanded. Once they were seated, Ludo could barely stop himself from throwing his arms around the German beauty's delicate frame immediately, so temptingly tangible a nymph as she had suddenly become.

They drove out of the city past the Royal Palace, the Bijenkorf department store and Central Station. Liza looked around in silence.

She was surprised that virtually none of the shop windows were lit up. How dull, she thought.

'There's another war on its way,' the taxi driver suddenly volunteered as they drove past the shadowy facade of Haarlem's lumber yard. He had had plenty of politicians in his taxi. My God, if they only knew what went on in Amsterdam of an evening! But he had no reason to complain. Yesterday, he had had another of those professor types in his cab. Two or three years tops, and the Russians would invade, he said. It was still a state secret. 'What do you think?'

'I've no idea,' babbled Ludo, recalling his conversation with Edo a couple of weeks earlier: the tide was turning and the clock ticking, but only Moscow knew the exact day and hour. It had all sounded very mysterious. Ludo was pretty drunk, but Edo's words suddenly resurfaced nevertheless.

'Nobody knows when, exactly,' the driver resumed mournfully, disposing of his cigarette butt with a vigorous flick out the window. He had been waiting four years for a council flat. He and the wife still lived with their family. He knew the score, that's for sure. And he figured, with the straightforward common sense he'd inherited from his mother, God rest her, that they were probably no better off than the Russians. If you ask me, they're very welcome. Why not give it a try, as an experiment? That's what he had to say, the man in the street. Where exactly in Haarlem did they want to go?

Ludo gave him the address and nestled his fingers in the blissful warmth under Liza's dress. In spite of the driver's booming voice, the German blonde had dozed off, her chin resting on her bare collarbone. Her nose and earlobes, where two golden daisy earrings glistened, looked as if they had been fashioned by hand. How old was she? Not a day over twenty. His lower body tensed. Boy, was she ready for it… Absolutely heaven-sent.

'Take the blacks in America,' the driver rambled on, now sucking on a lollipop that ticked irritably against his teeth. They were gorillas, of course, but the gorillas in Artis Zoo were better off than the blacks over there. He had been in the merchant navy for three years and had gone to a museum one day in New York where they had a stuffed nigger on display like a wild animal.

'Stuffed?' Ludo yawned. He could happily have wrung his neck.

People came from everywhere to see it, the museum's main attraction. And then he said, with his straightforward common sense, maybe those black buggers would be a lot better off under the Communists? What did he know? He was just the man in the street. But what he did know was that those politicians were no better than animals. The things they got up to here at night... But a flat for me and the wife...? Forget it... 'By the way...' The driver looked up at Ludo in the rearview mirror. 'Can I interest you in a watch?' He had quite a collection. Swiss. Real beauties. They were in the boot. No – was he sure?

As they approached the medieval edifice where Edo lived, the sound of the engine that had soothed her to sleep altered, and Liza woke with a start, wide-eyed.

'I'll be back in a jiffy, honey,' Ludo said, indicating that she should wait in the taxi. The hotel-keeper's son climbed the front steps under the grape-green lantern and pulled on a brass bell, shivering in the mist that had drifted in from the sea and engulfed the street in a milky haze. Edo opened the door, bleary-eyed. Ludo asked him for the taxi fare.

'Are you out of your mind?' What kind of bourgeois trick was it this time?

He would explain later; it was all for the cause. What did he think? An excellent catch!

'Oh, all right, then,' Edo muttered. He disappeared and returned a few seconds later with a note for the taxi driver. 'But if you're fucking with me, I'll haul you in front of the disciplinary committee. I'll be forced to.'

'Why would I fuck with you?' said Ludo. He took the money, gave his comrade a puppyish look of loyalty, and hurried back to the taxi.

Sucker, thought Edo to himself, but Ludo Bagman would never know.

31

Once the minibus had left the floral landscape behind and the characteristic Dutch countryside of open pasture, long straight gulleys and depressingly empty panoramas that did little for the imagination or emotions of the observer had resumed, Hans Matti was suddenly reminded of the day he had met Kati.

He had left Königsberg for Aachen a month earlier. The medical certificate that confirmed his weak kidneys dangled day and night around his neck in a felt sachet held by a cord. He was aware that he could still be called up for the army at any moment. But nothing could have led him then to suspect that he would soon leave, never again to see his family or the place of his birth, the yielding amber waves of the Baltic, the shadows of the Lutheran church where he had played as a child.

The German empire was then larger and more powerful than ever. He kept perfect track of advances on the eastern front on the newsreels. But when he thought about his brother, anxiety made him nauseous and his stomach churned, although the story of the weak kidneys was pure invention. In spite of the fact that the military doctor who had examined him was indebted to his father on account of some romantic complication, he still had to hand over every penny of his savings before he could persuade the man to sign the document declaring him 'permanently unfit for active military service'.

The young German with a passion for sausage-making had worked in a butcher's shop in Rauschen for nine uninterrupted years. Just as he had started to think seriously about opening his own business, the bloody war had erupted, and now he was penniless. Two more days and he would have to give up the attic room he rented above the baker's. He had applied for a job as the baker's assistant the week before, but the boss had just laughed at him hysterically. What could a baker do with a butcher?

Hans Matti wandered along, deep in thought, walking out from under the shadow of a chestnut tree on to the street, when, suddenly, he heard the sound of screeching tyres. He turned and saw death thundering towards him in the form of a black Mercedes. The car hit him at high speed. Hans Matti, who was blessed with a rare dexterity, flew up into the air like a feather and landed with a thud on a grass verge, where violets had been planted in the shape of a swastika and couples sitting on benches nearby kissed and messed around.

Kati, with little Liza, then seven, sitting like a queen on the red leather back seat, had yelled, 'Ulli, watch out!' But it was too late.

She would never forget his deadly somersault. It was almost as if the victim had launched himself from a trampoline.

The chauffeur was treated to an earful of abuse. How many times had she told him to watch out, goddammit? Thank God they had already dropped off the general in time for his meeting with the Italians at the town hall. What if they had been late? Unthinkable! Kati was about to prod the chauffeur to drive on when she was suddenly overcome by a wave of compassion. 'Ulli, go and see if the wretch is all right.'

Hans Matti rose from the swastika flowerbed, stretching himself as if he had just emerged from a refreshing nap, brushing off the petals and lumps of soil from his clothes. He then checked to see if his lucky charm was still around his neck. Jesus, what was that all about?

The chauffeur marched over to him in a rage, slapped him three times in the face with a pair of calf leather gloves and started shouting. What kind of idiot walked into the road without looking? Who was he, anyway? What was he doing in the middle of the street?

The unemployed butcher was about to produce his medical certificate when he noticed, in something of a dream-like haze, that the rear door of the classy car had opened, and a young woman in a black dress, her reddish hair partly concealed under a black hat, had stepped out elegantly. 'Ulli, get back here! I'll talk to the fellow myself!'

Hans Matti watched as the soldier turned on his heels and meekly assumed his place behind the wheel, and caught a glimpse of the little blonde girl in her white dress. She had wanted to follow in her black patent shoes, but her mother yelled at her to return to her seat. The woman walked over, and asked if he was all right; he had never heard an accent like hers before.

'I'm fine, thanks. Just a bit shaken.'

'You're quite the acrobat, I must say,' Kati observed admiringly, looking the young man up and down in quick appraisal. She was pleased by his physical proportions, the understated broadness of his chest and shoulders. The haze of his hair, black and spiked, looked as if it had been painted on his skull, as it did with wrestlers and athletes. Was he a circus performer?

'I'm sorry?'

'Do you perform in the circus?'

'Not at all!' Hans Matti exclaimed, tempted once again to show his certificate. But he changed his mind and told her he was a first-class butcher and sausage-maker, and that he was looking for a job.

'A butcher?' Kati snorted, disgust written all over her face, but then remembered the conversation she had had the week before with one of the maids in the kitchen. It was high time they replaced that beanpole, Frantz, who had been called to the Russian front. 'Where do you live?'

'Here in Aachen,' Hans Matti answered, a minor pain stabbing at his right thigh and left hip.

'We're looking for staff at the house,' said Kati, who had only moved from Dresden to Aachen six months before, along with her daughter. Had he heard of General Von Oberhaussen? He was a baron, world-renowned before the war for his love of wild animals and nature, had written no less than thirteen books, and he simply adored sausages and pâté. Could he make pâté?

'You name it.' The young man from East Prussia jumped in head first, 'There's French pâté, Ardennes pâté... but also Prussian pâté. Where I'm from in Königsberg, there's...'

'Please keep the details to yourself!' Kati silenced the handsome fellow with a grimace. She then took a white visitor's card from her handbag. 'Stop by tomorrow at noon. Ask for Fräulein Kati.' The chauffeur sounded the horn. The lady in black turned. The soldier behind the wheel pointed to his watch and guiltily raised his narrow shoulders, which were decorated with red epaulettes. 'Yes, yes, Ulli, I'm coming... We have to be at the town hall by two o'clock, I know...'

The good news made Hans Matti a little light-headed as he watched the Mercedes slowly disappear. The little girl had scrambled to her feet on the back seat, pressed her nose against the window, and looked at him curiously.

The gothic letters on the card read:

𝕶𝖆𝖙𝖎 𝕾𝖈𝖍𝖒𝖎𝖉𝖙

𝕳𝖔𝖚𝖘𝖊𝖐𝖊𝖊𝖕𝖊𝖗

𝕲𝖊𝖓𝖊𝖗𝖆𝖑 𝖁𝖔𝖓 𝕺𝖇𝖊𝖗𝖍𝖆𝖚𝖘𝖘𝖊𝖓

32

Amsterdam was a city raised on wooden stilts, Jacob Bagman expatiated, microphone in hand, as the minibus wrestled its way through the chaotic traffic on Nassaukade, heading towards the Rijksmuseum.

'How interesting,' Hans Matti mumbled. It was his first visit to the Dutch capital he had never heard about the stilts before. How exactly did they go about it? Did they just start building over the sea one day?

But the hotel-keeper was unfamiliar with the details. He took a bite of his salt-beef sandwich and pretended he hadn't heard the question. Maria had passed the sandwiches around; the whole lot had been wolfed down. They had stopped en route for a ten-minute coffee break, the white hotel cups now rattling in the basket at the back. Next time we stop, Maria thought, I'll wrap them in napkins. That clatter is driving me mad.

It was half past one and they still had a good part of the day ahead of them. While Jacob tried to remember where to find the pancake stall with the Hammond organ, thinking it would be a nice place to visit later in the afternoon, Ludo asked his father what he was planning.

'It's a surprise.'

The bridegroom-to-be had spent the last half-hour fighting an agonising craving in his ailing loins. He was horny. He had to have Liza, and as quickly as possible. With a rubber if he had to. Jesus, why hadn't they done it this morning? But where now? He would come up with something; that girl believed everything he told her.

Felix, meanwhile, spent the whole time looking out of the window with an open book on his lap. He was driving Ludo round the bend. He felt like giving him a good clump on the head, Felix and all the spoilt capitalist bitches he associated with.

'We're not going to see *The Night Watch* by any chance, are we?' Ludo fished, after a big gulp of air.

Jacob looked back at his son, an amused expression on his puppy face, and nodded. Yes, he wanted to introduce his future in-laws to the greatest work of genius their country had ever produced.

'What did he say?' snorted Kati at her husband. But the sausage-maker pretended not to hear his wife, raised his binoculars and stared outside, as if completely engrossed.

A sort of glasshouse crammed with tourists floated on tea-coloured water past canal-side houses with Dutch gables and granite stoops.

111

Hans Matti surveyed the windows of one majestic edifice, and in the room's dim light could discern chandeliers, antique furniture, bookcases full of books, and paintings. Not many barrow-boys and rag-and-bone men around here, he thought.

Ludo had clambered his way to the front in the meantime, hoping to arrange a tactical exemption from the planned itinerary. He still had some wedding business to attend to here in Amsterdam, and, as Liza was moving to the Netherlands, there was plenty of time for her to see *The Night Watch*, wasn't there?

Jacob whispered that he had something else up his sleeve for later that afternoon, a floating tour. You get my drift? He planned to board at the Damrak. Where would they meet up again afterwards?

Ludo suddenly had an excellent idea. 'The terrace of the Victoria Hotel?' he suggested. 'Four o'clock?'

Aadje Pruis parked his minibus in a street where the trees were full of deafening birdsong, happy he could finally read the sports page of his morning paper. He had missed an earlier opportunity when he had accepted Jacob's invitation to join the party on its visit to the Keukenhof. He had waited for passengers outside the gate hundreds of times but had never before gone in. Now he could claim to have seen the world-famous flower show at least once in his life.

Suddenly inspired, Ludo lifted his fiancée off the bus as if she were as light as a feather, his father and future father-in-law applauding enthusiastically. Her left shoe fell off in the process, and Louis carried it over to her meekly. The couple then disappeared in the direction of the Leidseplein.

This time the driver politely declined the offer to accompany the group. He wasn't really that interested in art. He had enough art at home every day with the wife and kids. On top of that, he would rather die than leave his valuables unattended in a city full of thieves and foreigners.

'You might have a point there,' said Jacob with an understanding nod.

Afterwards, the Bagmans, their two sons, the sausage-maker and his wife were strolling through the Rijksmuseum, their footsteps echoing along the tall green corridors as in a cathedral.

The building reminded Kati of the ministry in Berlin that she had visited with the general. There was a brass band, flags everywhere, and a buffet serving roasted wild boar – shot in the Black Forest – and capons from Poland. She had walked in a procession, General Von Oberhaussen at her side, his impressively decorated chest beside her black robe and pearl necklace. The Finnish granite structure was later destroyed by a bomb one night. There was nothing left now. Not a single stone.

'Was Amsterdam ever bombed?' Kati asked her husband, unable to restrain herself. Hans Matti was all at sea, gesticulating wildly, and trying to mouth his reply like a fish in a bowl: not another word, do you hear?

Shortly before they had left Cologne, he had carefully primed her not to mention the 'war'; the issue was still very sensitive in countries like Holland. It was better to be kind and obliging, let people see your human side, and then the world would understand that not all Germans were the same.

This was the most famous painting on earth, with the possible exception of the Mona Lisa, began Jacob in praise of *The Company of Frans Banning Cocq*, also known as *The Night Watch*, its subjects always at the ready to advance against the rabble with drums and halberds. The former antique dealer proffered a few casual details about Rembrandt's life extracted from a brochure earlier in the day. Sadly, the painter himself was only able to enjoy his fame and fortune for a very short time.

The sausage-maker stood close to the rope barrier, his jaw dropping in amazement. It was indeed a masterpiece, he exclaimed, although he was no art expert and had, in fact, never been to a museum of old paintings before. His factory, which he had built up from scratch, didn't allow much time for such things.

Jacob and Hans Matti then began a discussion on an entirely different subject, so often the case in the presence of art when the human capacity to free-associate is suddenly let loose. In the meantime, Maria asked Kati what she had thought of their visit to the Keukenhof.

'Just the best!' she said effusively, her head raised aristocratically. In truth, she had found the attraction mediocre, with the exception of the field of tulips on the way, with the windmill and its slowly turning sails.

The year before, she and Hans Matti had driven to Nice, where he had made his first cautious allusion to the possibility of moving to the area at some later date. They would probably... 'Over my dead body!' the sausage-maker's wife had interrupted, adamantly. The sea air was bad for her complexion, although the place itself was not unpleasant. They had passed villas with palatial gardens nestling romantically on leafy hillsides aside attractive lakes, compared to which the Keukenhof was a window box on a postcard.

'Yes, there's nowhere else quite like it,' the hotel-keeper's wife replied, her voice filled with pride. Flowers were a major part of the Dutch economy. The hotel also benefited indirectly on account of the many tourists that came to eat in the restaurant.

'I see,' said Kati, while Maria looked around, wondering where her sons had gone.

Felix and Louis had seen *The Night Watch* hundreds of times. It dawned on the biology student that his brother might enjoy Jan Steen's paintings, and their humorous and anecdotal content.

Louis had been obliged to hand in his magician's hat at the cloakroom. An elderly woman in a dust coat had winked and told him in a kindergarten voice that she had never seen such a beautiful party hat in all her life and that it must have been his birthday that day.

'Do they have those old-fashioned machines here with the sparkly wheels?' Louis asked as they walked along a corridor with enamelled floor tiles. They were suddenly forced to stop: a man in a blue suit, holding his false teeth as if they were rosary beads, lay flat on the floor with the face of a corpse. Two attendants in ill-fitting uniforms circled him in a panic, mumbling conspiratorially like whist players

Felix yanked his brother's sleeve, lead him along a side corridor, and they snaked along an interminable passage lined with black velvet curtains, greasy to the touch, which ultimately opened into an exhibition space bathed in dark green light, like a derelict aquarium. The machine Louis had meant was in Teylers Museum in Haarlem. Felix promised he would take him there soon. He looked around. Where in God's name were they?

The paintings in the room were far removed from the seventeenth-century collection. They were the strangest paintings that Felix had ever seen. An entire wall was covered with one naked woman. One canvas contained six hideously fat blondes hanging upside down with meat hooks through their heels. The painting next to it depicted a sleigh full of bearded men in fur coats in rolling snow-covered country, mint-green onion domes in the distance, their sleigh drawn by six brunettes in leather harnesses, deathly thin and gaunt. Was this modern art?

Whoever painted this must have been round the bend, Felix thought. Children of middle-class families tended to have conservative tastes when it came to art. He stepped forward to get a closer look at one of the panels, nevertheless. It depicted a glass container stuffed with naked girls, lithely intertwining like rollmops in a jar. A creature with a human body and a dog's head was just about to open the lid. Tears of terror trickled from the girls' eyes.

'Hmmm,' mumbled Felix, stepping backwards. To his right he suddenly heard a fearful yowl, swelling like a foghorn.

His brother was standing in front of a painting five metres away, trembling like a leaf, his tormented face convulsing in pain. Felix rushed over to him, fearing an epileptic fit. Louis stared, transfixed, at a painting, like a monk before the Devil, his arms stiff and motionless.

The painting portrayed a boy with a pumpkin head standing on a chair, having pulled his stiff member out from his breeches. He was surrounded by a group of emaciated ladies in evening dress drinking champagne, and gentlemen in dinner jackets, all laughing hysterically in concert, pointing their fingers at him.

'Th-th-that's m-me...' stammered Louis, plucking at his hair with a heart-rending shriek.

Felix took his brother in his arms and tried to calm him down. The guy in the painting didn't look like him at all. Surely he could see that? He should...

'It's me,' Louis said calmly. 'Why do you always make a fool of me?' He then pulled away from Felix, ran screaming into a shadowy corner, and collapsed in a heap as if he had been hit by a hail of bullets.

'Louis,' shouted his brother. At that, an inquisitive mustachioed attendant peered around the corner to ask what on earth was going on.

33

Lunch in the Victoria Hotel ran until three o'clock. Out of professional interest, Ludo studied how work was allocated between the waiters, how quickly the orders were taken, and the quality of the service after that.

But all he could really think of was the exquisite body of the blonde in front of him, Liza Bender, his future wife, who was carrying his child, and whose help he now urgently needed. Jesus, he couldn't contain himself any longer.

They had made their way from the Leidseplein to the Bijenkorf department store, where a shop assistant had sprayed three invigorating perfumes on Liza's wrists and a particularly sweet scent around her neck. Liza had then insisted that Ludo try on a navy-blue jacket with a white rollneck sweater and white trousers on the next floor. He now looked exactly like a filmstar, Liza gushed, whisking around him like a whirlwind. On the next floor, the generous groom eventually bought his fiancée a pink scarf for nineteen guilders. They then strolled across the Damrak to the Victoria Hotel, their fingers intimately entwined.

'It might sound silly, but I would kill for some tomato soup,' said Liza with animation, relaxing into a sea-green chair in the hotel restaurant, and glancing fleetingly at the menu. '*Und du mein Schatz?*'

Ludo examined Liza's smooth arms. She had picked up a slight tan yesterday on the beach terrace outside Bol's café in less than an hour and a half. Her legs and neck were also caramel. The cravings in his groin taunted him once again and he suddenly realised he'd overlooked something important. What should he do? He patted his chest, stood up, groped elaborately in his back pockets, and then said he'd forgotten his cigarettes.

'You had them with you a minute ago,' his fiancée remarked, slightly irritated, glaring at the pack of Lexington deep in his right-hand pocket. 'Would you like one of mine?'

'No, thanks, sweetie, I prefer my own brand. Order me a glass of whatever's on draught. On draught, OK...? I'll be right back...'

'A glass of whatever's on draught,' Liza practised, as Ludo hurried out, past tables of mostly elderly couples having lunch.

Where's a bloody chemist round here? the hotel-keeper's son muttered, darting into an alley off the Damrak, the warm sunlight replaced by cold air and the stench of piss. He found one immediately on Nieuwendijk, a sign above the door depicting a swarthy Arab with crimson lips. This was the place.

A grey-haired man in a white jacket lingered serenely behind the counter, where he was weighing out lozenges on low scales. He scooped the lozenges into white paper bags, and carefully pencilled the price on. Ludo told him what he was after.

'Helps me manage the stock. I don't have time to weigh them out otherwise,' the shopkeeper explained in a silky southern Dutch accent, glancing up at him for a moment. 'What brand did you have in mind, sir?'

'I'm not bothered,' said Ludo.

'We don't have "I'm not bothered", sir', the chemist responded, without batting an eyelid. He then pulled open a drawer, fished out a number of boxes, and plumped them down one by one on the counter with a hollow thud. Each box was different. 'We have contraceptives from France, Belgium, and let me see...' He proceeded to examine one of the boxes as a jeweller would a diamond, 'Germany, China, and – believe it or not – the home-grown variety...'

'French will be fine,' said Ludo agitatedly, digging into his trouser pockets. 'How much?'

'Yours for the taking, sir,' the chemist answered with a mischievous look on his face. 'They're samples from the supplier. It's forbidden to sell them.' His wife was Catholic, and they didn't usually carry that kind of thing. But he and his wife thought it would be wrong to just throw them away. He slipped a red box decorated with two golden doves across the counter. 'Can I interest sir in some throat lozenges?'

Ludo wanted to decline, but changed his mind. OK, the smallest you have. Not too many. That's fine...

'That'll be forty cents exactly,' said the chemist, rubbing the change on the palm of his hand a moment later as if it were gold dust.

Outside again, Ludo wanted to get rid of the lozenges straight away but couldn't see a bin nearby, so he just dropped them where he was and hurried off.

The tomato soup had just arrived, but the beer had clearly been standing for several minutes, if the lack of froth was anything to go by.

'Just what the doctor ordered,' said Liza, dipping her spoon in the orange broth to stir away the circle of cream and suddenly realising that she only ever felt like tomato soup when she was having her period. Pregnant women were all crazy about gherkins, but she had never once eaten a gherkin in Ludo's presence. Her mother was right about one thing: men were all the same – they never noticed a thing.

Ludo placed a beer mat over his glass, shook it a couple of times as if it were dice in a beaker, and guzzled at the froth as it dripped over his fingers and wristwatch. He then proceeded to shower Liza with compliments. He could hardly wait until the day after tomorrow, loved her more than anything else in the world, and would never leave her. Their wedding would be a glorious success, and he quite longed for her. Craved her. Wanted her. Now!

Liza's appetite suddenly vanished. She knew exactly what Ludo's hoarse voice meant, let the spoon sink into her soup, and fluttered her eyelashes. In the meantime, she frantically tried to work out her next move. She had been thinking about this moment for days and it came as no surprise, but his directness still left her speechless.

'What do you say?' Ludo took hold of her wrists and looked at her pleadingly, blood rushing to his pelvis. Oh, he could... Yes, he really could...

'What do you mean, dear?' Liza whispered, hoping for a miracle but not expecting one.

'I want you now. Do you know what I mean? There are toilets...'

Liza shuddered; her period was only three days old. She had slipped on a fresh pad that morning. What should she do? Her only way out was to say that the doctor had told her to avoid intercourse for the time being to protect the foetus.

'Sweetheart?' said Ludo. His burning eyes reminded her of an eagle's.

Liza realised that resistance was futile and feared that if she refused him, her secret – that she had made up the pregnancy, not only to commit Ludo to her for ever but, more importantly, to get away from

119

Cologne, away from her morgue of a home, away from the reign of terror that had nearly killed her, that had been worse than that of Emperor Caligula in the Middle Ages – would be exposed.

'Toilets?' Liza whispered, picking her spoon up again and glancing around furtively.

He had been here before. The gents were at the back, on the left. He would wait for her there. He was about to get up, stirred by the itch in his loins, when Liza, still preoccupied by the inconvenience between her legs, raised her right hand and said, in a submissive voice, that she would go first.

'I'll give you a sign. When I flush you can come in, all right?' Liza pushed away her half-full bowl of tomato soup, her lips hideously contorted all of a sudden.

'OK, hurry up...'

She got up, and disappeared down the corridor, her movements languid; when she caught a glimpse of herself in a golden mirror, the sight pleased her enormously and, all at once, her nerves were gone. A wave of tenderness washed over her. She even felt excited.

The sausage-maker's daughter passed an illuminated display of éclairs and various other pastries as she made her way to the cloakroom. She went down the stairs and almost bumped into a red-headed chef coming out of the gents, shaking his wet hands. The black rubber flap leading to the white tiled room was ajar. There was no one in sight.

She rushed in with the same impulsiveness with which she had jumped into a freezing cold swimming pool for the first time. She heard someone fiddling about with paper behind the first door, moved on to the next, and hastily turned the lock.

The smell was sickening. Liza grabbed a bottle of perfume from her handbag and squirted hysterically, as if exterminating an invisible swarm of insects.

The place was otherwise pretty clean. There was a basin with a mirror above it, and a shelf with a pile of linen towels. She had to be quick now. She pulled up her dress, pulled down her slip, and tossed the slightly bloodstained sanitary towel into the toilet with disgust. She flushed the toilet, and was about to hold a towel under the tap to freshen up a bit between her legs when there was an impatient drumming at the door. She heard Ludo plead, 'Open up, sweetie… Are you in there?'

Liza surrendered at that moment. She opened the door and watched her future husband slip inside, with the face of a kid in a candy store. He immediately threw his arms around her, smothered her with kisses, growled that she smelled fantastic, that he couldn't contain himself any longer, that his passion was unstoppable, and that he was going to take her and take her until they took flight.

'The door!' Liza panted, catching a hazy flash of herself in the mirror and turning the lock.

Ludo relaxed his vice-like grip. The tips of his trembling fingers danced down her spine and wriggled deftly under her clothes. His curved little finger headed down towards her buttocks. He buried his face in her breasts, licked his way up to her neck, towards her lips, hurriedly undoing his belt, his trousers falling to the floor with the dull clunk of keys and small change. 'Come on, take off your dress. I want you to be naked, completely naked…'

Liza pulled her red cotton dress over her head, praying to God that her fiancé wouldn't notice anything. Ludo planted a kiss on the soapy blonde hairs under her left arm. He attacked the first red nipple to appear with his tongue, asking her hoarsely if she wanted him, if she longed for him, Jesus Christ… didn't she? Was she horny?

'*Ja, lieber Ludo. Ich bin…*'

She groped for his member, which was hard and extremely thick, and pointing up towards the wilderness of his belly. But why didn't she bend over for once? Ludo turned her around, ardent. Liza suddenly remembered how Heinrich had once almost strangled her out of pure passion, his muscles of bulging steel. She was wet, tossed her hair back, and was about to lean forward willingly onto the wooden toilet seat for support, when the sound men's shoes entered the gents.

'That Van Klaveren with his miserable sanctimonious face is trying to screw us,' a deep voice boomed to the sound of two flushing urinals.

Ludo's tortured erection was already halfway up the blissful ravine of Liza's buttocks. They can all fuck themselves, he thought, and wanted to keep going, but Liza quickly turned round and placed her hand over his mouth. She stared at her lover with fear in her eyes, trembling like a cornered animal, which he found at once absurd and exciting.

'No, Gerard, we almost have them where we want them, I reckon,' the second man countered, the clatter of urine ongoing.

'Do you really think so?'

'Sure.'

'How come?'

'When we get back, we give him another drink,' resumed the second man, his voice deep, resolute. 'And then we say, Van Kleveren, either you accept our conditions or we'll offer the brickwork and plastering contract to Maupie Jansen. Then you'll see him sweat... Jesus, I needed that...'

The urinals flushed again, and the voices disappeared. Ludo lunged instantly into the trousers at his feet, and produced a yellowish condom which he unfurled over his penis, his fiancée looking on in amazement.

'What's that, Ludo?' she peeped, still afraid someone might hear.

'It's better like this, sweetie...' the hotel-keeper's son panted, his passion almost spent. 'You're pregnant. We have to be careful to avoid infection. For our darling baby... It's better like this... I read it in a book somewhere... Come on, bend over...'

'Oh, all right,' said Liza, and a couple of seconds later Ludo had pushed himself into her from behind. The Dutchman forced her fragile body up against the tiles with his powerful frame. A cold shiver ran down Liza's arms and legs, but she was delighted that everything was going so smoothly.

'Hot, eh?' Ludo panted.

Liza moaned something or other, her eyelids shut, captive to both pain and budding pleasure.

The hotel-keeper's son pulled Liza's hips towards him with full force and dug his teeth into the soft skin of her neck. The haughty face of a black woman with pointed breasts that he'd seen an hour earlier at the tram stop on Rokin Street came to mind.

He seemed to want to shout something, emitting a husky groan that sounded like a wail, and, in three or four thrusts, he came inside the body of his bride-to-be with a roar.

Somebody's pretty sick in there, thought the person who had just entered the toilets and walked straight over to the basin. It was the chef with the red hair again. He had taken off his engagement ring to wash his hands and forgotten all about it.

Fortunately, the ring was still there, in a puddle of water next to the soap. No one had seen it. He slipped the pricey golden circle onto his finger, thought about his fiancée and their date that afternoon to meet by the entrance to the Vondelpark at a quarter past six, and left with a smile on his face.

34

The Benders and the Bagmans were on their way from the Rijksmuseum to the Victoria Hotel to collect the bride and groom for the last event of the day: a canal trip around Amsterdam.

Louis sat next to his mother, stony-faced, apparently immune to the stream of sweet words she would whisper in his ear every now and then. The hotel-keeper's wife wondered what was wrong with him as she gently stroked his cheeks.

A little earlier, when her second son had collected his party hat from the cloakroom lady, he'd thrown it to the floor with a war cry and stamped on it as if it were burning newspaper. Kati had giggled, thinking that it was a joke, but took a hold of herself when she saw Maria's horrified face as she cried, 'Louis, darling, what are you doing? What's the matter?'

Felix had skulked to the back seat. He was troubled by an acute sense of powerlessness and compassion for his brother and felt sorry for the awful blunder he'd made. Maria glanced over her shoulder at Felix and asked again what in God's name had happened.

'Nothing, Mum, honestly,' was Felix's feeble response. Louis was probably just a little tired. He wasn't used to all this excitement.

Jacob nodded in agreement, declaring that not everyone was made for life in the big city; its impressions could sometimes be over-powering. Without any logical connection, the hotel-keeper then moved on to a story about a carpenter who had decided to build a boat in his attic. When it was finished, of course, he had no idea how to get the boat to the waterfront. A hoist wouldn't work. The whole project was a ridiculous mistake. The only solution was to dismantle the boat.

Hans Matti didn't understand the half of it, but figured the story had to have a humorous side and grinned throughout. Maria also uttered a cheerful noise or two – how could anyone be such an ass? – doing her best to cheer up her second son, but Louis was imper-turbable. He stared ahead, his eyes bulging fixedly, like those of a dead fish, his shoulders and arms stock-still, as if he had turned to stone.

Aadje Pruis had avoided encroaching on Jacob's territory until then, but his years of experience in the entertainment world inspired him to take his own initiative. Just before the Mint Tower, he turned to the right and thundered past a ribbon of picturesque facades along the Kloveniersburgwal, heading for the Red Light District.

'What on earth are you doing?' a shocked Jacob muttered, catching

124

glimpses of the canal that lead irreversibly to the labyrinth of lanes and alleyways the hotel-keeper knew all too well.

The Rokin was temporarily closed on the south side, this was the only road he could take, mumbled the driver, fishing for an excuse and turning away from his prominent fellow townsman whose trembling lips made him realise the enormity of his error. He could have kicked himself. There goes my tip, he thought, but there was no way back.

The first of the ladies – their naked legs and alluring cleavages – drifted past like water lilies in a ditch. Hans Matti, suddenly as bright as a button, groped feverishly for his binoculars, wrestled with the cord for a second, and set them in front of his mustachioed face. Kati immediately slapped them away from his eyes. 'You pig,' she yelled at the top of her voice. 'What do you call this?'

The sausage-maker's wife, already in great mental and physical distress because she'd been yearning for a glass of white wine for over an hour, surprised herself. Even Maria suddenly felt uneasy as, bright-eyed but demure, she observed the girls in their glass cages. She had often heard about the Red Light District and read this and that about it in the papers, but she had never been there before. Not a place for her, surely?

To make matters worse, the minibus got stuck behind a van delivering beer along the canal bank. A red-haired Neanderthal with tattoos on his arms was rolling barrels down a wooden plank on to the street. In the meantime, they all had ample time and opportunity to inspect the industry for which the capital had earned its international reputation.

It was pretty busy. Men in their prime, boys who should have been at school and pensioners with one foot in the grave swarmed all over the place, their eyes like rolling marbles, scouring the shop windows, which were all lit with pale red lanterns despite the afternoon hour and the plentiful sunlight.

Things a man would be hard pushed to imagine in his naughtiest fantasies were now taking place for all to see. A bald gentleman with snow-white sideburns, who reminded Maria of her teacher when she had been at trade school in Leeuwarden, marched purposefully and at a pace across the cobbles with a leather ring binder under his arm. He gazed greedily at the windows from the corner of his eye, and suddenly headed down a set of stone steps without looking up or down. The sideburns began their stately descent, the dark purple curtains of his chosen establishment pulled together in a jerk or two by a grinning whore with a gap between her front teeth.

What filth! Kati had wanted to scream, but she controlled herself. Her powdered eyebrows danced up and down like a jet fighter looking for a place to land. She disappeared into her handbag, grubbing around for a stray piece of chocolate. When she realised she had eaten it all, she asked Maria what she thought of the whole disgusting exhibition.

'I really don't know, dear Kati,' answered Maria, staring at her husband whose seeming disinterest was only thinly disguised. While she had profound compassion for these fallen women, she stated cautiously, she also found it interesting to see them with her own eyes for once.

Jacob heard a Teutonic grunt behind him and feared that his future in-law's excitement might be getting too much. The hotel-keeper suddenly remembered a book about Peter the Great he had read as a boy. He recommenced his storytelling, recounting the fortunes of the renowned Russian who had visited Amsterdam on no less than two occasions almost two hundred and fifty years ago. It was not impossible that the Russian monarch had actually stood where they were now. It had all existed back then, of course, the canals, the houses, the sun, the clouds, the facades. Could Hans Matti imagine it?

'Do answer the question, *Vati*!' Kati jerked her husband's sleeve. He had been innocently watching as a man with a face as flat as a pancake was welcomed into another sun-filled, glass-fronted kingdom by a blonde girl.

'What's that?' he asked.

'That all of this has been here for centuries,' Jacob repeated patiently – the canals, the clouds, the houses. He watched resignedly as the Neanderthal continued at leisure, now hauling empty barrels from an open trapdoor. The ominous roar of empty beer barrels being rolled up on to the street resounded deep in the minibus.

And it would still be there long after they were gone, the hotel-keeper continued in a sombre tone. The sun would rise and set every day, babies would be born, and young people would fall in love, without a care for what had gone before. It was unimaginable, really.

'How right you are, Jacob,' muttered Hans Matti, who was con-fronted by similar depressing ideas from time to time, more often now that he was getting older. It was enough to drive one mad, or to throw oneself under a train for that matter. Thankfully, nature made sure that such notions passed quickly, like a stabbing pain in the chest or heartburn.

All the while, Felix was cursing the artist who had painted *The Idiot* with its prick-wielding halfwit for the umpteenth time. Poor Louis must have seen the painting's name; it was printed in large let-ters on a card beside it.

He had an idea what was going on in his brother's head: Louis had seen himself for the first time in his life, not like in the mirror all the thousands of times before, but as others saw him – naked, piti-less. Art could be as powerful as dynamite, but worse.

Fifteen minutes later, the black plastic knob of the gearstick was finally shifted into first, and the party departed from the depraved district, just as a carillon in a bell tower with white wooden panels chimed an Offenbach melody, and Maria gently hummed along.

Kati started to complain loudly of a headache, and Louis still resembled a statue from Madame Tussaud's in the seat next to his mother. Jacob looked at his watch – four o'clock – and anxiously tried to decide on what to do next. In the circumstances, he couldn't possibly oblige Louis, who had a slight fear of water, to join them on a boat trip, and the idea of pancakes turned his stomach. The hotel-keeper now realised all the more how planning ahead was often pointless.

He decided to consult Ludo on what to do for the rest of the afternoon. The bridegroom-to-be was sitting next to Liza on the terrace of the Victoria Hotel, sunglasses on his head, smiling and looking remarkably relaxed.

Aadje pulled up in front of a pedestrian precinct, put on his warning lights and gallantly helped everyone off. He then drove his bus – both sides bearing the vermilion motto 'Wherever you want!' – to the land registry office and parked it under a tree. He was not to know that Jacob had once spent an entire afternoon behind that prominent facade, which now cast a bluish shadow over Aadje's piggy features, learning the ins and outs of property law, before purchasing the former Hotel Deluxe from its administrators.

'It's wonderful here in the sun, folks,' said Ludo, a cigarette dangling from his lips. He couldn't understand what they'd been doing for so long in that stupid museum. Museums are dead, out here it's alive. What did everyone want to drink?

'A glass of white wine,' said Kati directly, nodding at the half-bottle of Chablis in a cooler on the table. She fixed her eyes imploringly on the waiter, who moved like a pantomime character with a mouse-like face and stubby legs.

'So, what have you been up to this afternoon?' asked the sausage-maker's wife, turning to her daughter with feigned interest. Ludo had bought her a scarf, Liza replied cheerfully. She withdrew the gift from her handbag, looking up sweetly at her fiancé, who was still wondering why he had had to pay nineteen guilders for such a pointless rag.

'How splendid, my child. Will you try it on for us?' Maria requested. She then went on to order a coffee, as did Jacob and Felix.

Louis sat in silence like a scolded animal, his wicker chair creaking under him. What would he like to drink? asked his mother. Lemonade, perhaps? Or a coffee?

'Beer!' he barked, as if it were an order.

'Are you sure?' his mother cautioned, fearing that her son would be unwell on the way home. Alcohol usually made Louis nauseous.

'I want beer, dammit!' he barked again, his face trembling horribly.

Ludo looked at his younger brother in surprise and thought, What's up with him now, for God's sake? He, meanwhile, was in a state of pure physical bliss after the romp with Liza and the wine.

Half an hour later and they were on their way back to the coast. Jacob had decided to cancel the boat trip on Ludo's recommendation. Just as they passed the sugar refinery at Halfweg, Louis suddenly started to sing at the top of his voice. It was complete gibberish and sounded dreadful. Maria and Jacob clapped along hesitantly, followed by the kindly Hans Matti who even added an oompah or two, his lips pressed tightly together.

After throwing back two glasses of Chablis and snatching what was left of her daughter's wine, scolding her sternly for drinking during her pregnancy, Kati was completely carefree. Her private high made everything fly by in the most delightful manner.

Before long they were passing through the dunes on the wartime road, the same road that the Benders had followed to the resort a couple of days earlier. Once they reached the sea – a strange sea with violet waves and a silvery, dark sky – the wind picked up. Drops of rain appeared on the windows, running down like tears into the gutter. Maria mumbled something about rain not being on the agenda for Friday and that today's weather forecast had been completely different.

When they arrived at Hotel New Deluxe, an anxious-looking Mr Zwaan hurried out into the pouring rain, followed by two waiters with umbrellas who rushed into the slippery street, ready to escort the ladies to the door, as if they were guests at the Ritz.

The hotel-keeper accompanied his manager inside and asked what the matter was.

'This arrived an hour ago,' croaked Mr Zwaan, handing his boss a telegram. 'I don't understand a word of it.'

'Dear God!' the hotel-keeper exclaimed after reading the three lines of German text that were actually intended for Hans Matti Bender. Jacob had forgotten to tell him about the town hall's stupid decision. Now it was too late: The Flesh Tones were already on their way. Their bus was due to arrive at eight.

'What's wrong, Lucas?' Jacob asked when he realised his manager was still gaping at him in confusion.

'May I speak to you in private? There's something else we need to talk about.'

A high-pitched squeal sounded from the street. Both men turned to see Kati almost slip on the shiny wet cobbles, only to be rescued by Guillaume, juggling with his umbrella.

Her '*Danke schön!*' rang out over The Boulevard.

Jacob grunted something indistinct, and headed to his office, Mr Zwaan following behind.

Part Two

A New Future

35

The pragmatic depravity of their plan was as banal as it was simple. Six months after the wedding, Ludo and Liza would assist Hans Matti and Kati to shuffle off this mortal coil, their method of choice as yet unresolved, then sell the sausage factory, where everyone had long been exploited for a minimum wage, and take off with the money for—

'Florida,' whispered Liza, licking the letter L as if it were a lollipop.

'Do you really want to go to America?'

'Yeah...' Liza croaked, looking up at Ludo for one brief blissful moment, her eyelashes flickering, before nestling her chin once again on the pillow of his chest.

She was thinking about the delightful film that she had seen not long before at the cinema in Aachen. It was about three handsome young men and three blonde girls in a world of palm trees and perpetual sunshine, where life was one big holiday, and they all raced around in open-top cars, past bays filled with dolphins, and went swimming and played tennis. There were no parents, only an elderly black woman who served drinks and snacks from time to time in their villa, reminiscing about her own youth long ago. From then on, Florida was simply paradise, as far as Liza was concerned.

Ludo got off the blue tram in Haarlem, made his way over to Edo Novak's house, promptly handed him a bottle of whisky with its label printed upside down, which he had taken – without permission –from his father's stockroom. Edo accepted the gift irritably. How much longer would this farce carry on? Ludo shrugged his shoulders and climbed the stairs to the attic room where Liza had been in hiding for the past six days, a box of *Mon Cheri* chocolates at the ready.

The girl from Cologne could not even bring herself to leave the house without Ludo by her side. She was impressed by Edo, but still didn't know what to think of her curious host, who usually slept until the early afternoon and then spent half an hour in the shower.

By the time the hot water had crept its way up from the heater in the basement to the shower on the third floor, the pipes groaning and occasionally banging in the process, Liza had already been up for hours, sitting in the huge kitchen on the ground floor, poring over a plate with a couple of slices of stale bread and some jam, a pot of tea beside it, aching for the speedy return of her darling.

She had absolutely nothing else to do. In her head, she'd already convinced herself that her mother was dead. The slim newspaper with its hammer and sickle, which appeared on the kitchen table in the early afternoon, was all gibberish to her. By the third day, she had already resorted to counting the tiles on the wall; at 120, Edo had waltzed into the kitchen in his red silk jacket, unshaven but smelling of soap and aftershave. He had planted a stubbly kiss on her neck out of sheer contrariness, although she'd not mentioned it to Ludo, just to be on the safe side.

'Rio de Janeiro,' Ludo had determined, much to her surprise, yet another puff of cigarette smoke circling up towards the ceiling from his puckered lips. 'It's always warm... and they have palm trees and delicious—'

'If we're not going to Florida, I want to go to Africa,' Liza had responded resolutely; she would be twenty-four next year, but she had never seen a rhinoceros in the wild. Had he also heard that they were supposed to smell terrible?

The German blonde had eased herself away from him, purring like a cat, with a feeling of intense happiness. She wiped the sticky substance off her thighs with her slender fingers, seed from Ludo's potent and pitiless member, which now looked like a porpoise beached on curly seaweed below his waist.

'Why not a world cruise, sweetie?' was Ludo's flippant and fraudulent response. He had no intention of taking Liza anywhere. She was insignificant to his own plan; only her parents' capital would factor in what was a much grander design. He wasn't sure how, though, not yet. That was Edo's department.

But why was he so impatient and irritable all of a sudden? wondered Liza. He had the build of a boxer, but there were moments when his feeble, quivering lips gave him the look of a hysterical woman.

36

Edo was one of those rare people that always make an indefinably pleasant first impression. He appeared friendly and genuine, and his charm was impressive, generating a sort of addiction in others, a desire to speak to him again, to spend increasing amounts of time with him. The sort of thing that usually only happens between lovers.

Although only twenty-nine, the former history student had a past that read like a novel. He was the son of an emaciated orphan girl from Indonesia and a bon vivant with a weakness for fine clothes. His father's family background was vague to say the least. There were a number of different stories doing the rounds, but 'Flemish blood, with a touch of Alsace' tended to hold sway.

His father had arrived in Java by accident at the end of the 1920s, on a British passenger ship bound for New Zealand. He had stayed, and before long had amassed a small fortune by trading jewellery and perfumes. Edo grew up in fairy-tale houses, surrounded by swirls of servants, palm trees and trays tinkling with glasses of cool, refreshing lemonade, a little prince with curly black hair that straightened when he was twelve. These homes were later appropriated by others, illegally sold, or burned to the ground.

Edo's parents had sent their only child to a renowned surgeon in London in early 1939 for an operation to remove a lump of bone that had formed with ominous speed on his left foot. The operation was a success. Edo was obliged to spend three months recovering in rather frugal circumstances, looking out from his dreary bed on to a blank wall above a dry cleaner's. He still experienced a nagging pain every now and then, especially when the weather turned humid.

After the war broke out, one of the surgeon's nephews and his family generously took the boy in. Edo arrived in Vlissingen in August 1945 and stared out from the quay at the distant barren dunes that he knew of only from the songs they had sung at school. He was met by his one remaining uncle, who told him with astonishing matter-of-factness – his raincoat held tight at the throat against the blustering wind – that his parents were dead.

Edo was still a minor, and his uncle decided that he should finish his studies in the Netherlands. The family's possessions in Java had been entrusted to a notary, the sum transferred from Batavia every six months barely covering his expenses. He sent letters of complaint, but to no avail.

On a snowy winter's day early on in the war, Edo had wandered into a colonial supplies shop in Soho and bought the requisite light-weight uniform. Six years later, he had attacked the outfit with a pair of scissors, enraged, tearing it to shreds that he then burnt on the stove in his student room. He had found it impossible to cope with the unremitting stream of bad news from home. He wasn't allowed to fight or do anything else in the army because of his rotten left foot. One morning, on the station platform in Utrecht, he witnessed a battalion of baby-faced soldiers, kit bags on their backs, all singing at the tops of their voices, and ready to embark for Amsterdam and beyond. 'Why them…? Jesus Christ, why them and not me?' he had snarled hatefully through his pearl-white teeth.

The Americans, who had left his father and mother to die like dogs, were now trying to impose their rule on the world, while he was stuck in this eternally grey and miserable hole, like a rat in a sewer. After the Dutch East Indies were finally handed over, the money transfers from Batavia dried up completely, and his uncle had volunteered to pay for the rest of his studies. But this generosity, too, was short-lived. When he died, the family pounced on the inheritance like a pack of starving hyenas.

By the time Germany had capitulated, a sea of Japanese had been vaporised in a flash of light and the world had decided to embark on a new future with irrepressible courage. Edo Novak had virtually nothing he could call his own, notwithstanding his sun-flecked childhood memories, unusually sharp wit and bitterness at his current circumstances.

37

Ludo Bagman and Edo Novak had met by chance one evening eighteen months earlier, when they had both been sheltering from a downpour and awaiting the last tram on Spuistraat. The wind had howled like a dying animal.

'Late again,' said Edo, breaking the silence, having studied the handsome figure beside him for a while out of the corner of his eye.

'Typical Dutch tram,' Ludo replied, picking up the thread of a discussion he had been having an hour before in a bar with a guy from the stock exchange. 'God devised two punishments for mankind: being one of the chosen people or living in the Netherlands. I can't figure out which is worse.' He burped loudly. 'Excuse me, I've had a couple of beers... Ah, here it is...'

They carried on chatting in the silver light of the almost empty carriage, the light waning each time the blue tram began to increase its speed – shuddering like an animal – after slowing at a junction. Their handsome faces were reflected in the black windows; they could have been brothers. They turned out to have a lot of ideas in common too. They were in Haarlem before they knew it.

'I hope we meet again soon,' said Edo, pressing a piece of paper into Ludo's hand.

Alone on the tram a short while later as it thundered through the eerily dark dunes on its way to the coast, he glanced at the note with Edo's telephone number on it, the other side of which was the bill for a lunch or dinner at the Hotel Lion d'Or:

1 x Chicken Fried Rice + Prawn Crackers :		*fl 4,50*
3 x Beer	:	*fl 1,80*
2 x coffee	:	*fl 0,90*
1 x Double whisky	:	*fl 2,80*
Total	:	*fl 10,00*

After a bit of mental arithmetic, the hotel-keeper's son figured that the same meal would easily have cost one third less in their hotel. The Lion d'Or was little more than an old-fashioned hangout for snobs, and the kitchen was crawling with cockroaches.

While Ludo had spent that evening drinking, mingling with inebriated scroungers and idiots who often passed themselves off as artists and do-gooder idealists, and stared at every woman who came in, Edo had actually been trying to save humanity.

In a meeting hall close to Artis Zoo, where old-fashioned ventilator fans slowly circled overhead like a ship's propellers, he had listened to a report given by three of his comrades, who had recently returned from a field trip that had brought them from Moscow by way of seemingly blissful Odessa to the desolate tracts near Tashkent and Bukhara.

'To all intents and purposes, Uzbek women are equal to men. Any primitive belief in Allah or Orthodox Christianity is out of the question, and the present Soviet authorities...' A committee member was giving a lecture, his moustache the unhealthy brown of an uncooked shrimp. He snapped his fingers, the fluorescent lights went out, and the audience was treated to a series of slides.

Tea-coloured women in cotton dresses speckled yellow, their eyes like dates, smiled at their kindred spirits in the cold and distant Netherlands, revealing their golden teeth.

'But do they encourage the appropriate use of contraceptives?' enquired an unmarried woman as the projector hummed in the darkness. She was a secondary school teacher who raised questions of sex and hygiene at every meeting.

'Of course, Mrs Tempelboom. The State takes care of its women-folk from the cradle to the grave. Prostitution and other forms of physical exploitation have been abolished. But women are free sexually speaking, very free. Just like the men. Wouldn't you agree, Van Yperen?'

Another voice then muttered something incomprehensible from the stage and proceeded to rattle off statistics on income, production, births and deaths in the autonomous Soviet Republic of Uzbekistan, all in a distinct Amsterdam dialect, reading from a piece of paper with the help of a cigarette lighter.

On a plaster wall that served as a projection screen, mountains of dazzling white cotton and melons the size of rugby balls appeared, followed by local men with wilting, pitch-black moustaches, their features not quite Chinese. They sat cross-legged on single beds in the open air, and drank tea or gurgled on water pipes, and looked on, grinning, as teenage girls in short blue dresses, with red scarves over their white blouses, stoked the fire for mutton kebabs.

'The meat just melts in your mouth, comrades,' proclaimed Shrimp Moustache with infectious excitement. 'That sort of thing is impossible in this cold, damp and impoverished country of ours. But there is no reason to despair, comrades! One day our own streets will also rejoice!'

The dull pink fluorescent lamps flickered and fizzed, filling the room with light once again. A short applause was followed by the crackle and hiss of matches, as comrades right and left lit cigarettes.

There were roughly three times as many men as women in the hall. A gentleman with kind eyes and a crooked nose scribbled avidly in a notebook throughout the meeting with the stump of a carpenter's pencil. His name was Van Parijs and he was a roofer. He had always wanted to continue his studies, but had never made it beyond foreman. He hoped his son would get to university. When he arrived in the hall, his bicycle pump under his arm, someone had looked at his wind-blown face, and said in greeting, 'Hey, Van Parijs, how are things?'

Dockworkers, artists, primary and secondary school teachers sat fraternally alongside a philosophy professor, a shopkeeper, a bunch of bricklayers from Betondorp, an aristocratic young lady who had never needed to work (a fact she anxiously concealed) and boat workers with tattooed forearms, as well as members of other occupational and social groups.

Some were cheerful by nature, others tended to be more serious and complaining; animal lovers mingled with comrades more inclined to kick dogs, cats and any other short-legged creatures in a dark alley, anything rather than spoil them. There were party members and sympathisers present who would never be seen giving their seat up for someone else on the tram, but also selfless types who tried to help others wherever they got the chance, who lay awake at night pained by the sufferings of the world. The majority thought only of themselves, their children and their immediate families. Prioritise one's personal well-being, then consider that of your fellow mortals. It was always fine to lend a helping hand if it didn't have to cost one's own comfort, or lighten one's own wallet.

But one thing bound them all together: they had faith in a better life, in a new future, in the fight against exploitation and the dictatorship of money, against the pathetic philistine disciples of capitalism; they wanted peace and justice – short but sweet – all over the world.

Edo looked at the faces around him in silent disgust. He had nothing in common with most of them, and asked himself what in all conscience he was doing there, just as he had asked himself the same question a month earlier when he had attended a party meeting for the first time. He had intended to leave after the break, but something unexpected had happened: one of the committee members who had been to Russia, a man in his early thirties who went by the name of Kipman, recognised him.

After the exotic Central Asian diversion, Kipman had enthusiastically detailed the recreational facilities in Moscow, punctuating his spiel with broad sweeping gestures. He rambled on about the immaculate unisex youth camps in the surrounding forests, then about pastries filled with sour cream, and then the genius of Tchaikovsky and other such delights, warmly winking at Edo a couple of times from the podium. When he had finished, he immediately approached Edo and, smiling from ear to ear, placed his hand on his left shoulder as if they were old friends. What was his name again? the youthful committee member enquired in a refined, impeccably polite accent, which was only spoken in a few areas of the city.

'Edo Novak,' the former student replied. He had spent the previous months immersed in the lives of Stalin, Hitler, Napoleon, but also devouring books by Chateaubriand, Stendhal, Sartre, Bakoenin, Marx and Malraux in large numbers.

'Coffee's ready!' called a woman with a pallid complexion from the corner of the room. Everyone immediately descended upon a folding table laden with cups of steaming coffee and four large fruit cakes served by the secret aristocrat girl, who had had someone bake them for her the day before.

In the meantime, Edo and Kipman continued their conversation, sitting on the edge of the stage. It didn't take long for Edo to make his habitual strong impression, with his imposing build and keen expression. He said intelligent things – not just another dockland halfwit, but a young man you could talk to.

Edo summarised his youth in the East Indies and told Kipman how he'd given up studying history at university three years earlier. He could no longer bear the untainted egoism of his fellow students or the deceptive nonsense spouted by the professors, he said. He was now a free man, worked three afternoons a week in a bookshop, and wanted only to dedicate the rest of his life to the good of his fellow man.

'Is this really how you feel?' Kipman interjected, overcome by a satisfying feeling of confidence that was nowadays increasingly rare. In spite of their struggle for the abstract cause of good, party members were nevertheless paralysed by a fear of being in the wrong, or of saying the wrong thing.

Edo praised his lecture on Moscow and confessed that he couldn't wait to see the achievements of the USSR in person. He had heard that the Russians weren't only keen on sport but that they made communal visits to the bathhouse once a week. Was that true?

'Yes, yes... absolutely,' Kipman nodded, resting his hand once again on Edo's shoulder and lifting his pipe that spread the scent of rosemary to his vaulted feminine lips. 'But let's sit down, and I can explain... So many people just refuse to understand.'

A week later Edo was a member of the party, and less than six months after that he was on a train to Moscow to immerse himself in the Russian language, and all manner of other things besides, for a full six months.

He preferred to refer to himself as an idealist rather than a Communist. To everyone else, of course, he was the latter, and some avoided him for that very reason. He withdrew into his shell, nurturing the pointless rancour that seemed to grow within him with every passing day.

38

'Gentlemen...' Standing behind the lectern (in fact, a cutlery box covered by a length of black velvet), one December evening, Bastiaan Hermans looked out to see if any women were present – there were none.

A group of hotel and catering industry people had collected around the competition billiard table in Hotel Sea View, which failed to offer either views of the sea or any other natural phenomena. A fierce westerly gale was blustering outside. Everyone had arrived by seven – hats glued to their heads, cursing the Dutch climate – and Bastiaan Hermans had already popped out twice to see if his roof tiles were holding.

'Gentleman,' the hotel-keeper continued in his polished diction, 'the statutory duty falls to me once again, as chairman, to provide you with a concise summary of the events of the preceding calendar year. In spite of spending restrictions, increased taxes and the spiralling costs in all areas of our sector, and thanks to the exceptionally fine spring and a busy high season of innumerable foreign tourists, this year has been a reasonably successful one for our resort. After all, it is beyond dispute that – Jesus, Kees, quick – the window!'

A clear bubble glass window had been punched open by the wind, exposing the assembly to the unruly elements, knocking over a potted palm and sending a shower of rain all over the place.

A young man in a grey cardigan and a blue tie, a glistening golden anchor for a tiepin (inherited from his father who had spent his entire life at sea), raced from his folding chair to the open window. He was an apprentice chef at the hotel, but was attending the meeting out of personal interest, hoping to learn something from the discussions. He already had a child and wanted to improve his life. By the time he had forced the window shut and bolted it, the effort requiring all the strength he could muster, he looked as if he had just come back from a swim.

'Thank you, Kees... Please do take your seat... One thing is certain, gentlemen,' Bastiaan Hermans resumed, having written out his speech in full in a cash ledger with a fountain pen, intending to preserve it for the next generation, 'one thing is certain: if we are compelled to survive without our foreign visitors, it'll be a very sad day for our industry. All the more reason to meet the needs of all of our customers to the best of our ability, regardless of their nationality.'

'But if we have to go back,' he continued, his voice slightly raised, a tick in his hand-written text indicating this shift like an instruction on a piece of sheet music, 'if we have to go back to the days between the 1920s and the Second World War, when the summer was over by the end of July, and completely finished, for our purposes, by the 15 of August, then it will be impossible for seasonal businesses to survive, what with the misery of taxes, deductions and contributions of every sort, not to mention the recent spending restrictions.'

If the sun shone, there were plenty of visitors and business was brisk. If it rained, then they could whistle for it. Such was life. Fortunately, their own division was hale and hearty, the hotel-keeper elaborated, and greater cooperation with the national union was an encouraging sign. Membership was rapidly increasing nationwide, resulting in modern standards of service and organisation. In this annual review, he was pleased to concur with what the national chairman had concluded at the last general meeting. Everyone who pays his contribution on time is undoubtedly a union member. But all of those who attended the meetings – when possible, of course – and who let their voices be heard in a constructive manner, and who were justifiably critical of the leadership or policy at the appropriate moment, were also valuable members.

'So, my friends,' said Bastiaan Hermans, who had once attended a three-year further education course, which more or less guaranteed his re-election every year as chairman. Jacob, whose hotel was many times bigger, resented this state of affairs and in unconscious protest always sat at the back. 'Let us work to increase visitor numbers, for the benefit of all!'

A frail gentleman with an untamed head of black curls, familiar to all as the Italian owner of the ice-cream parlour at the end of The Boulevard, suddenly started to applaud. His command of Dutch was still poor and, as a southerner, he had let himself be carried along by the rhythm, melody and fervour of the speech, wrongly thinking it had reached its conclusion. He immediately realised his mistake, observed the many heads turning towards him, and resumed his listening pose with an expression that was both concentrated and theatrical.

'The committee has met a total of seven times in plenary session in the last year,' the hotel-keeper proceeded, nodding benignly to the Italian, whose name was Lamborghini, from behind his velvet lectern. They had also attended three regional meetings in Haarlem and the North Holland district meeting in preparation for the national congress, which would take place next year in the province of Zeeland. Their delegation, as everyone was aware, consisted of Wedekind the treasurer and himself. The national trade journal had recently published details of the previous annual congress, which the Middleburg branch had organised, exceeding their budget by no less than 305 guilders and twenty-five cents. They should have consulted our honoured treasurer Johannes Wedekind beforehand on how best to organise such an event!

All eyes now turned towards a diminutive figure sitting near the front, a leather folder on his lap. His hair was pasted in thin strands across his broad-bean skull. Wedekind was still visibly perspiring after a long day in the kitchen of his bistro, where truck drivers, travelling salesmen and others were welcome from six-thirty in the morning for toasted sandwiches, soups, Russian salads and the like. Rumour had it that he had overspent on a new delivery van and was now on the verge of bankruptcy.

'We are fortunate not to have suffered any loss of membership this year, neither by the resignation of any member nor by the demise of one of our community,' Bastiaan Hermans concluded. He expressed his hope that the coming season would be a prosperous one, not only for their own sector but for trade in the beach resort as a whole. 'Let it be a good year for all here present and for everyone else too.' That was their chairman's sincere wish.

145

39

In a different time and in different circumstances, Mr Zwaan would probably have made a perfect royal aide or imperial advisor, perhaps even counsel to a tsar. He was one of a rare number of people for whom tranquillity, fidelity and decency were more important than money and social standing, and although this characteristic may not have brought him far in life, there could be little doubt that he had found his destiny.

He had done his duty during the war, almost entirely unobserved, and without being thanked for it later, let alone decorated. After the war, he had moved from the east of the country to the beach resort for the sake of his little daughter, who suffered from a rare muscular disease and was confined to a wheelchair. Trees were scarce in his new home, and, unable to find work as a forester, he set out in search of alternative employment.

After a job with the Parks Department, he tried his hand as a book-keeper with a construction firm in Haarlem, where they had taken him on immediately thanks to his respectable appearance and unruffled demeanour. But Mr Zwaan was not cut out for office work. His wife, who also suffered from poor health, watched him grow more and more unhappy as the days went by.

During his regular constitutional with his daughter, he strayed one day from their usual path and happened to pass Hotel New Deluxe, where Louis was busy painting an outside wall under his father's supervision. Jacob had immediately approached the girl, who was encased between the rubber tyres of her wheelchair, a check blanket covering her legs, and, smiling, caressed her pale little face, before disappearing inside, only to emerge a moment or two later with a scoop of ice cream pressed between two waffles.

The eleven-year-old almost exhausted herself with words of gratitude, raising herself up as far as she could to give Jacob a kiss.

The hotel-keeper had seen the stranger and his unfortunate daughter several times before in the town, but this was the first time they had spoken. Jacob complained that it was proving very difficult to find a reliable person to supervise the waiters. If you didn't keep a constant eye on them, they would skive off, or do whatever they wanted.

'I'm your man,' Mr Zwaan had replied.

Jacob glanced at Louis, who was leaning over the disabled girl, enquiring if she was enjoying her ice cream every time she took a lick.

'Are you serious? Do you have any experience in catering?'

'Not as such,' the former woodsman confessed in his jovial easterner's accent.

They should talk about it, suggested Jacob. What harm could it do? He himself had made the move from antiques to catering and hotel management only a year and a half earlier. Before that, there was no way he would have been able to spot the difference between a Bordeaux and a Chablis.

A week later, Mr Zwaan had started work with the Bagman family, a decision he had never regretted for a single moment since.

Now, though, Mr Zwaan, who had followed his employer to his office after the minibus had returned from Amsterdam, was clearly occupied by something extremely important.

'Lucas, what on earth am I going to do with that bunch of hornblowers?' asked Jacob, only too well aware that there was no room in the hotel for The Flesh Tones. He collapsed into an antique chair, which was slightly incongruous beside his desk – a common café table covered with a green cloth. 'Please, do sit down. Let's ask my future in-law from Cologne to join us, then we can—'

But Mr Zwaan stood stock still. His hand moved slowly inside his black waiter's jacket and eventually produced a copy of *The Boulevard*.

'Lucas, why are you looking at me like that? What's the matter?'

'I don't believe a word of what they say about you,' the manager calmly replied, handing over the now unfolded newspaper to his boss. 'But what about the German? You know I'm prepared to do whatever you ask of me, but I'll be damned if I'll chase around after an ex-Nazi. Front page!' he added after a slight cough.

Jacob glared at the cover photo on the front page. A still youthful Hans Matti Bender, with a neatly trimmed moustache and shiny spectacles, was cheerfully marching along in an officer's uniform at the head of a procession of Georgian soldiers. The infantry battalion of the Wehrmacht, made up of prisoners of war from the Caucasus who had been given the choice to defect or face certain death, had been billeted for a time at the resort during the war. The soldiers were later transferred to Texel, where they played a heroic role in the revolt against the Germans and the liberation of the island.

When Jacob read the italic text printed beneath the photo his head turned crimson. It was as if his skull had split in two, one frozen half fully conscious of the horror of it all, the other prey to a burning rage that, untempered, would have set him foaming at the mouth like a madman.

The hotel-keeper jerked at his adjustable table lamp and studied the photograph once again, gasping in shock. Mr Zwaan asked if he would like a glass of water, regretting that he had not thought through how to confront his boss properly with the article

'No, I'm fine…' Jacob suddenly jabbed at the photo with his index finger as if it were a dagger, almost puncturing the page. 'What do you think, Lucas? Do you think it's him? My bloody reading glasses are upstairs…'

'Of course it is, there's no doubt in my mind,' Mr Zwaan confirmed flatly. 'But was there any truth in the—'

'In the accusation that I persuaded Jewish families to hand over their antique furniture before they were deported, is that what you mean?'

A clenched fist smashed the makeshift desk, sending a teaspoon into the air and then down towards a glass ashtray. The seething half of Jacob's brain had suddenly taken control.

'No, no... That's not what I meant...' Mr Zwaan cried, cringing with guilt since it was exactly what he had wanted to say.

There was a short silence; neither man moved.

'Fetch that Kraut right away,' the hotel-keeper said calmly, spitting the word 'Kraut' with some pleasure, as if it were a lump of phlegm stuck deep in his throat that had finally worked its way up and out.

Mr Zwaan sprinted out of the room like an athlete.

Jacob fell back into his Louis XVI chair, numbered ninth on the itemised list of treasures printed in a black frame beside the article with the tabloid headline: DAUGHTER OF NAZI MARRIES SON OF JEW PROFITEER.

He squeezed the gold-coloured inlay of the armrests, and could see once again the armchair standing by the fireplace in the Lauriergracht in his mind's eye. 'How're you doing, you old crook?' Benno Lemberg had greeted him countless times with his typical burr.

The hotel-keeper's mind suddenly went blank. It felt for a moment as if some merciful power was slowly drawing him down to the earth's core.

40

It was a month after they had been evacuated to Haarlem. Jacob and his family had been quartered in the house of a former guard at the panoptic prison, the guard having been promoted unexpectedly. Their mattresses, which had provided extra revenue every summer for years on end, had been confiscated the day before they left by an official waving a piece of paper heavily embossed with Third Reich emblems and swastikas. Jacob had been allowed to take the majority of his antiques with him, all the same. He stored them all in a barn that backed onto the River Spaarne, and hoped he could continue to run his business from there.

Deportation and forced labour in Germany were always lurking round the corner, but for the moment the occupier had other ideas: he was commandeered to work demolishing buildings along the coastline. Jacob made his way to the beach resort every day on his bicycle (and later on foot, which meant he had to leave the house at a quarter past five), and was forced to watch the area where his three children had been born and where he and Maria had been happy slowly crumble before his eyes.

Eleven months later, he was transferred to work with the concrete mixers in the dunes, where bunkers, underground corridors, walls and anti-tank defences were constructed at almost the same pace as the seaside buildings had been destroyed.

One Sunday afternoon he was sitting with Felix on his lap, teaching him a song from his childhood, when the doorbell rang. Ludo and Louis were still playing football in the field behind the fire station. Maria was busy in the kitchen trying to conjure up a meal from nine potatoes, six stalks of endive and any leftovers she could find, but without the missing magic ingredient: salt.

Jacob made his way to the door with Felix in his arms. A sturdy young man of twenty at most was standing on the doorstep, wearing a formal jacket, his black hair standing on end and looking like an upturned clothes brush, his hands steadying his bicycle.

'Are you Jacob Bagman?'

'Who wants to know?'

'Benno Lemberg sent me.'

'Come inside, please,' Jacob replied, relieved and smiling at Felix who was fiddling with his nose.

The stranger quickly shook his head and stuffed a piece of paper into Jacob's hand, which detailed an address not far from Ooster-park in Amsterdam.

'Long live Stalin!' cheered the lad, jumping onto his saddle and cycling away like a man possessed, his arms and legs flailing like a swimmer's.

The young man had an intelligent face with expressive eyes. Jacob would never see him again. The Netherlands may have been a small country, but it was always chock-full of people.

Two days later, he took the train to Amsterdam after work. He was nervous, apprehensive, tormented by recollections of his journey to Drenthe six months earlier with Uncle Simon.

He held the rain-soaked paper with the address in his fist until he suddenly realised how dangerous it was. He took a last look at the name of the street and the number of the house, tore the paper up, and let the fragments flutter away through the open window.

A moment later, the conductor stumbled into the carriage, directing his gaping yawn to the clattering panels on the ceiling: 'Tickets please.'

Benno Lemberg had been like a second father to Jacob for a long time, his guide and example in everything. They had first met on an autumn day, a blood-red sun setting beyond glistening rooftops, when Jacob had stopped to consider a silver ballet dancer on a little pillar at a market stall on the Waterlooplein. The statuette was all of eleven centimetres tall, but its beauty and grace struck the eighteen-year-old farmhand with such intensity that he felt weak at the knees.

'This fine young lady is actually old enough to have seen Napoleon. Pity such things can't talk. One of creation's big mistakes, if you ask me. It would surely be much easier on the ear than everyone else's drivel. Would you like to hold her?' enquired the stallholder, raising his ample head in an august fashion, his top hat skilfully balanced above a shock of chocolate-brown hair.

Jacob felt as if the salesman had caught him doing something un-toward. He touched his cap lightly in vague greeting, blushed, and continued on his way. A quarter of an hour later, though, he was back at the stall, compelled, enchanted. The eight rixdollars – each worth two and a half guilders – that he had brought with him to the capital to buy a new suit were burning a hole in his pocket.

With a mischievous glint in his eye, the salesman caught sight of him from a distance and greeted the young man as an old friend.

'So, young man, is love in the air? She's a particularly beautiful lady, even if I do say so myself.' The merchant ran his fingers down her matchstick-thin legs. 'The artist has exceeded in beauty what God already made fair. A masterpiece! If you would like to make an offer, I'll happily counter it. That's how it goes around here.'

Jacob worked for a gentleman farmer with a substantial farmhouse in the traditional Dutch style. He had been invited inside a couple of times and had been astounded on both occasions by the extensive silverware collection on display in antique cabinets, on sideboards and consoles. He had plates the size of palace windows, animals of every size and sort, letter openers, memorial coins, cutlery, and even a music box that played a French melody. But the farmhand had absolutely no idea of the value of such things. Once again, his provincial origins surfaced, just as they had when he had been evaluated for military service in Amsterdam.

'Eight rixdollars,' blurted Jacob, impulsively, trying hard to forget that his parents had saved the money from what little they had to buy him a suit.

'What, only twenty guilders? For such a superb little lady?' The salesman shook his head indignantly, gesticulating wildly in his ill-fitting, blue woollen cardigan and matching scarf, like a character from an opera, his feigned surprise and disappointment entirely convincing. 'Would you like me to hand over my life savings in a velvet bag at the same time?'

'It's all I have,' the farmhand replied, swallowing a mouthful of saliva, the salesman staring at the ground, frowning and silent.

In the meantime, Jacob's eyes drifted over the stall's other objects, all tastefully displayed: crystal carafes offset with grey pearls; a Lithuanian clock; a golden spoon on a bed of yellow velvet; various other antiquities that didn't really belong on a market stall but rather in the window of a shop with stylish flourishes and curlicues, the shop Benno Lemberg – after years of hard graft and saving – was, in point of fact, on the verge of setting up.

'Eight rixdollars? For this Parisian beauty?' the salesman suddenly resumed, briefly lifting the silver-plated trinket – which he had valued at three rixdollars maximum – from its plinth. Perhaps he should just give the poor young man his bank account details and be done with it. 'Make it nine!'

'Done, I'll take it,' Jacob relented immediately, with all the guilt of a criminal.

'Deal.' The word echoed through Amsterdam's cold October air.

Jacob started to fish the rixdollars from his pocket, which he had wrapped in a white handkerchief. He was painfully aware that he had walked into a trap with his eyes wide open, but at the same time he couldn't help but think how pretty the statuette would look on his bedside cabinet. His fingers trembled.

'Excuse me, sir.' Jacob looked bashfully up at the salesman and saw a strange glint in his eyes, a mixture of compassion and mockery, which made him shiver once again.

'Don't tell me this is stolen money, eh?'

The farmhand blushed and confessed that he had come to Amsterdam to buy a new suit, but had found the antiques displayed on the stall so magnificent, that it was his dream one day to possess a collection of silverware as fine as that of his boss—

'Put your money away,' Benno Lemberg interrupted in much the same tone he had used a year earlier when he had sent his son to boarding school. He didn't know who this farmhand was, but he was a good judge of character, and he was just about to give up this ramshackle market stall for a real shop. He had a proposal for Jacob.

A week later, Jacob burned his farmhand togs in a field that, in summer, grew strawberries, and started to work for Benno Lemberg. He was part of the growth of Lemberg's business from the very beginning. The shop was on the ground floor of a seventeenth-century townhouse in which a whaling merchant had once lived.

Negotiations ran like clockwork from the very start. A young lady who could speak French and English was appointed to work behind the counter, her soft doe-eyed look alone enough to make the predominantly male clientele surrender en masse. The business specialised in blue Delft pottery; people came from as far afield as Budapest and Berlin to consider their wares.

Jacob and Benno travelled the length and breadth of the country in search of merchandise, visiting auctions as far away as Lille, driving a Ford with a large boot. Jacob soon learned to distinguish Empire Style from Biedermeier, quickly became familiar with the Impressionists and the modernism of the Cubists, memorised all the silver hallmarks after an interval, and understood, in the meantime, that a good figurative painting – a landscape, or a portrait of anyone no matter how ugly – always made its price.

On Jacob's twenty-fourth birthday, Benno Lemberg appeared before him, a rustling envelope in his hand. 'So, now its time to start out on our own. We're not living in Russia, you know. I only wish I had a son as grateful as you. Now he's off chasing some shiksa to England. And he can't seem to find a steady job.'

Jacob opened a shop in Hoedemakersstraat. Three years later he changed direction, and, after his marriage to Maria, ended up in the beach resort, where the market for antiques was less lucrative than in Amsterdam. The focus soon shifted to curios and hire goods.

But the antiques gracing his window display remained top quality. They were his best advertisement, and he never gave up hope that times would change one day for the better.

41

His father had already been dead for some years by the time he found himself climbing the stairs, amid the stench of gas and damp newspapers, the shadow of Uncle Benno awaiting him, having, to Jacob's surprise, opened the door himself by tugging on a rope.

Retrospectively, however, Jacob could not tell which he found the more horrific: the sight of his father, lying like a bag of bones on a fold-up bed in the back parlour, barely breathing, his feeble voice constantly asking about the newspaper headlines, Death already painting its mask on his face, or the desperation written all over hale and hearty Benno Lemberg, considered by the occupier to be nothing more than an insect, a cockroach, to be hunted down, the rituals of hunting having been finely tuned.

'How're you doing, you old crook?' Lemberg greeted him, his lips grenadine, his enthusiasm feigned.

The last time they had met, just before the war had broken out, had been in the café at Schiller's Hotel. Jacob had poked fun at his former boss, telling him he'd become as fat as an elephant and giving him a friendly dig in his gloriously prosperous and elastic ribs.

All the weight had now gone, his face was gaunt, and there were startling charcoal rings under his eyes, though the boyish glint was still visible. 'Tell me, what's it like out there?'

Jacob followed the antiquarian into a room with only a settee and two chairs. The curtains were closed. A shaft of grey daylight filtered through a tall but narrow window in the kitchen on the landing, colouring everything in its path black and white.

'How have you been getting on, Uncle Benno?' Jacob had whispered, immediately aware of the absurdity of his question. What about Aunt Rosa and Gabriel? Was he here all by himself? Wasn't he aware of the dangers? Even of opening the door?

A tram screeched past on the street below; a coaster with an empty water glass shuddered on the window ledge. Jacob was silent, as if his tongue had been ripped out.

'I keep thinking about a story I heard as a boy,' Uncle Benno said, finally breaking the silence. 'It was a fairy tale. Everyone was poor and unhappy. Then one day a magic bird arrived, carrying a basket made from Viennese sweets in its claws, the basket full to bursting with diamonds. The people held a great feast. Finally, they were rich! But their joy didn't last long, for the diamonds turned out to be human tears. They had melted in the meantime and the basket had been reduced to sludge. It all took place in Vilnius. Actually, it wasn't a fairy tale, but a nightmare someone had transcribed. Poor souls! But what about you, and the family?'

Jacob told him about the evacuation to Haarlem, but kept quiet about the nauseating work he had been forced to do for the occupier over the past months. He went on to mention something trivial about Felix – he had swallowed a marble and they had found it in his poo the next day – and could have kicked himself: he had forgotten to bring anything to eat or drink for Uncle Benno. Who took care of him?

He had been stuck here for six days, Benno Lemberg related. Board cost him sixty guilders per day. And he had helped the woman who used to live there find a crib – and it didn't cost her a penny. She was staying with friend in Emmen, but she wasn't a snitch, he was sure of that. Still, he had to get away as quickly as possible. Rosa and Gabriel had already made it to Spain or somewhere else. All that mattered was that they had been safe for the past month. A contact he could trust had reassured him.

Maybe he still had a chance to fulfil his dream and become a grandfather. Gabriel had always been a spoiled brat – tell me about it – but he was healthy, thank God. Benno Lemberg had but a single wish: that one day someone of his own flesh and blood would tickle his toes. Grandfather – the word itself was simply glorious! He would buy his grandchildren toys and sweets by the truckload!

156

There was still an escape route to Switzerland, but there was so little time. He had handed over the last of his money and jewellery to get Rosa and Gabs to safety, even their wedding rings! What did Jacob think of that? But he still had his antique furniture from the Lauriergracht in storage in a shed on Javastraat.

'Dear boy.' Benno Lemberg turned to his former employee. 'I taught you the trade, now you must tell me what I should do.' He needed cash, and fast. Cash and jewellery were his only option.

Benno Lemberg shuffled over to a corner of the room where a chest lay open on the floor, leaned down and rummaged around for a piece of paper, shuffled back over the creaking floor, and handed it to Jacob.

'Items marked with an asterisk have already been sold,' Lemberg explained, flicking the list with a fingernail and plumping down into his chair. Could Jacob read in this light?

He had no idea what was going on in the outside world these days. Were people still doing business? Before arriving there, he had spent six months in hiding behind a bookcase without reading a single book. It had been as dark as the grave! Perhaps he could—'Wait a minute, Jacob, what are you doing?'

Jacob had plucked a fountain pen from his breast pocket, flattened the piece of paper on his lap with his fingers and quickly scrawled his signature on Lemberg's list of belongings. He scribbled underneath: sold to Jacob Bagman, Amsterdam, 12th October, 1941.

'Sold?' said Benno Lemberg, perplexed, still staring at the list.

Jacob told him what he had decided: Uncle Simon's gold coins, which he had hidden in the cellar between tins of furniture polish and sacks of dried peas, in the former prison warden's house where he now resided, should help Uncle Benno escape this pigsty. He would sell the furniture later or exchange it for food for his family.

'Are you sure you know what you're doing, Jacob?'

'Completely sure.'

Benno stood, swaying, and then fell into his friend's arms for the first and last time, sobbing silently.

42

As Mr Zwaan marched with a military gait towards the stairwell leading to the hotel rooms, grim determination written all over his face, Hans Matti and Kati, on the floor above, were in the middle of one of their marital quarrels, quite oblivious.

After three glasses of Chablis in Amsterdam, the sausage-maker's wife was in the mood for more, and uncorked a crisp bottle of Moselle, four of which lay swaddled in white cloth, as if they were babies, at the bottom of her suitcase.

'Do you think that's a good idea, dear?' Hans Matti tried to curb her impulse without success. Jacob would surely offer them all a glass or two with dinner. Couldn't she wait a little? He was certain Jacob would—

'Jacob, Jacob, Jacob,' his wife interrupted, stingingly. It was as if he was Jacob's bloody lap dog! Kati looked outside and suddenly felt like an animal in a cage, unable to move. Jesus, what a godawful country! Look at that bloody rain. She simply longed for a warm bath. A hotel without a single bathroom! Gabi was right. They used to have a bath at home in Dresden—

At that moment, there was a demure single knock on the door. Hans Matti found Mr Zwaan on the threshold, his back rigid, his jaw firm.

'*Bitte kommen Sie mit, Herr Bender,*' he said in a measured yet cryptic tone, Mr Bagman wished to speak with him.

'Everything OK, dear?' said the sausage-maker, smiling sweetly over his shoulder. Jacob wanted a quick word. She should try to get some sleep; she looked a little pale. He closed the door behind him.

'*Der Jacob, der Jacob,*' Kati aped her husband, her head bobbing, her lips coiling in her mealy white face like worms in the rain.

She knocked back the rest of her wine, placed the glass on the green lino floor and collapsed on to the bed, a screech of tortured bedsprings protesting at her ample bulk. Her brain functions lagging, she registered only now the cold click of the door closing. The cage was suddenly transformed into cold storage. The rain continued to pour with the sound of falling pins, which they used to weigh and sell in hundred gram packages in Dresden.

Kati wriggled underneath the blankets and before long was feeling drowsy. She suddenly recalled a day in May – just how long ago was it, exactly? – when she'd gone for a week on Rügen Island with two of her girlfriends; she wearing a white cotton dress, her curious horror of anything to do with the beach or the sea fully developed even back then. She was the thinnest and prettiest of the three, still under twenty, a deliciously fragrant German flower, a pulsating edifice of vein and muscle, overflowing with vigour and *joie de vivre*.

A man had approached her on the lukewarm boulevard that first evening (Hermann? Heinrich?). God, what a beauty she had been in her day. The sun had had a different colour then – warmer, fuller – and the sky was a different shade of blue. Kati dozed, but woke with a jolt a few seconds later. The image of her dark, curly-haired waiter, his umbrella at the ready, hovered before her eyes in an evaporating opal haze, like the breath of a lover at the window. She recalled his scrumptiously muscular buttocks, and his gleaming smile, charming, but also suitably mean, in her view.

The sausage-maker's wife lifted her skirt and slipped her awkward hand, a charitable countess visiting a neglected orphan, cautiously towards her crotch.

Kati panted and gasped. The colour slowly returned to her cheeks as she wheezed and groaned, and, her wrist clenched between her thighs, a flood of blissful despair coursing through her, she implored Jesus and all of the saints to help her, although, in truth, she just wanted to swear.

'Lead on,' Mr Zwaan instructed, in the same tone he had once used to order a traitor across a rustling bed of leaves, a revolver between his shoulder blades, following him deeper and deeper into the woods, to where someone else had finished the job with three dull thuds.

'Where are we going?' Hans Matti enquired, shrewdly sensing that something was amiss.

'Keep moving, please, *Herr Bender*.'

'Isn't this weather terrible?' the sausage-maker remarked as they headed down the stairs towards the vestibule, where the clatter of the rain and the rumble of thunder could be heard.

Mr Zwaan accompanied the German in silence to Jacob's modest office. The hotel-keeper had lit a short cigar, and was puffing at it nervously, as if it were his first.

Hans Matti stared admiringly at his future in-law in his sumptuous chair. Jacob hadn't mentioned that he smoked. He had a few fine cigars with him upstairs. He always took them with him to the annual butchers' fair in Hamburg.

'Is this you?' Jacob asked abruptly, holding up the front page of *The Boulevard* to Hans Matti as if it were a charge sheet.

'What do you mean?' the sausage-maker asked, a shiver running down his spine.

Jacob translated the caption into broken German and asked a second time if the picture indeed showed Hans Matti marching at the head of a battalion of Georgian soldiers. The whole town now spoke of nothing else. Why on earth hadn't he said something? How could he do this to Liza and Ludo?

Hans Matti snatched the newspaper, and raised his glasses to examine the photo closely, his fingers trembling. It was as if all the muscles in his body had been suddenly severed, like the ropes at the launch of a ship. A feeling of horror surged through his body, bringing him to the point of nausea.

'My brother, my dearest brother,' he murmured gently, his voice choked with tears.

'What did you say?' scoffed Mr Zwaan from a corner of the room. He stepped forward and adjusted the desk lamp, shining its pale light through the circles of cigar smoke directly in Hans Matti's face. His eyes were almost blinded by tears.

'This is my dearest brother, Otto. I never thought I would see him again. When was this photo taken? Where can I get information about it? I would like—'

'Brother?' bellowed Mr Zwaan scornfully. He was reminded of a pair of cowards that he'd seen squirming like eels, crying out to God and their mother, before they were summarily executed by the Resistance.

Hans Matti asked for a cigar, took a small one – a Corona, unprocessed tobacco – from the box proffered by Jacob, and began his account of the past. His brother had volunteered for military service in 1939. Otto had just disappeared one day, to Siberia or Africa, he had always thought. But here, in this very town, where his daughter was about to marry…

'Who's to say it isn't you?' thundered Mr Zwaan, his tone that of barely disguised accusation.

'Me?' the sausage-maker exclaimed, almost jumping from his chair. Where in God's name did he get that idea?

'The man in the photo is your spitting image,' the former Resistance worker charged. Your twin brother? The manager's customary restraint collapsed, and he laughed out loud, incredulous.

Hans Matti removed a calf leather wallet from his breast pocket, his hand still trembling, dug out a snapshot, and passed it to Jacob.

'This is me with my dear brother Otto,' Hans Matti announced. 'It's the only photo that still exists of the two of us together. It was taken during our last year at technical school in Königsberg.'

'Impossible!' Jacob mumbled under his breath, examining the sepia print meticulously, overcome with relief. Indeed, they were like two peas in a pod!

'There's only one difference between us,' Hans Matti added. He took his foldout magnifying glass in its chamois case from his pocket and held it over the photo on the front page of *The Boulevard*. Yes, yes, it was him... Otto had a mole the size of a four-leaf clover above his left eye... He had loved his brother so much. Otto was born only fifteen minutes after he was, but had always been Hans Matti's little brother.

Jacob looked at the man before him sobbing like a child, and was overcome with compassion. What an extraordinary thing! But how had the local rag managed to get hold of Uncle Benno's inventory? What should he do? Insinuations were easy to refute, but an accusation was often worse than a condemnation, particularly in the Netherlands, where an ingrained Batavian spinelessness systematised people to take refuge in numbers whenever any individual appeared to threaten the group.

43

After the day trip to the Bollenstreek and Amsterdam, Felix had escaped immediately to his room. He freshened up at the sink and then went to the family kitchen to tell his mother he would be staying in Leiden until the day after next.

'I thought you were going to stay here,' cried Maria disappointedly, still wondering why her husband and Mr Zwaan had abruptly hastened to the office. Her intuition told her that something was definitely up.

Meanwhile she prepared the family's evening meal, not wanting to bother the chefs who already had quite enough work preparing for the wedding dinner.

'I have a phrenology class tomorrow and an important practical,' the first-year biology student informed his mother, not having to lie.

'Phrenology?'

'The study of the skull,' Felix explained.

Goodness, the courses they offered nowadays! But would he be there on time on Friday? They had to be at the town hall by ten-thirty. And where was his good suit?

'I'll take it with me,' Felix replied, caught unawares by a profound feeling of love for the woman in her apron who had borne him.

'See you Friday, Mum!' he said, kissing her firmly on the cheek.

'OK, my dear, I suppose, if you must go…'

Maria dipped chunks of stale cheese, brushed with whisked egg yolk and lightly seasoned, into a bowl of breadcrumbs.

Six bright red meatballs soon sat on a flat plate ready to be fried in good butter.

All day long Liza's proximity had intoxicated Felix, the after-effects of which still held his body captive. He felt queasy and feverish and painfully aware of his desperate position yet again, although refusing to accept it, like a patient in his hospital bed surrounded by a host of grandchildren who thinks he's fit and healthy and will live to a ripe old age, unable to accept his doctor's fatal diagnosis.

Felix stuffed his good suit, hanger and all, into a bag and headed for Louis's room. Before knocking, he took a couple of deep breaths, like an unfaithful husband about to make amends.

Louis was sitting on his bed, half-naked, his knees pulled up to his chin. In the attic window, raspberry storm clouds careered past like warships. A blissful smile spread over Louis's face. He didn't look up.

'How's it going?'

His brother was engrossed in a book bound in Moroccan leather that Felix had bought from an antiques shop a month earlier to learn more about the magical world of minarets and flying carpets. It had disappeared the following day. Hmm, so that's where it went.

'How are you, Louis?' Felix repeated, looking anxiously at his brother, whose cheerfulness was sometimes as scary as his frequent lengthy silences.

'Death doesn't exist!' Louis burst out. Everyone simply went to heaven, which was full of beautiful girls! A million virgins! Girls by the dozen, ready and waiting—

163

'Louis, I want to—'

'You can do whatever you want with them,' Louis mumbled to himself, 'and there is food and drink...' But suddenly he looked up at Felix with a strange glint in his eye and asked him why the world was full of bastards.

'Bastards?'

Did Felix think he was stupid? He had deliberately taken him to see that painting this afternoon to punish him. Just like Ludo used to force Felix to punish him. Ludo was always threatening him with the Devil. But there was nothing to be afraid of. Nothing! A million horny virgins!

'What do you mean?' said Felix, completely confused by Louis's irrational nonsense. He walked over to his brother and tried to calm him down.

'Get away from me, Jesus Felix Christ!' Louis exploded in a sarcastic peal of laughter. 'Get out, d'you hear...? Go on, fuck off!'

He jumped to his feet, his body sickly pale, and threatened to throw the book at his younger brother as if it were a stone.

44

The history of the world is only partly written – a single colourful grain in a vase full of sand – but since humanity had reached adulthood, there can have been few fathers as desperate, with their eldest son's wedding so close at hand, as Jacob Bagman at that moment.

The hotel-keeper had thought the morning before that everything was ready for the big day. Now, with little more than thirty-six hours to go, he realised he would have to start from scratch.

Mr Zwaan had sloped off fifteen minutes earlier, muttering that he had something to organise in the restaurant.

'Well, I suppose I'd better send my band back right away,' fretted a crestfallen Hans Matti from behind a curtain of cigar smoke.

'What? I won't hear of it!' Jacob exclaimed, suddenly churlish and emboldened. They can all go to hell! The band might not be allowed to play in public, but what went on in his hotel was his decision. What time was it?

The sausage-maker looked ostentatiously at his watch, a white-gold specimen that his wife had bought him the year before as a Christmas present from Maximiliaan Metz, a jeweller in Antwerp and a craftsman who greeted his clients in every language you could think of, including Russian and Polish.

'A quarter to six. God almighty, doesn't time fly. Before we know it, we'll be a couple of old men!'

Jacob briskly lifted the Bakelite earpiece. He had arranged so much by telephone during the previous weeks – the crates of champagne from Okhuysen's, the appearance of Ivan Poestash, and a hundred other things besides. Thank God it was still low season. How many people needed rooms? Was it a very big band?

'Twenty-six, give or take… Two or three to a room is fine. They're a healthy bunch. Twelve of them work in cold storage. It's minus twenty down there, even in the summer! I'm proud of them. They're like sons to me…'

Jacob opened a drawer and fished out a grimy, well-thumbed address book from among the clutter. The hotel-keeper leafed through it, flipped it open at H, started to dial, but slammed the receiver down after the third digit. He flipped the book open again and redialled the number, the telephone propped between his sagging chin and collarbone.

'Bastiaan, my friend, how are you? Well?' he began. Listen: as he knew, his eldest son was getting married the day after tomorrow. He was looking forward to welcoming him to the festivities as chair of the local trade association. It was going to be quite a party, and he had organised a special attraction too. He wouldn't believe his eyes! But he had a small favour to ask… Are you still there? He had a German brass band that needed accommodation. You could call it

165

an orchestra of sorts, twenty-seven all told... Oh, he knew about it already... Good... They were arriving that evening around eight... His own place was full of wedding guests already, and he thought... What? He was also fully booked? But it was still so early on in the season... Aha! He had read the article. Yes, yes, terrible, terrible... But surely he didn't believe such nonsense...? Oh, but his wife had been taken ill...? So he wouldn't be able to make it to the wedding after all? But... Sure, of course, he understood...

'Jesus Christ, the miserable coward!' fumed Jacob, slamming the phone down, his nostrils flaring.

'What's the matter, Jacob?' asked the sausage-maker, who had understood almost nothing of the conversation and, after his cigar, was now in the mood for an ice-cold beer.

'They've all gone completely round the bend in this bloody town!'

Jacob could no longer avoid the subject, so he explained to Hans Matti that he was also referred to in the article. Without going into detail, the hotel-keeper briefly told him about Uncle Simon's gold, and the plight of his former boss Benno Lemberg.

'But that puts us both in the same boat,' the sausage-maker summarised the situation, his eyes like saucers.

Then the telephone on the desk started ringing.

Jacob answered, hoping his colleague from Hotel Sea View had had a change of heart. Instead, he heard the lilting tone of Willem de Rover, proprietor of the local cinema, The Monopole. The business had been closed for some time by order of the mayor, its windows masked by wrapping paper, a poster of a slender girl in a white leotard, jumping like a lion through a burning hoop, still taped to the door. Underneath, the caption read 'Coming Soon', although the American film it advertised had long since been released.

Willem de Rover had also come to the beach resort from Amsterdam. He had just read the article in *The Boulevard* and found it a worthless piece of scaremongering. He should take the editor-in-chief to court.

'Do you think he's behind this?' Jacob pried, the unexpected support like balm to his soul.

Willem was absolutely sure of it! Joris Pakhoed was a foul little bastard, a heartless careerist, playing around with the mayor's daughter on the side. And the mayor, he didn't want to get started about that miserable bureaucrat! Just because he had let a bunch of youngsters dance to jukebox music in the foyer one Monday evening, the bugger had withdrawn his licence indefinitely – illegal to jive in this town after ten, apparently. Public order! Jesus, the place was getting more like Russia by the day!

'I know, Willem,' Jacob interrupted. 'I know.' And the local taxes were going up, year on year.

Anyway, that wasn't why he'd called. The cinema proprietor suddenly changed the subject. Did Jacob know his Joey? By whom Willem de Rover meant the coloured lad who had graced the lobby of The Monopole last winter, dressed in a cherry-red liftboy's jacket with gold epaulettes. The African had delicate lips like poppies, which were of no use when it came to speaking Dutch. He did his best to greet every cinemagoer with a 'Hello, sir', women and children included. He had become quite an attraction, a bit of a teddy bear.

'Of course,' Jacob replied. He had been to see a Doris Day film with Maria that December.

The poor devil needed money, De Rover explained. He wanted to bring over his wife and child from – where was it, where the Belgians were always running amok? Couldn't he make use of him on the wedding day and give him some pocket money?

'As what?' asked Jacob, who couldn't fathom what De Rover had in mind.

As a porter, of course! He had tried to find a job for his former employee, even in Amsterdam, but nobody wanted him. Incredible, didn't he think? A nigger on the door always gave a good impression.

Jacob agreed, partly because De Rover appealed to his unwavering social conscience, and partly just to be rid of him. His brain was suddenly overwhelmed by a multitude of things that had to be reorganised.

'God will reward you!' said the cinema proprietor, a curious remark for someone who had been the subject of all sorts of unsubstantiated local gossip, mainly in relation to women and young girls. Perhaps that would explain his unconditional solidarity with Jacob, the latest target of unfounded allegations.

During a sermon on the sins of the flesh in the local Dutch Reformed church – a diminutive building behind Kostverlorenstraat, haunted by the spectre of death from dawn till dusk – allusion was made in guarded terms to townsfolk like Willem de Rover, his cinema and his debauchery.

Fortunately, De Rover was oblivious to it all. He had been raised on the streets of Amsterdam and would probably have yanked the minister from out of the pulpit, robes and all, had he heard about it.

45

Kati had never understood why they had had to come to Holland three days before the bloody wedding in the first place. She longed more than ever for a hot bath, a glass of white wine between her breasts, but all she had to look forward to was a day of long dreary preparation, while everyone around her was busy with chores.

The arrival of The Flesh Tones last night had given her a bit of a boost. They had broken down somewhere north of Arnhem and had been stuck at the side of the road for nearly two hours. It had been close to eleven-thirty by the time they had parked outside the hotel, the old bus vomiting soot and trembling like a maltreated animal.

Maria had prepared a tray of sandwiches, which Kati had immediately taken from her to pass to the band members like Florence

Nightingale with the troops at the front. But within fifteen minutes, the sausage-maker's wife had had enough. She informed Maria with a yawn that her headache of that afternoon had come back with a vengeance, and went to bed.

In the hours before the band's arrival, Jacob had called three of his fellow hotel-keepers locally, but for some unknown reason they were all fully booked, and their wives all seemed to have fallen pray to some strange virus or other, making their attendance at the wedding the day after next highly unlikely.

To satisfy his suspicions, the hotel-keeper had asked Mr Zwaan to telephone Bastiaan Hermans at Hotel Sea View, pretending to be someone else.

'Hello. My name is Van Zanten,' said Mr Zwaan, the mouthpiece wrapped in a linen napkin.

Hermans was completely taken in. 'Good evening, Mr Van Zanten, how may I help?'

'Would you happen to have six double rooms for a group of sales representatives from Leuven?' asked Mr Zwaan, pretending to be calling long distance.

'Certainly,' Bastiaan Hermans cheerfully replied. All of his sixteen rooms were unoccupied. He could put up a whole football team, if necessary. Would he like to make a reservation?

'I'll call you back in five minutes.' Mr Zwaan hung up, nodding in silence at his boss.

Jacob felt tarnished and miserable, like a broken toy on a rubbish dump.

'What now?' said Mr Zwaan, looking at his watch.

Jacob took a decision on the spot: the band would be accommodated in the rooms that had already been prepared for Maria's Friesian relations, who were expected the following day. The musicians for whom there was no room upstairs would have to sleep on mattresses in the restaurant.

'And tomorrow?' said Mr Zwaan.

'We'll just have to see,' the hotel-keeper responded with a sigh, suddenly craving a glass of ice-cold Jenever, although he never normally touched a drop.

Jacob had only managed to inform his wife of the claptrap in *The Boulevard* over supper.

Maria went to the kitchen for a moment, splashed her cheeks a couple of times with tap water, and returned to the table with a dazed look. When her husband spoke of his intention to go to the editor-in-chief the following morning and demand a printed apology, Maria snapped at him sternly in response. 'You'll do nothing of the sort, Jacob! You'll only make matters worse! Let people think whatever they like. More broad beans, anyone?'

Louis hadn't said a word over supper, and had merely glared from time to time at his brother Ludo, who was constantly making jokes. Liza spent much of the meal giggling, her wrist to her mouth, as if she were back at school with her girlfriends, Herr Doktor Posendorff bleating on about the culinary predilections of the Romans who, among other delicacies, were apparently crazy about mice stuffed with finely minced pork and pine nuts.

In the meantime, Hans Matti savoured his meatball, heaping praise on the quality of the meat and its preparation.

'Would you like another?' asked Maria.

'No, thank you, dear Maria… Really, I couldn't…' But his protest was in vain. The meatball originally intended for Felix was transferred from the pan to the sausage-maker's plate, and he gobbled it up with as much pleasure as he had the first.

Kati poked and pecked at her deep-fried cheese, and eventually managed to clear her plate. She had gathered from the conversation that her daughter's future father-in-law had not been altogether trustworthy during the war. The papers never just published any old nonsense. But she didn't find the idea so appalling, all the same. Regardless, every word of Dutch spoken during the meal irritated her intensely. Now and again, she would walk over to the window, her calves quivering, peer down on to the street below, and mumble, 'I wonder what's keeping that bus, and my dear Flesh Tones?'

46

It was eight-thirty in the morning. A couple of band members were washing and shaving at the hand basins in the gents, their backs to a bank of six urinals (one of which was out of order and had been converted in the meantime into a receptacle for cigar butts). A narrow neon tube of light in the shape of the Greek letter omega turned their naked torsos a pistachio green.

In the corridors, on the stairs, in the communal showers, on the landings leading to the rooms and in the café, German musicians had taken over just about every part of the hotel, creating a high-season atmosphere. Instead of twenty-six, no less than thirty-six Germans had arrived, much to the shock and consternation of the Bagmans. No single member of The Flesh Tones wanted to let this chance of a lifetime pass them by. It was their first international per-formance, and Hans Matti had agreed to cover costs and expenses.

A pungent odour of French cheese filled the restaurant as the first band members began to stir at around seven-thirty, coughing and snorting, chilled by the thin blankets and tired after a short night's sleep. Some had already set about their various stretching exercises in the early morning light. One skinny individual in white flannel long johns even performed a series of somersaults on to his mat-tress, clapping loudly at the same time. He had clearly performed the trick before and few of his roommates paid him any attention.

The previous evening's storm had drifted eastwards. The sun was radiant in the sky, casting a delicate orange glow over the dunes, as if at the end of a long summer's day. The weather for the wedding looked promising.

Mr Zwaan had drawn the bulky curtains back with a long pole and opened all the windows on the street side for maximum ventilation. The briny sea air, which some of the band members had never experienced before, poured into the room and roused their appetites.

As soon as breakfast was ready, the musicians descended upon the platters of sliced cheese and cold meats, the baskets of soft and crispy rolls and the pots of tea and coffee, like a plague of locusts. They seemed particularly keen on the sliced meats, which they were able to purchase at discount from *Benders Fleischwaren*, and which they were accustomed to consuming in large quantities.

Poor Maria was going round in circles. The hands on the clock in the vestibule had somehow sprung forward to nine-thirty. She only had an hour and a half to clean the hotel rooms left in disarray by the Germans. Her family had called from the station in Leeuwarden; they would arrive on the eleven-thirteen.

The chefs were surrounded by pots and pans, chopping, stirring and slicing anew to the sound of steaming, clattering lids. Lunch was to be a thick asparagus soup followed by a light meat dish and sautéed potatoes. Her Friesian family were used to eating a hot meal at lunchtime, and Maria didn't want to run the risk of them going to the wedding banquet with upset stomachs. But how was she going to feed The Flesh Tones? And where, for that matter, were they going to stay?

'I think I've come up with a solution, dear,' Jacob reassured his wife.

A little later on, they went into the restaurant accompanied by Hans Matti and Kati. The musicians were already wearing their pale blue uniforms. Slices of sausage, the colour of liver, decorated the sleeves and lapels. The men greeted Hans Matti as one, rising to greet him and standing just in front of their chairs, unobtrusively.

The sausage-maker gestured proudly towards Jacob, introducing him as the owner of the magnificent family hotel and as the future father-in-law of his darling daughter. The Flesh Tones cheered politely.

The bandleader was dressed in a white uniform with gold buttons and red epaulettes. On account of his considerable stature and maize-coloured moustache, his colleagues from the slaughterhouse nick-named him 'Bismarck', although his real name was Ludwig Morgensenf. He approached Hans Matti ceremonially, his pro-truding belly preceding him, and clicked his heels to report for duty, as if he had just returned from an expedition to the South Pole, having endured every hardship.

A bony little musician then glanced furtively to his right and left, his Adam's apple bobbing up and down in his mottled throat, and suddenly produced a clarinet. An overfed colleague beside him, his eyes like a child's, still full of sleep, chewed on a tinned Frankfurter sausage (Maria having quickly heated and served these up) the same width and colour as his fingers. When he had finished, he rummaged around on the floor and lifted a bashed and dented French horn to his lips, phlegmatic and unhurried. A third band member had propped a drum on his lap, meanwhile, and was fidgeting with the sticks like an impatient customer in a Chinese restaurant. The first musician then issued a shrill cry of '*Fünf, vier, sechs!*', and the trio played a drinking song from the northern Rhineland. Everyone joined in at once, excitedly drumming on their plates with their cutlery as if the wedding had already begun.

Ludo and Liza had taken advantage of this distraction to sneak out of the hotel and sit under an imposing chestnut tree on the square.

The weather was blissful; the blackbirds twittered happily. They made their way to the tram station, where the blue tram would depart for Haarlem in six minutes.

'What a farce!' sneered the groom, more and more convinced that he really had nothing to contribute to his own wedding. Liza nodded in agreement. She had always utterly hated that oompah band. It was all the idea of her conceited mother.

Maria truly loved brass bands and the like, revelled in the music at her husband's side, and toyed with the idea of calling one of the chambermaids to give her a hand. 'Have you seen Louis this morning?' she asked Jacob, smiling broadly. 'We should fetch him. He would really enjoy this.'

But Louis was still in bed, immersed again in the book bound in Moroccan leather, drifting through a breathtaking landscape of palm trees populated by virgins with hips like harp strings, fully intent on staying where he was, come what may.

47

Business had been brisk for some days now in Mr Monjoux's gentlemen's tailor's, The Colours of Mozart. A remarkable number of people had bought new shirts or ties, even new suits. The turnover in stockings, socks, belts and braces had easily been twice as high as usual in the past week. The slender shopkeeper with the melodious voice knew how to play it smart, particularly with the ladies who escorted their husbands to the shop, some of the men looking as agonised as if they were going to the dentist. Now, though, Mr Monjoux had a serious problem.

Following the first article about Jacob Bagman in *The Boulevard*, there were clear differences of opinion among his clientele. Some had chosen to insult the hotel-keeper openly, others were diplomatically silent, and others still took his side, praising his selfless efforts on behalf of the elderly and his always cheerful disposition.

But there seemed to be no logic to who would think what. He had a devil of a time trying to work out which camp each customer was in, and adjust his sales technique accordingly. To top it all off, he was expected to attend the reception the following evening at the Hotel New Deluxe: in short, a major dilemma.

Mr Monjoux had more or less fled the village where he grew up in May 1945, abandoning his parents' home in Limburg, where the garden even produced a crop of grapes every year. Before her untimely death, his mother used to ferment the grape juice in vats, which she would later bottle and distribute at Christmas among the poor and the local clergy. His family had played a prominent part in the community for centuries, but then they had backed the wrong horse. His father had committed suicide, followed three weeks later by his brother. No one needed to tell Mr Monjoux how things could change.

To the outside world, the shopkeeper effused grace and charm, but his private life was plagued day and night by hidden storms. There were only two things left in the world he knew he could rely on: the tinkle of the cash register and himself. And because pragmatism was one of his more valuable talents, his attendance at the wedding remained an open question, however much he liked Jacob as a person. Business came first, no matter what.

Bagman and Monjoux had once spent an afternoon together in Paris and had let themselves be immortalised by an artist in Montmartre later that evening. The hotel-keeper had beamed with delight – his own portrait rolled up, tied with a red ribbon, and carried under his arm like a baguette – as the artist gave Mr Monjoux's eyes a romantic touch with a final rub of the charcoal. 'Good man, Raymond! Now it's time for a drink. The night is still young!'

They hit the town like two teenagers, moving from one establishment pulsating with accordion music to the next. They guzzled litres of red wine, and, having descended a flight of granite steps, the glow of their cigars intermittent in the sinuous darkness, they bumped into a couple of Danish girls on a side street. One was blonde and slender, the other plumpish with a proliferation of dark brown curls, three of which Jacob discovered on the collar of his shirt at breakfast the following morning, his lowered eyelids aquiver already betraying enough.

He sipped at his *café au lait*, simply unable to comprehend that the night before – the squeals of excitement behind a white door, the gurgling bathtub in a haze of steam, the evanescent contours of voluptuous flesh – had actually happened.

All at once, he started to fidget wildly, his hands searching all over his body like a monkey in Artis Zoo. The other members of the trade association, much amused, made all sorts of insinuations. Mr Monjoux and future councillor Herman Nederleven, on the other hand, remained silent, apprehensive.

The memory of Paris rose up like a flare now and then in his otherwise blackened mind, like the light on a drowning man's life jacket. Although Monjoux was married to a girl from Limburg twenty-two years his junior, slender and blonde, the diminishing prospect of his original ambition to be a doctor still pained him, the likelihood fading with each day spent among rows of suits.

A honeycomb structure of shelves was piled high with shirts; a basket full of paired, unlabelled socks (bought from a factory that had gone bankrupt) dangled beside the till; a glass display case of luxury accessories – tiepins, rings, silk cravats, gold and silver cufflinks – had the highest mark-up in the entire shop, but the lid with its heart-shaped lock was opened only on the rarest of occasions. The people here tended to be more restrained and less inclined to outward show than their southern compatriots.

Two male customers came into the shop: Engel Holboom and his younger brother Klaas. Engel said that he was looking for a new suit, preferably blue, something simple but high quality.

'You'll have read the article, no doubt?' Engel Holboom enquired after a while, his posture defenceless, arms outstretched like a scarecrow's.

Monjoux darted constantly back and forth between the cash register and the adjustable mirror, a tape measure around his neck and a row of pins between his narrow lips.

'What do you mean?' uttered the shopkeeper, who played dumb like a virtuoso.

176

'About Bagman,' said his customer.

The brothers had taken over their father's automobile company three years before Holboom senior had died. They were unmarried and lived together in a detached house on the edge of the dunes. Their relationship was like that of a husband and wife in an unhappy marriage to which both were resigned. They never agreed with one another, which was another reason for their constant carping, although it did also establish a curious balance between them.

'Isn't it a bit too old for you, Klaas?' asked Engel, who was the only one of the pair who would go dancing in town once in a while.

'It's nothing of the sort, Engel. It's just what I was after,' retorted his brother with eyes downcast.

'Easy does it, gentlemen, we're not done yet by a long chalk.' Mr Monjoux then took to his knees like an altar boy and started to fiddle with a piece of cloth.

'I've known for years that Bagman was no good. No good before the war, during the war, and after the war,' Engel Holboom went on, desperate for a word of support.

'He was one of the first to be evacuated, don't forget,' his younger brother countered dryly.

'Mmm...' The tailor stuck a pin in the sturdy Twente fabric close to the groin. 'If we let these trousers out a couple of centimetres at the waist...' (here he squeezed his index finger between the trousers and a fold of flab) 'and take them in a couple of centimetres here and down there in the leg...' (here he ran out of pins and had to return to the tray by the cash register) '... they'll fit like a glove, yes, like a glove... virtually made to measure.'

'Tell me, would anyone with any decency open a business in the former central office of the National Socialists?' resumed the Opel car dealer, long irked by Jacob Bagman's preference for Ford.

'What are you talking about?' mumbled Mr Monjoux, genuinely surprised. This was news to him.

A smile brightened Engel Holboom's face. 'Didn't you know?' Hotel Deluxe was closed in July 1940, he explained, and became the party residence of the National Socialists a month later. The things that went on in that house! A consignment of Polish schoolgirls was spotted there only days before liberation, the car dealer related with a glint in his eye. The bastards got them drunk and made them dance around naked on the billiard table, bottles of champagne spouting between their legs. And to think the Allies had already liberated South Brabant.

'My brother went for a look a couple of times,' Klaas Holboom added in his perpetually dry tone.

Engel pretended he hadn't heard the remark and directed his reptilian eyes down towards Mr Monjoux who made a few last tugs and prods, unperturbed. 'So, there we are... All done!' he concluded, twirling around his client like a dancer, as the shop bell tinkled and Councillor Nederleven walked in. 'I'll be right with you!' the shopkeeper announced with easy politeness.

The councillor, who was already sifting through a rack of fashionable, high-quality jackets, remarked almost to himself that he had all the time in the world.

48

Turn into Gorki Street from Red Square and the renowned Hotel Tsentralnaya is just a couple of hundred metres on the right. Only one of the porters, all of whom wore pale blue kepis on their smoke-aged heads, and all of whom were seated to the left of the door like a company of parrots, could point to the Netherlands on a map.

'Our tsar was there once,' an elderly man with a white moustache informed Edo Novak, staring at him with unnaturally bright eyes. The others – Tartars, for the most part – didn't seem very interested in the world beyond the Soviet Empire.

The porter with the white moustache had spent much of his life in the port town of Murmansk. He had worked at sea as a young man and had once spent eleven days in Le Havre, where his ship had docked for repairs. The memory of those days was wrapped in the blankets of his subconscious, soft and warm, like a cuddly toy. He could recall a few words and phrases – *merci beaucoup, je vous veux, combien, potage* and *au revoir* – and still had a taste for hearty red wine, which was virtually impossible to find in Moscow.

The porter's name was Igor Igorovich, and he was the most senior of the company that kept an eye on the comings and goings of the hotel guests, usually from the comfort of their creaking bentwood chairs. They worked in shifts: two days on, two days off. Every eight hours they would sleep for an hour on a plank in a cubby-hole behind the lift shaft, each of them taking his turn. Now and then they would scribble something in a ledger with a fountain pen. In extreme cases, which were particularly rare, they would grab the telephone, a bright red Bakelite device on a nearby stand with serpentine legs, and rattle off a message into the receiver.

Edo entered the foyer one December day, light brown suitcase in hand, wearing a herringbone jacket and covered in snow. He was exhausted from his long train journey, but relieved that he didn't have to spend a miserable Christmas in Holland. Igor Igorovich graciously offered to help him with his luggage, but Edo refused with equal grace.

They became friends immediately. Just a month or two later, the porter saluted him enthusiastically: 'What a clever and lucid mind you have, sir. You remind me of one of those intellectuals from the old books! I'm very proud to have made your acquaintance!'

'Call me Edo, please,' replied our young fighter for a better future in capable Russian.

'*Chorosjó Edo!*' the porter cheered, his chest lifting like the bow of a schooner. '*Merci beaucoup!*' he added politely.

The language and ideology programme was taught in a factory-like building on the eastern edge of the city, one hour each way on

179

the metro. The course started a week later than planned, owing to the late arrival of comrades from South America and Belgium for reasons unknown.

The day after his arrival, Edo woke up – in a foetal position as if he were still in the claustrophobic sleeping compartment of the train – with the receptive brain of a child who had decided to love his step-father, no matter what.

Utrecht, Berlin, Warsaw, Brest, Minsk: they were all behind him now. With every kilometre of his journey eastwards through Europe's bleak landscape he had felt lighter and lighter, like a prisoner being set free of his chains link by link.

A hitherto unknown energy immediately seized hold of him, a pulsating and driving desire. At the buffet restaurant on the third floor, he ate a greasy fried egg and a hunk of black bread, washed down with piping-hot sweet tea. He then made his way to Red Square in a whirl of snowflakes that fell to the pavement like slivers of porcelain in a snow globe. That he omitted to wear a hat drew some strange looks from passers-by.

With the reverent steps of a pilgrim, he crossed the snow that carpeted the world-famous square from corner to corner, its crackle underfoot as he headed towards the mausoleum. Edo's heart was in his throat, and he was sweating in spite of the ice-cold conditions that chafed his skin like a blunt razor. There was no sign of the notorious queue of visitors. He passed a sentry with rosy cheeks, who stood like a statue by the entrance, his rifle bolt upright between his boots.

Once inside, Edo could immediately detect the humid aroma of everlasting life. He turned right along a dusky corridor, descended a flight of stairs, and for a brief moment was privileged enough to glimpse the embalmed bodies of the two leaders through a haze of bluish glass, their faces the colour of freshly served lobster in the darkness. He felt a surge of energy rush through his body, a convulsion that laid waste to any final remnants of doubt.

He stiffened. The shadow of a soldier in a corner by the marble tomb suddenly came to life. The Dutchman heard the stern Slavonic command and realised he should be moving along, even though he was the only visitor.

Outside, moments later, he gasped for air like a man possessed, and his thoughts ran round and round in circles, as if he had spent the entire time underwater. The clock on Spasski Tower chimed eleven. The Communist looked up at the ruby stars on the Kremlin's turrets, his eyes smarting in the fierce light. Their radiance dissolved amid the growing blizzard, like fresh blood concealed beneath swathes of bandages.

Back in his hotel room, and feeling as sick as a dog, Edo retched and vomited in the basin. He took it to be some kind of catharsis in the classical sense. A voice cried out from within him: Only a child wouldn't grasp that history is always expanding! Everything is still possible. Especially now!

He rinsed his mouth with lukewarm tap water, and got rid of the rusty taste with a lick of the salt on his skin. Who would ever have suspected that he, the child who had only had to snap his fingers to obtain everything he desired, would now be standing here on Gorki Street, in the heart of the USSR, a miserable wreck, throwing up, and playing all or bust with the rest of his life?

Edo thought of the books he had read about Lenin's exile, the hardships he experienced and the successes he ultimately achieved, Lenin, now clad in a glass overcoat as a macabre attraction, alongside Stalin, his mastodon successor, lying in state for all to see. A man who had lived life, not just survived it, but *lived* it.

'Jesus,' he barked at his quivering reflection, 'life is for living!' And he retched for a second time. He even managed to regurgitate the green chunks of undigested pork chop and peas that he had wolfed down in the screeching and rocking restaurant car shortly before his arrival in Moscow.

49

The weeks that followed were terrifying. Edo made his way to class every morning at eight, in a metro crammed with lines of rigid faces, bodies pitilessly creamed off from the masses on the platform by the closing doors.

He did his homework in the early evening like a good student and then headed to the third-floor buffet, where the food had the same indefinable taste and vile colour as the lunch served by the ladies in paper hats in the institute canteen. Much to his relief, Edo was told he did not have to exchange his hotel room, with its pleasantly creaking parquet and Karelian birchwood furniture, for a communal residence in the Lenin Hills, as most students did.

'Lucky you,' said a Russian with purple hair in a bell-shaped mound, who resided in the hotel's administration booth, where he was supposed to have his visa initialled each week. 'Nothing new, of course: Amsterdam always has its own room in the Tsentralnaya.'

Edo bought a beaver-fur hat and a pair of fur gloves from a shop close to Kievsky Station, but he had been born under Java's tropical sun, and remained constantly cold whenever he went outside. He found it hard to believe how people – even the elderly – could spend entire afternoons in the biting cold, chatting on a bench in the park, as if they were watching the sun go down in Tuscany. The climate made him worry continually about his bladder; his morning erections disappeared for the first few days after he arrived, causing him to panic.

He only really came to life when he was in his room. The heating was turned up to the highest setting, but it got so hot that he was forced to crack open the window on the street side every now and then, allowing the white whirling icy clouds inside for a couple of seconds.

The pile of books next to his bed was his only entertainment. There were no cafés in the neighbourhood, and the theatres were always sold out. During his single visit to the cinema, where they were showing a film set in a Siberian mining town, the complicated plot diminished his enthusiasm halfway through, and he fell asleep.

There was an absurdly cheap restaurant on the ground floor of the hotel, its imposing colonnades and chandeliers rarely accessible to the general public. The place was packed day in day out with men in grey suits, party officials and Communist captains of industry from the provinces, the majority wearing huge spectacles on their fat, oleaginous faces. They moved slowly, like tortoises, especially when drunk.

The tempo was raised when the whores arrived, shepherded discreetly inside by the porters at ten o'clock sharp. The girls left their spectacular fur coats at the cloakroom, swapped their boots for the elegant shoes they had brought with them in linen bags, disappeared into the ladies for at least a quarter of an hour, and re-emerged, painted, ready to be taken upstairs, or back out into the cold night, by whichever party member fancied them. Sometimes they would be back within fifteen minutes or so, and the whole procedure would start again from scratch.

Igor Igorovich, who never missed a turn, scurried to be first to accept the tips that the ladies had already counted out in their taxis, their snakeskin leather handbags crackling as they stuffed the money in his trouser pockets. This was all much to the consternation of his subordinates, who only received a small proportion of the kitty. The senior porter justified the procedure by insisting that he had to hand over most of his takings to his superiors, which was, in fact, true.

The dining hall was rented out at least three times a week for weddings, the same men in the same grey suits appearing, this time with their rich and vulgar wives, harping on like old hags. Waiters with

Tartar features glided gracefully between the white linen tables bedecked with trays of food, bottles of champagne and carafes full of vodka. The curtains on the street side were always carefully closed, obliging the less fortunate passers-by to speculate as to what was going on inside, in view of the steamy windows and the dull drone of music. The majority had lost interest long ago.

One evening, when Edo had come down to the lobby for a chat with Igor Igorovich, he was dragged into a wedding party by a pair of female tentacles. The partygoers quickly realised that he was a foreigner and a curiosity, and he was whirled around the room in a deluge of alcohol. Then the bride pulled him onto the dance floor with her right hand. The Russian blonde fell in love instantly with the handsome and exotic apparition. She kicked off her shoes, screamed something incomprehensible at the trumpeters, and, with real Slavonic passion, set about a brazen sort of courtship dance, which she finished by forcing her drink-sodden tongue into Edo's mouth.

The groom's fist appeared from behind a pillar and punched someone with a pockmarked face right on the nose. There was a sudden collision of flesh, fisticuffs loudly encouraged from the wings, the crowd like that at a boxing match. By tradition, a wedding was not a wedding without a good punch-up, so the party continued to the sound of breaking glass, the remains of red and black caviar and plates inscribed on the back with the hotel's name in hazy blue enamel smashing to pieces on the floor.

Jesus, what have I started? thought Edo, looking out of the window at the swirling frost on Gorki Street at midnight.

The young Communist was suddenly overcome by a troubling nostalgia for the paradise of his youth, and even for a certain morning in Amsterdam when he had walked – slightly intoxicated but also anxiously alert – among the trees of the Haarlem lumberyard while everyone still slept and nature had told him that everything would be all right in the end.

His moment of euphoria in the mausoleum on Red Square only a couple of days earlier now seemed like a very long time ago, and even left him with a sense of having been deceived.

50

Three weeks later, his melancholy vanished in an instant with the arrival of a group from Latin America, all in their twenties and thirties, who considered the entire course to be just a necessary evil. They wriggled out of class whenever possible, sold their dollars on the black market for outlandish exchange rates, and mocked the fanaticism of their lecturers and the occasional witless passages in their textbooks.

The Latinos avoided the buffets like the plague, seemed to take taxis everywhere, and their sex lives were enough to make an ordinary person dizzy. Their notebooks were crammed with girls' names divided into categories: Masha, Dasha, Natasha, Natasha (blonde), Julia (blonde), Zjenja, Dasha (skinny), Natasha (3), Julia (screeches like a siren), and so on, all the names followed by telephone numbers.

They were a carefree and athletic bunch, but on special evenings in the canteen, with pictures of Marx, Engels and Lenin on the wall, they revealed their nascent potential as the political leaders of tomorrow, wildly gesticulating in their elegantly tailored suits, anticipating the revolution in their respective fatherlands as an inescapable fireball thundering ever closer.

This was already the third time the Latino group had participated in the Moscow programme, and their Russian was close to perfect. Neither did the charming Dutchman escape their attention; in fact, Edo quickly became their favourite. What an idiot he had been before they arrived! It turned out that the grotesque city he had come to know had another face. A scintillating parallel reality lay hidden behind the depressingly grey facade, a world of mirrored recesses filled with glittering light, colour, and forbidden pleasures of every kind. At least, this reality existed for those who knew how to access it.

The Latinos were the playthings of the daughters of the elite; Edo quickly joined their ranks. As soon as their affluent, immensely influential parents departed on, say, an official trip to a distant Soviet Republic, the private chauffeurs were dispatched to pick up their South American friends. They would be transported to apartments with unbelievable views of the city, villas where the antique furniture of the previous inhabitants (dead or émigré) still decorated the dining rooms and other areas, or dachas buried deep in pristine snow in the woods outside the city. The freedom fighters and revolutionaries were treated to imported bottles of liquor and mountains of food, prepared with the very best butter and sour cream.

The host's girlfriends usually remained seated, like shy little kittens, ready to metamorphose into sluts, an archipelago of bedrooms and the banya – a standard feature in every house – awaiting them all.

Edo had once screwed a girl from Kazan in a sweltering banya. She squirmed with pleasure beneath him on a towel, winking at a Chilean boy, who had suddenly emerged from the steam, to join them. Edo was liberated from a terrible secret in one fell swoop. In the days that followed he felt as light as a feather, dreaming idly of the future, and had begun to hate the Netherlands more than ever.

Spring was in the air. One evening, as they sipped sickly-sweet Crimean wine in the garden of a student whose father had just been appointed ambassador to some African country or other, a chubby Georgian girl leapt to her feet to propose they take the family jet to Tbilisi. She waddled into the house and returned with a telephone on an endless extension lead.

One hour later they were making their way to the military airport in a convoy of Volgas. Three hours later they were racing across

Rustaveli Boulevard in the Georgian capital, where the girl from the Caucasus had a wood-built palace on a mountain at her disposal, with a terrace that looked out over the sulphur baths that the city was famous for, all of them tired from the flight and drink-addled. The bacchanal continued, local wines and delicious hors d'oeuvres dripping with fresh garlic were served, and when the sun came up over the mountain ridge like a ruptured pomegranate, the temperature quickly exceeded that of Moscow by fifteen degrees.

The Communist universe of private chauffeurs and other servants in which Edo now found himself catapulted him back to the world of his childhood in the Dutch East Indies. Once again he was part of a privileged class, guarded by a protective shell that gave his life renewed meaning. He decided there and then to improve his Spanish. The imminent insurrection in Latin America was like a ripening fruit. One only had to wait for the right moment to pluck it. He would help his new comrades to spread the revolution as soon they were at the helm in their respective homelands.

The ex-student seldom thought about his former comrades, kneading their caps, who had gathered in the meeting room in Amsterdam before his departure to wish him luck and express their fervent hope that he would return a fully-fledged Communist and a devoted party activist. The poor idiots! When it came down to it, their fantasy didn't reach far beyond a new moped, a caravan in the country and meat seven days a week – a juicy T-bone steak at best. Were these not the very same desires as the average bourgeois pig, born out of frustration and rancour?

No, his former comrades were totally unimportant. One day he would take part in the true struggle and ball his fist to the sun in the midst of the revolutionary masses. But he still needed his base in the Netherlands for the time being. He wasn't stupid, neither was it in his nature to bet all his money on one horse.

51

Jacob Bagman was still searching for somewhere decent to accommodate The Flesh Tones that coming night.

'Are you sure it's not a question of money?' enquired the sausage-maker, after Jacob admitted that accommodation for the musicians was proving something of a problem.

'Not at all, dear Hans Matti,' the hotel-keeper assured his guest.

Kati was in bed with another migraine, chewing on a dried prune to ease her constipation. When Hans Matti informed her that he was taking his men to the beach for a breath of fresh air, she emerged from under the blankets, growling that they weren't *his* men, they were *hers*. The mild-mannered sausage-maker merely shrugged, and told her they would be back in an hour or two.

Shortly after they had headed off, Jacob drove his blue Ford to the estate where Baron Xavier Van Tates lived; he was his very last hope.

They had become friends before the war. The quasi-aristocrat in an artistic vagabond's hat would often pop into Jacob's shop in search of porcelain. Nothing about the recluse suggested that he lived in a country house with thirty rooms or more. The baron had once confessed that it was actually all stuff and nonsense, and that a person could only fill his belly or make love in one place at a time, and a corpse did not require much space for its journey to the afterlife.

The Van Tateses had arrived in the Netherlands from Scotland at some point during the previous century. They were arms dealers who had made a fortune on the bulk delivery of weapons and the provision of loans to the fragile Dutch kingdom. Entirely owing to the mercantile spirit of the monarchy, the Van Tateses were soon rewarded with an aristocratic title by the very country that had enjoyed its greatest prosperity due to its republican and egalitarian disposition.

Van Tates owned the best part of the dunes surrounding the town, and maintained a good relationship with the prince consort, who, at least once a year, always early in the morning, would race at staggering speed up the driveway in his sports car, two or three cars of courtiers following. Shortly afterwards, gunshots rang out and clouds of smoke rose from the misty dunes as if from medieval weaponry. The prince consort and his entourage would leave the protected nature reserve just a few hours later with a large consignment of pheasant, hare, rabbit, the occasional fox and, exceptionally, a deer, all of which ended up at the royal stables, only to be forgotten and later burned on a compost heap.

The hotel-keeper wanted to ask the baron if he could use the residential barracks in the dune park on the edge of the town for the musicians. These were concrete constructions from the Nazi period that the Van Tateses had rented out for a number of years to summer visitors from Amsterdam.

'Stop right there!' yelled a rat-faced gardener after Jacob had driven just a couple of metres up the drive, past the open gate. The man slapped the bonnet and pointed at a blue noticeboard detailing Article 461 of the Penal Code that was nailed to a knotty old beech tree. 'Who are you?'

'A close acquaintance of his lordship,' the hotel-keeper smoothly replied. Would the gardener kindly let him through?

'Not on your life.' The handyman stood his ground, his crazed-looking eyes rooting Jacob to the spot.

The next thing they heard was a dog barking: woof, woof, woof. His lordship strode towards the gate, brandishing a walking stick and dressed in an olive green smoking jacket, his shock of grey hair unruly. The sunlight sparkled on the white pebbles underfoot; a brown dog reeled around him in circles, barking and jumping up against him constantly.

'Well, look who it is! It's been years,' said Van Tates, shaking the driver's hand through the open window with confident ancestral charm. 'Don't tell me you've found the French biscuit-ware statue of Anna Pavlova that I've always wanted? I've been looking for the last six years. Am I in luck?'

'I'm afraid not,' Jacob mumbled, and he explained that his antique business was a thing of the past, and that he had concentrated exclusively on his hotel in recent years.

'What did you say?' bawled Van Tates, groping maniacally at his skull as if he had just been stung by a wasp.

Jacob was about to repeat himself when his lordship seemed to undergo some kind of strange attack. He slapped at his left ear with his hand, revealing a flesh-coloured plastic hearing aid that looked like an unsightly growth.

'Bloody thing! My eldest brought it from America last month. Supposed to be state of the art, but the batteries aren't worth a damn. Down, Tudor! Tudor! What was it you said?'

Jacob stepped out of the car and smiled at the dog with as much charm as he could muster, the dog spinning round the back of his legs like a tornado, and told the Baron once again that he had been out of the antique business for several years now and that he—

'Oh, I know all about that, old man.' Van Tates looked relieved; apparently the hearing aid was functioning again. Surely they had spoken about it at an auction in Amsterdam a couple of years ago, hadn't they?

'Yes, of course,' said Jacob, although he had no memory of the fact.

Van Tates looked at his watch, his bushy eyebrows twitching, and invited his former supplier of fine porcelain to join him inside for a cup of tea.

Jacob graciously accepted the invitation and the pair were about to head for the house when he noticed the elderly aristocrat's face darken, like a summer sky before a storm.

'Evert,' he thundered, waving his walking stick at the gardener. 'When in God's name are you going to do something about that

190

damned pond? Jesus Christ! The duckweed's a metre thick! Are you waiting for Tudor to drown in it?'

The dog, whose existence had become the main focus of attention in the house after the accidental death of the baron's wife in the south of France fourteen years earlier (she was buried in Grasse), was sitting at his feet, looking up at his master adoringly.

A moment later, Jacob followed his host by way of a marble lobby to a room with a trapezial conservatory that gave a view onto a sun-drenched corner of pine forest.

Van Tates invited the hotel-keeper to sit on the very same divan on which prince consort would recline, tired from the hunt, a beer in his hand, heartsick for some Parisian model or other of barely twenty.

The baron collapsed into an armchair, its leather so dog-eared that the stuffing protruded through several holes, as if through bulging, jaundiced eyes. He slapped a colonial side table with the palm of his hand, an elderly maid, wearing a long, pewter-coloured dress with a high white collar, and looking like a guest at a nineteenth-century sanatorium, arriving in silence with a tray. The aroma of strong tea filled the room.

Jacob consulted the grandfather clock standing against the wall: it was nineteen minutes past twelve. What if his plan didn't work? He could put up The Flesh Tones for one more night in the restaurant if necessary, but then what?

'A lot of blackbirds this year,' Van Tates remarked, gulping down some tea. A trail of saliva trickled slowly over his chin towards his craggy turkey neck. He had counted sixteen that morning. So, and to what did he owe the honour?

'My son is getting married tomorrow.' Jacob had decided to begin at the beginning, but the elderly aristocrat now jumped to his feet in distracted alarm once again.

'Ow, its screeching! The bloody thing's screeching! Damn those

Americans...' He slapped at his left ear for a second time. 'Buried? What did you say? But when did he pass away?'

'Married,' Jacob corrected his host, and patiently elaborated the events of the last few days. Could he rent the summer barracks for a day or two? He had to find somewhere for the German brass band to stay.

'It's a strange thing,' Van Tates mumbled, massaging Tudor's cartilaginous left ear. He had known Jacob for years, but when he had read yesterday's copy of *The Boulevard* and seen the photo, it really made him think... Yes, he really believed...

'What, you already knew all about it?' queried Jacob, blushing all over.

Jacob could use the barracks free, the baron told him, even if he needed them for a week. He only had to ask Lodewijk Edelweiss, who took care of everything there... And now, dear Bagman, Van Tates declared, leaping up, panting, then leaning on his walking stick for balance, now it's time to show you my collection of Soviet porcelain. He was curious what Jacob would make of it. One of his granddaughters had visited last year: dreadful place, but their porcelain was superb – skaters, bathers at the beach, skinny athletic girls, delightful, refined... Come along...

They walked along a glass corridor, grapevines outside waving gently in the sunlight with an almost palpable satisfaction, while Van Tates explained that summer residents were not expected until the end of the month. A ludicrous business, that article! Those damned socialists were to blame. Give them a couple of years and they'll be manning the barricades! He had the gift of second sight – he could see it coming – it was indisputable. Jacob had to make sure that he had shares in America by then. Free advice, take it or leave it! An appalling country, but of all the appalling places on earth, it was perhaps the least so.

Jacob nodded but said nothing. Nodding and saying nothing was often the best policy.

The Friesian delegation arrived at the terminal on the midnight-blue eleven thirty-three train instead of the eleven-thirteen.

Empress Elizabeth of Austria had arrived at the same station on a couple of occasions, tormented by bouts of melancholy, aching for the salubrious seawater baths and the beach walks that were supposed to relieve her depression.

The party had missed their connection in Amsterdam, because Uncle Bouke had quite suddenly thrown up in the middle of the platform. Advanced in age, Uncle Bouke was the only surviving brother of Maria's mother. He hadn't left Friesland in thirty years or more, and had spent the entire journey looking out of the window, bearing the expression of a soldier in a tank moving into enemy territory.

The more nervous he became, the more he had a damp feeling around his bottom. He had made his way to the toilet when the train was passing Zwolle, took a gulp or two of lukewarm water from the tap and blew his nose. He then folded his handkerchief with care, and slipped it into the back of his trousers up against his buttocks.

But having just arrived in the capital, the platform swarming with people, a few dark-skinned foreigners included, his system couldn't take it any longer and calamity struck, emerging literally from the other end: his breakfast gushed out in waves next to a telephone box, a man inside with a small suitcase wrinkling his pockmarked face in disgust.

Maria had quickly pulled a summer jacket over her apron and had left for the station alone. Meeting her beloved family always made her nervous. She hadn't seen some of them for four years. The hotel-keeper's wife was reminded of when she used to meet Jacob off the train late at night before the war, after he had enjoyed a night on the town in Amsterdam with his antique dealer friends, often stinking of booze, tobacco and the occasional whiff of perfume. Would her husband, her splendid Jacob, with his good-natured puppy-dog face, ever have...? No, of course not, impossible! The very idea! And she remembered the previous day behind the rosebushes at the

193

Keukenhof, and a flush of warm contentment reddened her shiny cheeks. He was the best husband in the world. But when she thought about Ludo and a terrifying moment from her own distant past – consigned to the deepest recess of her consciousness – her face became sombre and rigid for a fraction of a second, assuming an expression that no one had ever seen, not even her husband...

She was startled by the hissing and screeching made by the train as it came to a standstill under the wrought-iron canopy, half a metre from the buffers. Maria wove through the stream of arriving passengers, already discerning her fair-haired nephews and nieces head and shoulders above the crowd. There was Tjitske and dark-haired Jetske, and how long had it been since she had last seen her sister Femke?

'Femke!' Maria called, falling into her arms a moment later. 'Femke, my dearest sister, how are you?'

'Uncle Bouke was taken ill in Amsterdam,' came her modest reply in a dialect unfamiliar to most mortals in that part of the Netherlands.

'Not at all. That sister of yours is talking nonsense,' Uncle Bouke declared, ill-tempered, raking his fingers through his shock of octogenarian hair. He sniffed at the sea air warily, as if it were roasted garlic. 'Is it far?'

'About seven minutes on foot,' Maria reassured him, before decorating the rest of her relatives with hugs and kisses, the glow in her cheeks restored. Her oldest niece, Tjitske, had lost her husband to cancer a year earlier, and was now living on a sort of pension; Tjitske's sister, Jetske, six years her junior, was a handicrafts teacher who had yet to marry despite her baby-faced good looks, and who went to the Catholic church every Sunday in black, although she had been raised a liberal Remonstrant and had grown up a dyed-in-the-wool tomboy. Only wide-hipped Femke had produced any offspring: three handsome lads, Wubbe, Wierd and Wiebe, born exactly thirteen months apart. Maria treated each of them to three welcoming kisses.

Wubbe and Wierd worked as joiners for a shipbuilder in Harlingen. Wiebe, with his blond locks, was by far the best-looking of the three. He worked in an ironmonger's shop in Leeuwarden, although he dreamed of a job in the catering trade after working for two weeks as a barman the previous summer. He couldn't wait to see his oldest cousin Ludo; his greatest desire was to go out with him in Amsterdam.

'I could eat a horse!' yelped Uncle Bouke suddenly, mumbling that it must have been the water he drank on the train. What else could have upset him? He hadn't thrown up in over half a century, for heaven's sake.

The party proceeded in the warmth of yet another fine spring day to the Hotel New Deluxe, Maria and Femke leading the way.

The northerners were already dressed for the wedding, the men in dark, sober suits with black shoes, the women in breezy dresses of printed cotton. Jetske wore a gossamer hat decorated at the rim with artificial fruit, which had been made by a pupil who had a crush on her – a secret she tried to dismiss every morning before the statue of the Virgin Mary in her bedroom by making a swift sign of the cross, as if swiping fluff off her nose. Tjitske shouldered a leather bag full of make-up and essentials – face powder, lipstick, sanitary towels and perfume, and shaving gear and a change of underwear for everyone. Her accommodating nature and desire to spare the boys inclined her to undertake the task willingly.

Wierd was the odd man out. He was wearing a pair of dark green dungarees that made him look twice his size. An unidentified object sheathed in chamois leather rested against his right shoulder. Everyone knew that this was a hunting rifle. His suit was folded neatly in Tjitske's bag.

Weird was a fanatical hunter and poacher. He had read a newspaper article about the abundance of game that inhabited the dunes thereabouts, and was determined to try his luck there early the next morning, the day of the wedding.

They passed through the streets of the beach resort and inspected the shop windows and signs – some of which were in two languages – with great interest. The ladies were immediately struck by the fact that products were considerably more expensive here than in Friesland. A loaf of brown bread was six cents dearer!

Halfway along Zeestraat, the wedding party was suddenly confronted with a sight they had never seen before: a platinum blonde of no more than twenty, sunglasses propped like a tiara in her hair, was turning out of a side street in her brilliant red, open-top sports car. The girl's ample bosom was stuffed into a tight dress, shamelessly displayed like exotic fruit.

'Dirty whore!' Femke muttered through her teeth, casting a menacing look at Jetske and Tjitske, as if they were somehow in the wrong too.

If a pilot had flown his plane northwards from where they were now standing, crossing a stretch of boggy land reclaimed from the grey-blue sea, crossed the Ijsselmeer and its dam, the Afsluitdijk, which looked like an electric eel with rigor mortis, he would have seen Friesland looming in the distance after a mere eleven minutes. But the northern party already had the feeling that they were far from home, and all succumbed to consuming homesickness, one after the other.

Wiebe was the only one to separate himself from the procession, doing his best to relax and walk like a local.

53

Hans Matti's impotence proved less problematic than he had feared. He was a regular visitor at the annual butchers' fair in Hamburg, where he stayed every year in a hotel with views over the Elbe. Strictly speaking, his presence was no longer necessary. Orders were streaming in from every corner of the country. At a particular point, as his accountant had advised, he had appointed a chief of exports, a financial administrator from Munich, who also attended to the lion's share of national distribution issues, leaving Hans Matti free to devote himself to his favourite activity: developing new products.

At least three days a week, Hans Matti could be found in a yellow-tiled room lined with cleavers and grinders, dressed in a white lab coat, experimenting with freshly minced meat, herbs, garlic, vegetable extracts and such like, an alchemist in his laboratory, his moustache aquiver with creative bliss, the radio at full blast. One day, listening to a discussion programme about Picasso, he suddenly had an idea for a recipe, a new and delicious salami sausage, which became available for purchase all over Germany within two months, packaged in a colourful wrapper and sporting the name 'Picasso'.

In the early years, he had visited the Reeperbahn every night, along with all the sailors and the other guys, dressed in a trench coat and trilby. He was disgusted with himself every time he clambered on top of Gretchen or one of the other girls, invariably in a hovel stinking of wet mushrooms. They were young... very young. One day, to his horror, he realised that he might as well have gone to bed with his daughter.

Some time later, Heinzmann, a business contact from Hanover, who dealt in intestines, offered him an address from his leather pocket diary with a nod and a wink. The dear girl's name was Marlène; she only received visitors at home. She worked as a secretary in the offices of one of the city's more important magnates with whom she had once had a brief affair. She had grown accustomed to life's little pleasures, like expensive outfits with matching shoes, nylon stockings, menthol-flavoured filter cigarettes, fresh cream cakes from Christiansen's and other such luxuries that her own income didn't permit. The financial responsibility she bore for her daughter weighed heavily upon her. She had had to move back in with her mother in the village she left when she was sixteen, and was constantly afraid that her child would meet the same fate.

Hans Matti's mistress irritated him a little at the beginning, especially after one of their orderly sex sessions, he pausing in her kitchen on the fourth floor to look out, glassy-eyed, at the dreary warehouses opposite, Marlène prattling on and on about something or other, or rather about nothing at all. It was like being at home with Kati!

But after six months he could barely live without her. He had become addicted to his haughty little German plaything, to her slender ankles, to her high and mighty public persona, Marlène who would not read an unseemly word in the newspapers but who was, nevertheless, a total harlot in bed, where she would squeal sometimes like a helpless child, reminding Hans Matti of the paternal feelings that had never fully developed when it came to Liza. Above all, his relationship with this woman twenty years his junior introduced a certain structure and tranquillity into his life. Hans Matti's Mercedes headed for Hamburg with increasing regularity, Kati left behind at home with yet another excuse.

What else was he supposed to do? Kati's fire had gone out after a few short years. It probably had something to do with the way women were made. Erotic decline had invaded her feeble body like a slow-acting poison. In the past, on one of the rare occasions before going to sleep, and after switching off his bedside light, when he would lay his hand gently, deliberately, on Kati's belly, she would promptly ensnare him in her tentacles like an octopus around its prey, his body drawn ever closer to hers. Now, she simply pushed him away with a growl, turned her back and fell asleep, and would soon be snoring and filling the room with her putrid breath.

The early years of their romance now seemed longer ago than his adolescence. Hans Matti still cherished the unrealistic hope of being able to walk along the coast of Rauschen again, visit the garden of the house where he was born, which, by some miracle, had managed to survive the wrath of the Soviets.

He had employed a history student, whose father was in charge of the purchase ledger at the office, to investigate a number of family matters for a substantial fee. All he could find on his brother Otto was a copy of his birth certificate, which now hung in a silver frame above Hans Matti's desk. The student committed his findings to paper – in fountain pen in very refined German – and even managed to produce a photograph of the sausage-maker's former home. The Russian text on the back of the image explained that the house was now part of a military hospital named *Zarja* or 'Dawn'.

The day after the strange car accident that had almost cost him his life, Hans Matti had telephoned Fräulein Schmidt on the stroke of twelve, and was summoned to General Von Oberhaussen's villa that very afternoon. Kati wore a black gossamer dress and received him with fussy pomp in a hall with stags' heads mounted on the wall. She drew him swiftly by the sleeve through an arched door and down a spiral staircase to the immense kitchen below.

The young sausage-maker was immediately set to work. He received a magnificent new chef's uniform, with a black eagle embroidered just above his heart, and got to work on his sausages and pâtés right away, full of enthusiasm. It was as if he had died and gone to heaven. He had only to submit a list of ingredients to one of the nine maids – all of them suffering in silence under Kati's yoke, she having been promoted a couple of weeks earlier, out of the blue and much to everyone's surprise, from servant girl to housekeeper – and they would be delivered an hour later.

The kitchen worked round the clock. Hans Matti had five colleagues: a chef for hors d'oeuvres; another for soups; yet another for fish dishes; a pastry cook; and an expert in desserts. The East Prussian butcher took his place on the treadmill, producing superior lunches and opulent dinners. The general's breakfast consisted of liver sausage cut in oval slices and served with mustard and a large glass of weissbier. In the evenings, the general drank French red wine that was delivered monthly by army trucks from the occupied territories in tin-covered, felt-lined boxes marked 'Handle with Care'.

Two weeks later, the general marched into the kitchen, cupid curls atop a pear-shaped body squeezed into a dazzling white parade uniform.

'Which one of you is Bender?'

In the process of sprinkling freshly chopped parsley over a veal stew, Hans Matti felt the blood rise to his head. The sausage specialist turned, wiping his hands on his apron, thinking it was all about to end. He raised his index finger timidly.

'Oh, my dear fellow!' the general proclaimed, overflowing with admiration. 'Your sausages are simply delicious. Just like Mummy used to make!'

Kati watched from the side, her arms folded. The general instructed her to double his salary. He also received a room in the service quarters next to the villa, a sizeable space for one person and with hot and cold running water, something he had never experienced before. Kati and Liza lived in the same building.

Hans Matti had already noticed after the second day that the general paid occasional visits to Kati in her apartment on the ground floor of what was the former coach house. It was a topic of much whispering and knowing grins among his fellow chefs in the kitchen and the servant girls who enjoyed a bit of gossip. The girls could chatter for hours, sitting on the kitchen counters, clean tea towels under their skirts, their hands flat by their hips at right angles, constantly swinging their white-stockinged legs.

One evening when the general had gone out to dinner, allowing Hans Matti an early night, he was woken by a series of strange noises. He heard the sound of chairs being dragged violently over a tiled floor, then something falling with a thud, then an irregular tapping sound, giggling, and then chairs scraping tiles again. After a while, all the noises combined in an orgy of sound. Hans Matti didn't have to guess its source.

The noises were coming from the room directly below his. The curtains were closed. Everything around him was pitch-black (this is how a blind person must feel, he thought) but he suddenly caught sight of a square of light by the sink that he had never noticed before. Hans Matti slipped out of bed in his flannel long johns and crawled with bated breath towards the source of light like a nocturnal wild animal.

He pressed his eye up against the spyhole, scraping his cheek against the wooden floor. To one side of the art nouveau lamp of dark-green glass that cast its light downwards in perfect conical form, the sausage-maker had a bird's-eye view of a section of Kati's room.

He could make out a single slipper discarded next to a three-quarter-length bed, a piece of white lacy underwear and a spinning top with a clown's face. Suddenly General Von Oberhaussen came into view, tottering along in red boots, his wild grey hair all over the place. From above, his naked back looked like a platter of cold meats.

The general was being chased by Kati, who had let down her firebrand auburn hair. Her breasts were strung up in a vivid green brassiere, a ribbon of cloth disappeared between her buttocks. Otherwise she was stark naked.

'You're a very naughty little boy!' Kati squealed, threatening him with a wooden cane.

'No, please, no!'

A vicious whack followed that sounded to Hans Matti like a meat cleaver beating a Wiener schnitzel before being smeared with egg yolk and dusted with breadcrumbs.

'No, Mummy, please don't!'

Kati chastised the general for a second time, the whack eliciting groans of pleasure. The scene ended with him collapsing from exhaustion at the foot of Kati's bed. With a blissful smile on his sweaty face, he started to jerk at a half-erect bulge that was hidden like a worm beneath the folds of his colossal belly. Kati made encouraging noises, as a mother might when her child takes his first steps or draws a nice picture.

This event in fact took place twice a week, on Wednesday and Sunday evenings. The young sausage-maker was now head over heels in love with Kati, feeling like this for the first time in his life, and intoxicated by this heavenly, dream-like state, like a dragonfly drunk

201

on the perfume of a flower, humming and singing, Hans Matti produced the best sausages and pâtés he had ever made. At the same time he was overcome by fits of deep despair, given the hopelessness of the situation.

Hans Matti did not yet know that time could be a person's best friend as well as his worst enemy.

54

It was easily five degrees warmer in Haarlem than on the coast. The sight of boys and girls on scooters in fashionable sunglasses transported Liza instinctively to Rome or Monaco, to all those wonderful places she had never seen. But everything was about to change.

Edo had telephoned Ludo an hour earlier and more or less ordered the hotel-keeper's son to bring him twenty-five guilders without delay. Ludo still had to return to the chemist's for a second round of penicillin and, accordingly, Liza wasn't exactly welcome company, but the arrival of The Flesh Tones had irritated his future bride so much that she had insisted on joining him. When she sensed that her darling was still stalling, she had whispered, 'You do love me, don't you?'

Ludo tried to fob her off with a lie about having to go to the jeweller's in Haarlem to collect the wedding ring they had chosen a month before. According to Dutch tradition, this was a job for the groom alone.

'But I'm still going with you,' protested Liza, determined to hold her ground, completely unaware that the rings had been hidden in Ludo's bedside cabinet for more than a week. She could look after herself in the city for an hour, no problem.

They sat arm in arm for the entire journey. Liza caught sight of a doe or a deer bolting into a hollow in the dunes and droned on about it for a full fifteen minutes. They drank coffee on a terrace on the main square, overlooking the medieval city hall.

Such a naïve little creature, smirked Ludo, having left Liza to her own devices and walked off in the direction of the fish market.

He picked up his medication, cursing under his breath the Fokker bitch who had given him the pox in the first place, and made his way through a series of alleys and back streets to Edo's place, where he had to ring the bell six times before there was any sign of life.

The young Communist opened the door, his face cadaverous, and asked Ludo immediately if he had the money. The former student had fallen prey to the malaise that tended to engulf him when he missed his daily snort of cocaine.

Edo had tried the stuff for the first time one winter's night in Moscow with his South American comrades and a group of Kalmyck girls with hairless cracks and bodies like panthers. He could no longer recall their perverted Asian faces no matter how hard he tried. Although the coke had stung his nose and burnt the roof of his mouth like scorched rubber, the powder produced complete and utter ecstasy in all his senses from the outset, the warm explosions in his head and veins sizzling like sparklers.

The Kalmyck girls were so on heat that, at some point, the entire thing descended into an orgy. Everyone did as they pleased with everyone else, entranced by the most honourable feelings that all of humanity would share with the break of the new dawn. Edo felt tongue after passionate tongue, gliding over his chest towards his neck. 'Hello, what's your name?'

Pleasure spread over him like feathers from an emptied pillow. The delightful kaleidoscope of light and bodies took Edo back to the sensations of his childhood. As a young girl slurped the nectar from his navel and another maternally caressed his cheeks, he even babbled a word or two in Malay. The deep dejection and insatiable hunger that inevitably followed every high were unbearable, but, when he returned to the Netherlands, he immediately went in search of the magic powder, tortured by restlessness and irritable sleepless nights.

One scorching day in June, a comrade had taken him to his rooftop apartment that had a view of Anne Frank's House, by then a tourist attraction. He had descended into the blissful cave once again, and after a few minutes (hours? days?), he found himself outside by the canal, a couple of addresses in his pocket.

Before long, he had been sucked into a vortex in which everything – the least effort, the most worthless idea – was focused exclusively on financing his indispensable escapes. His monthly salary in the bookshop was only enough to meet his needs for a week. He stole increasing amounts of money from the till.

The solution to Edo's problem presented itself one evening as he returned from a party meeting where the consequences of the uprising in Budapest were again discussed. He was with a sympathiser from a particularly well-to-do family in Gooi, a young guy named Bastiaan Kromhout, for whom Edo Novak – with his experience of the Soviet Union – was almost divine.

'Is it true?' the boy asked cautiously as they passed a typical North Holland coffee house.

'What are you on about?'

Bastiaan Kromhout detailed the rumour that was doing the rounds in party circles: Edo had apparently obtained an influential position within a number of partner organisations in South America. Edo was flattered but alarmed by this. What kind of idiotic conclusions had they drawn simply because he occasionally used party stationery to send a letter to Buenos Aires? He first wanted to shrug his shoulders and say it was all nonsense, but then had a flash of creative genius.

'I'm not allowed to talk about it,' he said in a hushed and secretive tone, searching for a reaction out of the corner of his eye.

'I would love to join!' Bastiaan Kromhout exclaimed enthusiastically.

What was the name of the organisation? Could he become a member?

He approached Edo again on the same subject the following week. Edo had learned in the meantime that, his drearily bourgeois blazer notwithstanding, the nineteen-year-old had an artistic temperament and aspired to be a dancer on a stage with lights everywhere and standing ovations from a multitude of admirers. But he was trapped in his father's family business – they had been bed manufacturers since 1867 – though some party members expected great things of him nonetheless, given his dedication. Hadn't Marx had a capitalist background, after all?

'Can you keep a secret?' Edo enquired from behind a conspiratorial cloud of cigarette smoke in a carefully chosen café.

He was indeed a member of an underground revolutionary association, Edo told him. Plans for them to disperse all over the world were at the ready. Bastiaan could be part of it all one day if he wanted, but it was still top secret at this stage and furthermore – Edo hesitated slightly for effect – the organisation was in financial difficulties. Some kind of financial contribution was necessary, otherwise...

'How much?' asked the millionaire's son, who had learned the dull reality in early childhood that everything under the sun had its financial aspect.

Edo alluded to an amount, and, in view of the reaction, immediately doubled it. He would collect the donations monthly. There would be no proof of payment, as he could imagine...

'Of course,' Bastian Kromhout agreed, his hand disappearing into the inside pocket of his blazer for his wallet.

On the congested train back to Haarlem, Edo was overcome with anger and self-hatred, constantly avoiding the gaze of a young workman, his dungarees covered in plaster and paint in the seat opposite. He feverishly tried to justify his moral collapse, but to no avail.

Suddenly, he was reminded of the suffering the world had inflicted on his parents, and his body swelled with rage, like a mould filled with boiling lead, and he heard the rasping voice of Igor Igorovich, the porter at Hotel Tsentralnaya, who had invited him to his house in Moscow one evening.

Igorovich lived alone in a three-bedroom apartment in a district full of former merchants' houses and abandoned churches. The fur of a polar bear with its jaws wide open was spread out on the floor. He had shot it with his own rifle north of the Arctic Circle. Edo's host invited him at least three times to feel one of the beast's yellow incisors.

After the umpteenth toast to one another's good health and the future of their respective homelands, Igor Igorovich started to talk about when he had fought in the army, lowering his voice to a whisper. He had been there when the Soviet troops had entered East Prussia, he said, proceeding to deliver a treatise on the anatomy of German women, grinning at every disgusting detail, rubbing his hands, and looking frequently at his foreign visitor as if for validation.

'And before that, my son,' the porter continued, turning towards Edo with a scowl. Before that, he had been a guard in an encampment north of Leningrad during the construction of the White Sea-Baltic canal. 'That was something, let me tell you. The prisoners died like rats. I finished off a bunch of them myself.'

Edo's Russian was pretty fluent by then, but he still thought he'd misunderstood, and asked him what he meant, just to be sure.

'You heard.' The porter brought his snorting, bulbous, alcoholic nose to within an inch of Edo's face. Biff, bang, wallop! With serrated steel pokers. They worked a lot with pokers. A shot in the back of the neck now and again, but munitions were sparse. That's how it went! There were real bastards among them, alcoholics, criminals, rapists, thieves, political scum, the occasional beggar. He could still see the look of fear in their eyes. But sometimes it was as if it had never happened.

'You get my drift?'

Edo felt sick. He looked at his watch and wondered how he would get home in the snow. And then, perhaps from fatigue or confusion, he asked the stupidest thing one person can ever ask another: if he was sorry for what he'd done.

'Sorry?' The Russian shook with laughter, as if he was about to throw up. Why should he be sorry, and to whom? To God, who didn't exist? To the Devil? To his parents, who were beaten to death in front of his very eyes in a barn in the Ukraine? Sorry?

'Some hunt, and some get hunted,' he continued philosophically. 'It's the only way.' It was the same everywhere else. He had seen enough in Germany and France! It was the same the world over. And didn't the ends justify the means? Igor Igorovich coughed and rose to his feet, his belly brushing against the table, an almost empty bottle of vodka in his hand, 'Eh, foreigner, am I right?'

'Absolutely,' Edo concurred, as an overcast sky settled over the now troubled landscape of his mind.

55

The boy from Gooi wasn't the last. In six short months, Edo had assembled a group of three young men around him, all gloriously handsome and from decent families, and all of them craving a new life.

Two of them had made contact with him through mutual friends. Ludo was the only one he had met by accident and was not really in the same league as the others. Nevertheless, Edo had invited the hotel-keeper's son to join him for lunch a couple of weeks after his return from Moscow, taking the opportunity to sound out his politics without arousing suspicion. He saw through him in an instant.

Ludo had spoken of the unmitigated monotony of his work, told him he secretly hoped that there would be another war, that society was full of egotists and profiteers, above all the politicians. They were bleeding everyone in the country dry, factory workers, small business owners trying to keep the hounds at bay, you name it. And then there were the Americans: the worst of the lot.

'Absolutely! The bottom of the pile,' Edo concurred, gnawing at his pork satay.

The hotel-keeper's son remembered Betsy Prins, barely seventeen at the time, tossed like a ball from one Canadian soldier to another. Dozens of so-called liberators had penetrated her, and they were forced to cart her off to St Mary's Hospital in Haarlem, rife with infection and burning with fever, the doctors initially unwilling to treat her because of her tainted background.

'The world is on the brink,' proclaimed Edo, raising his hand and ordering two double whiskies.

He told Ludo about his amazing time in the Soviet Union and about his close connections with influential comrades in South America, where all hell would soon break loose. They could certainly use men like Ludo. He sketched a universe of freedom and future pleasure. The revolutionary advance guard were naturally the elite in a world of free love. There was no God, and you only lived once! After Edo had elaborated in a similar vein on his time in Moscow for a while, Ludo – grinning – asked, 'Are you serious? Was it really like that?'

A week later Ludo paid his first contribution, on condition that his name never appeared on a list of any kind. The young Communist promised to take care of it.

'Have you got the cash?' Edo asked for a second time, staring at his comrade from the corner of his darkened room, his eyes like glowworms.

Ludo showed him the banknote.

'Good, excellent!' The bookseller snatched the money, lunged at the telephone and dialled with quivering fingers.

'Rudi, is that you? No? Where is he, then? I need to speak to him right fucking now! Amsterdam? Tell him to call me back as soon as possible... Edo Novak... No, not Bovak, Novak... N for nobody... Please! I'm begging you...'

Ludo looked at the wall clock, thought momentarily about Liza, and told his friend that he'd never seen him in such a state.

'It's the stress,' Edo whimpered, his face translucent and shiny. He couldn't think straight without coke – it was the price he had to pay for creative genius! He had to give a lecture in a couple of days, a treatise on the situation in Africa, and he hadn't been able to write a word of it. Once he felt better, he was going to need every second.

'But surely you're coming to the wedding tomorrow?'

'Wedding? Hah! If you can call it that!' snorted Edo, laughing derisively.

Suddenly the telephone rang. Edo darted to pick up the receiver with all the speed of an iguana's tongue.

'Rudi, my friend,' he cried, his face lighting up. 'Come as quick as you can please! Oh, half an hour... Can't you make it sooner? I'm fucking dying here, man.'

Bastard, thought the hotel-keeper's son, returning to the main square a few minutes later. Edo had just laughed in his face! But where was all of his money coming from? Not Edo, for sure!

Ludo figured that he no longer needed him, all things considered. He would get out of this dump soon enough without the help of Edo's revolutionary buddies. Give it a year, maybe two... then he would take control of the Kraut's sausage money and be free for ever. And why should he go to South America? Like Liza, he wanted to go to Florida, to drive along the palm-lined streets in one of those American limos. He would take her with him, just as someone to screw along the way... English, of course. He had to improve his English...

His reverie was abruptly interrupted when his thoughts turned to how to dispose of Hans Matti and that old bag of his. He had taken up reading detective novels a couple of months earlier, flipping greedily through the pages to see what happened next, but the culprits always seemed to get caught. Edo had alluded – sphinx-like but with conviction – to the long arm of Moscow, an arm that could reach around the entire globe, flawless and effective, faking car accidents, inducing heart attacks, providing vials of untraceable poison. On reflection, he might need Edo after all.

Liza was waiting obediently for her future husband to return, sitting on the terrace where he had left her, her beautiful legs elegantly crossed.

'Don't tell me you were bored, sweetheart?'

'Would you believe it, I just saw a camel!' piped Liza, bursting with things to say. 'There's a circus in town.'

Ludo left a couple of guilders on the table and led his fiancée by the arm towards the Prinsenhof, looking furtively at his watch.

'What's the big hurry?' Liza complained, clattering along beside him in her Dr. Scholl's.

They were expected back at the hotel. His Friesian relations would have arrived by now and they were supposed to be joining them for dinner. 'Let's get it over and done with, eh?'

'Oh, yes, I see,' said Liza, looking up at him, more in love than ever.

They had to run to make it on time for the tram, and something fell out of Ludo's breast pocket on the way.

'The rings!' yelped Liza gleefully, before realising that it was, in fact, a dark yellow vial of medicine.

'What's that?'

'It's valerian,' Ludo spluttered, quickly returning the vial to his pocket. He was so terribly in love with her, you see. It was affecting his nerves.

'Me too, dear Ludo,' sighed the sausage-maker's daughter.

As the tram rattled through the dunes fifteen minutes later, Liza looked out at the shiny world around her, as deeply contented as a princess in a royal carriage on her way to her stately home.

56

When they got back, Ludo noticed Arno Prins hanging around in front of the town hall on the square, in more or less the same spot as he had once seen his father drag a young girl like a ventriloquist's dummy out of his official car.

Ludo took Liza by the elbow and made a beeline for the other side of the road, pretending he hadn't seen the ghastly prole. But as they passed the gushing municipal fountain, his former Nationale Jeugdstorm cohort suddenly grunted, 'Trying to ignore me, Bagman?'

Arno Prins stared at Ludo in silence, painfully aware that the German blonde by his side was looking him up and down in disgust. He then said he'd read the article in *The Boulevard*. Interesting. But what if he were to stir up some shit as well? What would Ludo think of that?

'What do you mean?'

'"This is what the dirty Jews did to Jesus,"' Arno Prins quoted, his tone formal and measured.

Ludo was fuming, but he also knew that the only way out of this was to keep his calm. He turned to Liza and asked her if she wouldn't mind nipping to the shop for a pack of Lexingtons.

'I haven't any money,' she replied.

'Here, take this sweetheart, it should be enough. Three packs, if you can. It'll be a long day tomorrow.' He pointed at a touristy tobacconist's opposite. Under the Nivea awning, to the left of the entrance with its bamboo beadwork curtain, there was a revolving rack of shiny postcards.

'Nice piece of crumpet,' Prins drooled, unashamedly following the voluptuous blonde with his eyes.

Ludo bit his lip and looked calculatingly over at The Great Wall, a recently opened Chinese restaurant, with an inset doorway. He slowly walked towards it, hoping Prins would follow.

The story of Arno Prins began with his sister, the only surviving member of his family besides himself. Paul had been shot in the stomach in the autumn of 1944 in a pine forest near Leningrad. He had lived for three days after being shot, and had just managed to write a letter home, informing his family in faint handwriting that he was in love with a Russian girl called Tanja, who had blue-grey eyes and a pug nose, and who took good care of him. He was only eighteen when he died.

Their father had been arrested just outside Brussels and deported as a fugitive to Holland where he served eighteen months behind bars for treachery and as an accessory to murder. He was finally executed one morning at dawn in the dunes at Scheveningen. His extremely attractive wife, meanwhile, had moved in with a lawyer in Amsterdam, refused to have anything more to do with her children, and died three years later at home on Stadhouderskade from flu, which suddenly became pneumonia and led even more suddenly to her death.

Ludo would be marrying that rich German tart the next day, Arno Prins charged, disgruntled. Everyone was doing well except for him. Even Betsy had managed to make something of herself. But she could tell him all about it in person tomorrow at the party.

'What?' said Ludo, who still couldn't bear to hear Betsy's name spoken.

Hadn't he heard? His sister had moved in with Dr Bodisco over three months ago now. Twenty-six years his junior! Her marriage in Overijssel had been a total disaster, and the children were in some sort of home. Besides, Bodisco had had his eye on her for a long time. Everyone was fucking thriving, but he was stuck loading fish carts for pocket money. He had known about them all along, by the way, Arno Prins added mockingly.

'About what?' asked the hotel-keeper's son, looking out for Liza over his shoulder.

About his old man's shady deals, about him swindling the poor Jews out of every last penny. *The Boulevard* would certainly be interested in even spicier information, didn't he think? Deserting his own baby brother on the street... tut, tut, tut. How much—

'Get to the fucking point, Prins!'

He was leaving in a month on a container ship bound for New Zealand, but he needed money to set himself up when he got there, plenty of money, if he got his drift. His lips would be forever sealed... But Ludo would have to—

With his all his might, Ludo threw Arno Prins against the doorway of the Chinese restaurant, buried his fists in his kidneys, and then kneed him in the crotch.

'You filthy rat! Are you trying to blackmail me? Nobody around here would believe you, not any more, understand?' Ludo punched him again, this time hard in the stomach. Arno was too stunned by the shock and the pain to make any form of reply, and just stood there, whimpering, crumpled and weak. Ludo wanted to hit him again, but Prins begged for mercy, groaning. The hotel-keeper's son let him go, watching with satisfaction as his victim hobbled off in his white clogs like the hunchback of Notre Dame.

'They were out of Lexingtons,' said Lisa, prettily. He hadn't noticed her arrive. The shopkeeper had checked especially for her, but they were completely sold out. She had bought Caballeros instead. 'Hey, what was up with that creep?'

'Must have eaten something that didn't agree with him.' Ludo smirked, lighting a cigarette from the packs she'd just given him and smoking it to the filter in just a couple of puffs.

When they arrived back at Hotel New Deluxe five minutes later, Liza almost had a fit at the sight of a black man dressed as a circus monkey standing in the hall, grinning from ear to ear.

'Hello, sir!' he exclaimed.

Ludo summoned Mr Zwaan and asked him what on earth was going on. The hotel manager shrugged and said that the gentleman had appeared an hour ago quite out of the blue. No one could get any sense out of him, and he refused to leave.

'What the fuck are you up to, then?' Ludo asked the black man, lifting his chin and standing on the tips of his toes as if he were looking over a wall.

'Hello, sir!' Joey the porter repeated.

57

An increasing number of local people were now claiming to recognise the German on the front page of *The Boulevard* from the occupation, his small circular glasses and square moustache in plain view as he briskly marched at the head of a legion of Georgian soldiers.

The newspaper's offices were sited in a former dairy and only open as a rule on Tuesday mornings. But Joris Pakhoed was at his desk for the second time in succession that day, reaping the rewards of his scoop.

The editor-in-chief and former geography teacher had the look of a nineteenth-century bureaucrat, with a pallid forehead and long sideburns, although he was known to be particularly progressive, a modern man. His admiration for his predecessor at the vocational school was unreserved. In just a few short years, Herman Nederleven had risen to the dizzy heights of Councillor for Public Works, had moved into a delightful new home with a double garage – *Huize Cortina* – on the other side of The Boulevard, begun to send his daughter to piano lessons, and had insisted that she attend a French-language school, although she was only seven.

Pakhoed, at thirty, was an optimist at heart, and convinced that those who did right by others would be rewarded for their efforts in this life. He had rejected the Protestant value system of his parents as quickly as some people lose all their hair or turn grey overnight.

A wonderful task had been set aside for his generation, he believed. After reading a book, the title of which he could no longer remember, the young geographer had thought for a long time that he was a Communist. The system still seemed superior, at least in theory, to every other vision of society developed over the centuries by philosophers and political thinkers. But since that book he had learned something else about the world. He now knew that base capitalist powers would always exist and always work for the destruction of the incredible human experiment undertaken by Moscow. This was why the Soviet Union had isolated itself, and was forced to defend itself with terrible weapons in response to the aggression of the West; all those millions of people – marching joyfully forth over sun-drenched squares bearing their red flags aloft – would doubtless have preferred to conquer the globe with olive branches.

A couple of months earlier, he had become a member of the only party that was still able to bridge the gap between idea and reality, but he had also made up his mind to continue to work for the poor and underprivileged and help wherever he could. From his first day as a teacher, children of railway workers and general labourers were seated in the front row of the class, the small number of wealthy pupils who hadn't made it to the grammar school or the academy, in spite of parental influence, were strictly confined to the back. This was his way of compensating for the injustice inherent in society.

How could he have known that Jacob had delivered pamphlets as a young man for the Socialist candidate, Domela Nieuwhuis? It also came as something of a shock when Herman Nederleven had telephoned to inform him that the hotel-keeper had been a respected member of the party for years.

'But shouldn't we expel him?'

'On what grounds?'

Joris Pakhoed read him part of a letter that had arrived from California quite unexpectedly a couple of weeks earlier.

'*I have hesitated for a long time,*' Gabriel Lemberg wrote in justification of his decision to send the list of his father's possessions to the local press. '*Of course, I don't want a penny of the money back. I simply want justice to be done. It is for this reason that I enclose the original documents. As far as I'm concerned, Bagman can go to hell, and the rest of Holland. The so-called healthy sea air is a deadly poison, like gas in a coalmine. Sincerely, Gabriel Lemberg.'*

How could anyone be so despicable? Joris Pakhoed reasoned for the umpteenth time, peering out of the window for the paper boy. He cherished the hope that his colleagues at the *Haarlem Times* would pick up his story and run it on their front page too.

Licking his lips, he examined the article and the photograph once again – the layout was truly excellent – and could scarcely believe that he was responsible for this publication. He dreamed for a moment of a professional career in journalism. Readers would heap praise on him for his insightfulness, his sense of justice and, perhaps, after a little study and a lot of hard work, even his journalistic style.

The tram ground to a halt. Joris Pakhoed looked up in anticipation, but instead of the paper boy with his duck-billed nose and club-foot, he saw the beaming face of Herman Nederleven as he got off his bicycle with studied elegance and walked into his office.

'You've set the cat among the pigeons and no mistake!' The councillor could barely contain himself. Was the story all true? People had to know where he stood, as a figure of authority. The wedding was less than twenty-four hours away, and he had just heard that the Kraut in the photo wasn't the father of the bride after all, but his twin brother.

'Twin brother?' Pakhoed's face exuded contemptuous disbelief. 'If you say so… A shameless lie, if you ask me.'

At that very moment, Jacob Bagman pulled up in his Ford, parking its front wheels right up against the pavement, wormed his way out of the car and tapped the window to indicate that he would like to come in.

'Good morning,' said the hotel-keeper evenly, as he entered the room and was engulfed by the smell of printer's ink. He nodded at Councillor Nederleven, his eyes squeezed tightly shut, and came straight to the point. He declared that the front page of yesterday's paper was the result of a terrible misunderstanding, that—

'Mr Bagman, I have all the evidence right here,' Joris Pakhoed quickly interrupted, doing his best to make the 'Mr' sound as fractious and contemptuous as he could. He grabbed a feather-blue envelope from his desk and held it up for all to see. *Air Mail*.

'Christ Almighty!' cried Jacob a couple of minutes later, trembling with disbelief, Gabriel Lemberg's missive in his hands.

The letter, too, was the result of a terrible misunderstanding, the hotel-keeper awkwardly tried to explain. He had actually done the father of this gentleman a favour—

'By cheating him out of his antique furniture, no doubt!' the editor-in-chief interjected, his voice rich with disgust as he picked up the list of antiques, and tapped it with his finger.

Councillor Nederleven slowly stood up, walked over to Jacob and placed a hand on his shoulder. Why was he so upset? If it was all simply a misunderstanding, as he claimed, it would all turn out just fine. Wasn't this a democracy after all? But there was something else that troubled him. He had heard that the German brass band they had spoken of had now arrived in the town. Jacob was well aware of the local council's stance on the matter. He wasn't planning to do anything stupid, was he? Public order directed—

'Drop dead, Nederleven!' Jacob barked furiously, turned on his heel and stormed out of the building.

The councillor turned and looked at the editor-in-chief, whose face glistened with triumph, as if to say, Didn't I tell you? Jacob Bagman is an arsehole, pure and simple, a complete shit.

58

The plot of ground known as Kostverloren Park – something of an exaggeration, given its size – was an extension of the hundreds of

217

acres of dunes that had belonged to the Van Tates family for as long as anyone could remember.

In the 1930s, an enterprising individual opened a teahouse in the park, a romantic rock garden complete with ducks quacking in the pond and an enclosure for apes as its crowning glory. The foundations of all of these constructions, along with the bones of the ape, were now buried beneath the sandy soil. On that very spot, in the shadiest and most sheltered part of the town, work had started at the beginning of the war on concrete bunkers intended as sleeping quarters for troops sent to work on the erection of the Atlantic Wall.

Since the opening of the railway line from Amsterdam to the coast in 1881, the local population had been exposed to the presence of foreigners in small numbers, but the arrival of the Free India Legion in 1943 served as a major attraction for the wives and daughters of families that had not been evacuated. British Indians who had defected to the Nazis were the first to occupy the bunkers, their eyes as black and shiny as wet charcoal. In the evening they filled the town's blacked-out bars and restaurants. Abortionists were soon summoned to eradicate serious errors but, according to the local authorities, the soldiers had become such a threat to the town's moral virtue that the legion had to be relocated to the Gulf of Biscay, allegedly on health grounds.

Shortly afterwards, the beach resort was swamped by a second wave of exotic men, this time seven hundred Georgians, who had been billeted all along the coast. They marched daily in a recently cleared yard in front of their barracks, all dressed in Wehrmacht uniforms, except for three in Caucasian national costume, who always marched at the front.

The insane idea that Hans Matti's brother Otto had not been sent to North Africa, or the primeval forests of Lithuania, or the olive groves around Baku, or the cornfields of Ukraine when he left Latvia, but here of all places, to the very town that was to witness the wedding of his niece – later, yes, but only a little later, a tiny grain of sand in time's unending hourglass – had now been haunting the sausage-maker's thoughts for a full twenty-four hours. It was simply beyond him.

Hans Matti had taken The Flesh Tones to the beach, like a grandfather with a gaggle of grandchildren. Before long, one of them produced a leather football and they immediately split into two teams, using their uniform jackets as goalposts. As bandleader, Ludwig Morgensenf insisted on acting as referee.

Hans Matti was soon standing at the side of the makeshift pitch, cheering on his football-crazy compatriots. To the outside world he was proud and blissfully happy, but in his head he was preoccupied, despite the turmoil, with one thing and one thing only: the fate of his beloved twin brother. What if Otto had survived the war? Maybe he was still... somewhere... No, of course not... Madness... Don't even think about it... One thing was certain, though: he had to contact the journalist who wrote the article as soon as possible.

When the brass band arrived back at Hotel New Deluxe at around three, all ruddy-faced and with shoes full of sand, Jacob informed the sausage-maker of the new accommodation plans.

'What? Bunkers?'

'Outstanding holiday homes,' the hotel-keeper responded, sugaring the pill.

'Morgensenf! Prepare the men for departure. We're moving out!'

'*Jawohl, Herr Bender!*' The slaughterhouse foreman's voice echoed around the main corridor of the hotel.

The busload of German musicians attracted plenty of attention as it trundled through town. The delegation was met at the park gate shortly afterwards by Lodewijk Edelweiss, who could barely disguise his revulsion for his guests.

Edelweiss wore a grey military moustache and a ruthless expression, and his often drunken mien was apparent even during the day. The steward tried nevertheless to appear more aristocratic than the man he had served for the best part of twelve years. He came from a renowned family of industrialists – his father was the last to live a life of idle leisure – and had a deep hatred for the local middle classes, all of whom he considered plebs with aspirations or common money-grubbers. They had disturbed his domestic tranquillity more than once. He would never forget the day he had had to put up with crowds of screaming proles on his own doorstep, combing the stalls of a dreadful bring-and-buy organised by none other than Jacob for one of his dim-witted good causes – a day out for the elderly.

He had read both articles in *The Boulevard* keenly, with eyebrows raised. He had thus been completely taken aback when his lordship had called him an hour earlier, asking him to assist the proprietor of Hotel New Deluxe – with his shady war record – by providing accommodation for his German guests.

'*Wilkommen! Welcome!*' Lodewijk Edelweiss cried, demonstrating the extent of his knowledge of modern languages. He then narrowed his eyes and saw to his horror that the Krauts had what looked like special symbols on their uniforms. It was difficult to make out from a distance that they were actually just slices of sausage, advertising *Bender's Fleischwaren*. The steward produced a jangling bunch of keys from his riding coat and asked Jacob how many nights the band would be staying.

'Probably just the one,' the hotel-keeper replied, suddenly remembering that he had visited the place before the war with Ludo to see the monkey.

Hans Matti trudged along after Jacob and Lodewijk Edelweiss past a forest of lilacs and up onto the dunes where a whitewashed concrete box with an iron door and bolted shutters appeared above the reeds. The steward prised open one of the iron doors with considerable effort, a musty mixture of damp and rot greeting them all. Jacob peered inside and was overcome with shame in the presence of his future in-law. This was not at all what he had expected!

220

The bunker contained a bunk bed, two metal chairs and a table with a couple of dried pieces of orange peel left behind by the previous inhabitant. It looked more like a prison cell than holiday accommodation.

'Where is the basin?' Jacob enquired.

'Next to the pump,' Lodewijk Edelweiss replied.

'And the toilets?'

The steward gestured with his arm towards the surrounding dunes, staring at the morally tarnished hotel-keeper at once knowingly and mockingly.

'My men are used to working in cold storage!' said Hans Matti, sensing his future in-law's embarrassment. But did they have bed linen by any chance?

'I have enough bed linen for a hundred orphanages,' Jacob declared, looking at his watch and realising that he still had to arrange some form of dinner for the men that evening. He asked Lodewijk Edelweiss if there was a telephone nearby.

'There's a payphone behind the clubhouse,' the steward responded, pointing to an orange bunker with a mosque-like domed roof.

The booth was as hot as an oven, and there was no telephone book to be found, only a couple of torn pages on the floor. The hotel-keeper fished a coin from his pocket, put it in the slot, and tried to remember the number for The Rotonde, Johannes Wedekind's bistro. It was a simple five digits. He closed his eyes and pictured Wedekind's shiny red delivery van, the monthly repayments for which had almost bankrupted him. Of course: 12111!

He hurriedly dialled the number.

'Kruisbeen Fishmonger's,' chirped a friendly female voice at the other end of the line.

'Oh, e-e-excuse me,' Jacob stammered, not giving his name. 'I thought this... eh... But isn't this the number for The Rotonde?'

'That's 12211, this is 12111,' the woman grumbled in reply, and hung up.

Jacob took a second coin from his trouser pocket and popped it in the slot but it seemed to get stuck. He had to tug the cradle up and down a couple of times and then thump the side of the contraption before the coin dropped into the tray.

A moment or two later, Johannes Wedekind picked up against a backdrop of sizzling pans and tinkling cutlery. The hotel-keeper enquired if Wedekind delivered hot meals. With his son's wedding so imminent, his own chefs were all working at full tilt, he could not ask more of them.

Of course, Wedekind replied excitedly. He delivered hot meals every day to the town hall. Jacob asked if he could arrange thirty-six dinners for delivery that evening.

'Thirty-six, eh? What about roast chicken?' Wedekind suggested.

'I'm not sure. They're Germans.'

They soon agreed to a dinner of veal cutlets with fresh green beans and sautéed new potatoes, and a 'house dessert' that consisted of two slices of tinned peaches floating in their own juice, and a waffle with a blob of whipped cream on top.

Johannes Wedekind had, in fact, received a phone call from Bastiaan Hermans a couple of hours earlier, nosing around for information about the wedding. He had played his cards close to his chest, of course, but now he knew for sure: Jacob Bagman was one in a million and an excellent customer. He would certainly be going to the wedding.

Hermans, the proprietor of Hotel Sea View, despite his sonorous voice and golden fob chain, had never earned him a penny.

59

The Friesian branch of the Bagman family had made their way to The Boulevard after lunch, waddling like geese along the coastal town's sweltering streets. Their formal attire drew a fair amount of attention. The visitors avoided the beach to protect their shoes and Sunday best.

Young girls were basking in the sun, stretched out on beach towels, shamelessly exposing their naked limbs. Femke muttered something about the unconvincing airs and graces of women from the west. Jetske peered demurely from behind the decorated rim of her hat at the goddesses before her, struggling with a sense of powerlessness and despair at her own midriff, her heart pounding as she uttered a quick prayer.

The men entertained themselves in the meantime by peering in turn through an enormous pair of binoculars. The contraption was attached to an iron plinth and could be turned in all directions. The viewer snapped shut every three minutes, though, and all you could then see was the shadow of your own eyelashes. It had to be fed another five cents. The boys zoomed in on all the naked flesh they could find, sucking on the five-cent coins between their lips. Wubbe couldn't keep from grinning when he caught sight of something funny through the lens: a woman, all skin and bone, who wore her hair in a grey bun, her face as white as parchment, pushing a girl in a wheelchair through the sand towards The Boulevard with all the strength she could muster. The girl's legs waggled back and forth like those of a rather tall, plucked chicken.

Uncle Bouke pushed his nephew out of the way, so that he, too, could take a look, and he also started laughing; the crippled, feeble and the mad were always a source of amusement.

Wiebe, meanwhile, was upset because Ludo had responded coldly to his question about Amsterdam's nightlife. That he was leaving the following evening for his honeymoon in Paris was a serious blow. His long-held hope to hit the town with his favourite cousin was history.

Wierd detested everything about the seaside, but had other things on his mind to keep him occupied. As he planned to sneak out early the next morning to go hunting, he had asked Louis to show him the dunes at the southern edge of town. They had crawled under the barbed wire fence into the grounds of the Water Board. Louis, who was no stranger to this area, pointed out where explosives from the war lay still buried in the sand, and tugged strands of copper wire that poachers used to catch rabbits in huge numbers from beneath the bushes.

At some point, Weird had stuffed his hand in his trouser pocket and pulled out a small revolver.

'What's that?' Louis asked, full of curiosity.

This was what you used to finish them off at close quarters, Wierd explained with a grin. He could usually pick them off with a single shot, of course.

The two cousins were startled by a dry rustling sound behind them. Wierd immediately hid the gun. They turned around.

A boy in a white shirt and short trousers, not much older than fourteen or so, was making his way towards them. His jet-black hair had a neat side parting, and seemed wet, as if he had just left the barber's. He had a serious, extremely intelligent look about him, and had an owl resting on his outstretched arm, a jangling chain attached to one of its talons. The bird looked strangely like a pussycat.

'Nice owl. What's his name?' asked Louis. He vaguely knew the boy from town.

'None of your fucking business,' was the gruff response, the boy falconer carrying on his way, sovereign and silent, as if he owned the place and the halfwit with the chubby cheeks and his lookalike side-kick were mere trespassers.

Jacob and Hans Matti only returned from the bunker village around six that evening. He had felt like a performer in a show running back and forth all day, trying to keep myriad plates spinning on top of swaying rods. He had done a decent job of it, all things considered, as none of the plates had come clattering to the ground.

The sausage-maker immediately went upstairs. Jacob telephoned Johannes Wedekind again, this time to order thirty-six cold meat platters for breakfast, to keep The Flesh Tones happy the next morning.

'Cash on delivery as usual?'

'Certainly.'

Jacob found his wife folding napkins in the linen cupboard. She told him that the hotel had been hit by a wave of tiredness – almost everyone had gone for a nap a couple of hours ago.

Jacob told her all about his successful visit to Baron Van Tates. Maria listened attentively, curious to know all about how the stately home looked on the inside, all the while continuing to fold napkins like a virtuoso. After she had folded the last napkin into what looked like a shell, Jacob suggested that then might be a good moment to run through the schedule for tomorrow.

They headed for the kitchen. The head chef wiped his hands on a check tea towel hanging from his apron, and met them with a smile. Willem Jansen was an extremely friendly local man, with the dark features of a southerner, and going slightly bald.

'Ship still on course?' asked a cheerful Jacob Bagman.

'Aye, aye, captain!' came the chef's reply, his spotless white hat at an angle.

Willem Jansen ushered his employers over to the fridge. He opened the bottom right-hand door and pulled out a stainless-steel platter halfway to reveal the pièce de résistance: magnificent chunks of veal already sliced into perfect portions and lightly marinated. Towers of mashed potato had been piped through a sack and now emitted a pale shimmer on the shelf above, ready to be brushed with butter and baked tomorrow.

'And the vegetarian dish?' Maria couldn't help but ask, just to be on the safe side.

Willem Jansen opened a second door and removed a Pyrex dish containing a glossy white substance, wet and slightly tremulous, like some kind of cheese of unknown origin.

The head chef explained the cooking process: after fifteen minutes

225

in the oven at a low heat, the tofu was drenched with a deliciously spicy sauce, along with some crunchy fried vegetables. It drove them crazy in the Far East.

He then showed them the various tiers of the wedding cake, steeped in apple cider and riddled with slivers of glazed fruit, as well as the marzipan roses for decoration. He was planning to put his finishing touches to this masterpiece in confectionery early the following morning. A highly artistic sous chef had also fashioned the happy couple out of marzipan, the bride more successfully than the groom.

Jacob and Maria thanked their head chef and then went to the banqueting hall where the tables were already set for the dinner. Only the menu cards were missing. Streamers attached to the high ceiling converged on a central chandelier, making the place appear from below like the inside of a circus tent. A backcloth depicting a romantic castle somewhere in Hungary, surrounded by sprouting weeds and a rain vat, which had been used for the second act of Strauss's *The Gypsy Baron* in which Dr Bodisco had displayed his vocal talents a couple of months earlier, adorned the stage.

'Are you sure we haven't forgotten anything?' Jacob asked his wife, as they made their way back along the corridor.

The hotel-keeper only now caught sight of the black porter standing by the front door in his cherry-red uniform and told Maria about the promise he had made to Willem de Rover.

'He's been there all afternoon,' Maria interrupted. 'But when I brought him a cup of coffee and a snack an hour ago, he was nowhere to be seen.'

Jacob approached the African with a paternal smile and tried to explain to him in Dutch, in imaginary German, and then in a jumble of several languages that, while his presence was much appreciated, he did not need to start until the next morning.

'Hello, sir!' Joey the porter responded.

'*Tomorrow ist früh eenuff*,' was Jacob's final effort.

The amiable-looking foreigner looked at him, clasped his hands together, placed them against his right cheek with a smile, and nodded at a sofa in the cloakroom where he hoped to sleep that night.

'Just leave him be,' said Maria resolutely, pulling her husband away by the sleeve with a kindly wink at the black man.

It was nearly half-past seven, high time she woke up the rabble upstairs. Her family weren't used to the sea air and would probably be hungry. And weren't they all always so cheerful, black people?

60

The ruins of the city sneered in delight at the passengers for the only train that still might depart.

They had fled just in time, apparently, Liza lagging behind them like an obstinate dog. In the sweltering spring sunshine, Hans Matti had almost given himself a hernia lugging the two suitcases that Kati had stuffed at the last minute with candlesticks, bonbonnières, cutlery and other silverware from the general's cupboards, cursing all the while the slob who had abused her for years and then disappeared without a trace.

Gaunt women descended like birds on the rubble, rummaging for household effects, clothes or a solitary photo that might have survived the explosions and the inferno that followed by some miracle or other, completely unaware of the extent to which they resembled their fellow sufferers in the devastated Russian cities so many thousand kilometres to the east.

Without orders to follow or obvious motivation, some had started to clear up, tossing debris from one pile to another with barely comprehensible resilience. Young girls sold their unwashed bodies in cellars and doorways for food. Their mothers stood guard or watched, absent and broken, as lust defiled their daughters, chewing on the bit of bread or scrap of sausage that the bloke had used to pay for the privilege. Streets where the sky was once blue now looked like soiled shirts smeared in soot. They were no longer streets.

Hans Matti muttered something about not understanding why they had come to Dresden, of all places. 'Shut your bloody mouth,' Kati snarled, tugging sternly on Liza's arm.

Although the bonds of authority had been severed for some time, the former housekeeper still treated the butcher as her subordinate. Kati was looking for her father, having heard that he was still alive, and wanted to see if the house he had transferred to her name was still standing.

Hans Matti stared in horror at the lifeless world around him and tried to match what he saw with the stories that were circulating about the devastation of his homeland, where the Russians were now running the show. The cathedral in Königsberg was gone for ever, the castle damaged by fire, entire districts had been wiped off the face of the earth. It was as absurd as it was incomprehensible.

The young butcher was pulled into a vortex of anxiety, and yet he couldn't believe his luck. From all of the general's staff, Kati had chosen him to join her on her expedition. He was walking on air.

It transpired that her father had died three years earlier, and the street where she had lived after moving from her childhood home in Bavaria was nothing but a burned-out shell. Kati took it all in for thirty seconds or so from a verge at the side of the road, her mouth drooping, the vigorous young grass that had shot up through the black grit tickling her bare legs. Then she tugged at Liza's arm once more. 'We're leaving tomorrow!' she declared.

They slept that night in a spacious apartment where everything was still in one piece and even the ceiling was undamaged. The woman had asked for a silver spoon as payment, one of the few without a swastika. Kati reluctantly agreed. When Hans Matti finally declared his burning love for her the following morning, sunlight flooding through the white curtains, birdsong all around, General Von Oberhaussen's former mistress gave in to a fit of hysterical laughter. Love? Nobody talks about love any more.

Kati began to undress him, slowly and without the least feeling, as if she were peeling a banana. The sausage-maker's inexperience and long-standing desire for her were such that he came within three seconds of penetration. He was still a virgin, he conceded.

'What?'

'I'm a virgin,' Hans Matti repeated sheepishly, looking like he had said something wrong.

At this, Kati had started to cry with laughter, briefly waking Liza who was cuddling her teddy on a sofa in the room next door. The little girl's nose twitched, as if someone had been tickling it with a straw, and then she fell asleep again.

The Friesians refused to speak a single word of German over dinner, but perhaps they were simply unable to. Kati ignored them completely.

The curly-haired waiter was off that evening, and Kati had just learned that the boy lived in a rented room on the second floor of a villa with a red roof just opposite the tram station. Fortunately, the town was not quite the size of Paris!

Jesus, what a dull idiot her husband was, she thought as she watched Hans Matti's repeated attempts to charm the Friesian family of their future in-laws with smiles and lame hand gestures. He was a man of industry, an independent entrepreneur with over one hundred and fifty employees. Where was his pride, for God's sake?

It was as if she were dining with the dead. Although everyone breathed, talked, laughed and produced related noise, it barely reached her. She suddenly remembered that she had promised to telephone Gabi, the only person who understood her futile life, which had been nothing but a struggle from the very moment she was born.

In the Bavarian village where she grew up, Kati and her father lived next door to a civil servant. His two daughters, the only other children in the neighbourhood, avoided young Kati as if she reeked of shit. She always had black and blue bruises, and grazes from her father's drunken rages, but his moments of remorse, when he would press his daughter close to his powerful chest, sobbing hysterically that he was going to kill himself, were strangely full of comfort, warmth, even a fearful sort of bliss. She loved him with an intensity and devotion that she would never experience with another man.

After primary school – girls only – she worked as a cleaner, an apprentice hairdresser and a waitress. She had slept with hundreds of men, perhaps eleven of whom could have been Liza's father. Her daughter didn't appear to be interested, however. She had never questioned her mother on the subject. On the one occasion, when Hans Matti had been prying for information, Kati had simply ignored him. What had she done with her life, though? Spawned a monster of a daughter, whose childhood was filled with all the things she herself had never had. Married an impotent husband and given him the best years of her life. Where would he be now if he'd not had her ideas, and her leadership?

The money made from the suitcases of silverware and cutlery was used to buy meat mincers and pay the rent on their first butcher's shop. Kati Bender née Schmidt had groped around for days on end in basins of lumpy meat, adding ground cloves and other spices to the sausage mixture, fighting her disgust, as the last remnants of her youth had faded.

After dinner, Kati had quickly changed into a red dress, and left the hotel around nine o'clock. The courteous black porter had opened the door for her.

'*Danke schön*,' said Kati, with a burst of warmth. His frame lingered in her mind's eye, like morning dew clinging to a spider's sticky web – well-built to a man, those Africans. But was it true that they smelled?

His one remark in English barely registered, however. She had drunk three glasses of wine and a shot of Friesian bitters. Her blood coursed through her body. Her sole thought was of Guillaume, his shoulders, his cruel chin. What should she do? Ring his doorbell? What the hell? After tomorrow, she'd be gone for good.

It was warm outside. The leaves of the chestnut trees rustled in the sky above her head, the sky itself remote and fragile. She detected strange perfumes, and the May breeze penetrated her thin dress. Ecstasy! The sausage-maker's wife suddenly felt alert, attractive, free. She would throw herself into his arms, yes, press her lips against his, just as she had always done...

She drifted past shopfronts, all closed for the night, and passed an ugly church with gravestones on the grass in front of it, heading for the square next to the tram station. But when she finally gazed up tearfully at the window on the second floor of the villa with the red roof, behind which she thought she could make out his silhouette, her body would go no further, had suddenly ceased to function. What if he rejected her? What if he refused to open the door? Jesus, she would rather just throw herself under this passing tram, with no passengers on it, its bell clanging away. She looked up at the glowing window again. Her cheeks suddenly became numb, dull and lifeless like papier-mâché, and her entire body began to tremble. This was ridiculous! She didn't dare to ring the bell. She was afraid of being rejected. Jesus Christ, she didn't dare! A terrible shiver ran up the length of her spine from her bottom to her throat. Drink, if I don't get more drink I'm going to die, she thought. Wasn't there a bloody bar somewhere around here? She looked around in panic but couldn't see anything. Kati resolved to telephone Gabi.

She made her way to a phone booth under a chestnut tree, shut the door behind her, rummaged in her handbag, and tried to stuff the largest coin she could find – a two-and-a-half guilder rixdollar – into the slot, without success. The guilders likewise refused to go in. Only the ten and twenty-five cent pieces, which she dug out from between the tissues, lipstick and foundation in her bag, did the trick. She dialled the number and listened as the line clicked and crackled, as if it were trying to connect with someone in Timbuktu.

'Gabi, is that you?'

'Kati!' her housekeeper replied, stifling a yawn, as if she was just turning over in bed. 'How are you?'

'Terrible, terrible,' the sausage-maker's wife moaned, and told her friend all about the nightmare that had engulfed her. Gabi had been right! Holland was indeed a dreadful country, and, Kati added, making no mention of her own agony over Guillaume, her daughter was about to marry into a family with a retarded child. The father of her future grandchild had a brother with protruding eyes and a head like a pumpkin.

'Call it all off, immediately, while you still can!' shrieked Gabi, who understood Kati's caprices better than anyone.

'That's exactly what I said,' Kati hastily replied, the coins dropping one by one into the box below. Then she heard the sound of a man clear his throat – an unmistakable sound, a man in her house in Cologne – immediately drowned out by a fit of coughing.

'Gabi! What was that?' screamed Kati, panic-stricken. Surely she didn't have a man with her? It was strictly forbidden. She knew the rules well enough! Surely she wasn't...

'No, not at all, I have the flu!' the housekeeper retorted, barking as hard and as deep as she could. She had—

The line was suddenly cut off. Kati groped madly around in her handbag but had run out of coins. Jesus Christ! She was going to search the entire house from top to bottom! Couldn't she even trust her own housekeeper any more? The whole world was full of nothing but lies and deception!

She wriggled out of the phone box, ran through a maze of lanes and alleys in the direction of the hotel, and then suddenly stopped, beholding a sign above a bar, the word 'Heineken' in bold white letters. It was dark by now and a welcoming strip of light beckoned through the curtains. Drink! She walked in amid a hubbub of chatter and thick smoke. Her arrival induced a brief silence. Then the ivory ricochet of billiard balls, and the murmur and the shuffle of cards, like the fluttering wings of a dove, resumed.

'*Ein Schnapps bitte!*' Kati placed her order with the barman, after settling demurely into a chair by the window. A waiter brought a glass of Dutch Jenever on a wet beer mat swimming in a puddle of water on a round flat tray. She took the glass, emptied it in a single gulp, and ordered another.

Men nervously looked at her, one after the other. Everyone knew very well who this elegant creature was, her pearl necklace around her neck, her gold bracelets dangling from her wrists, boozing all by herself like a tramp. The picture served to support the majority in their belief that something truly rotten was going on at the Bagmans'. Wasn't his eldest getting married tomorrow to that blonde Kraut?

'*Noch ein Schnapps bitte!*' Kati yelped, having guzzled her second in under ten minutes.

She took her time with the third schnapps, inadvertently smearing lipstick all over her face with her wrist. By her fourth, the sausage-maker's wife clearly had no idea where she was. She applauded eagerly every time the red ball hit a white on the green felt billiard table. After downing her fifth, she winked at the barman, and then spent the next hour slumped forward in her bentwood chair.

Kati had taken a one hundred guilder note from her handbag with an exaggerated gesture. There wasn't as much money as that in the cash register, and a couple of the regulars had to be called upon to make up the change. It was dark when she staggered out into the street, but still blissfully balmy. What was that rustling sound? Ah, the sea! And there was a full moon, too. An ideal moment to take her leave of this life, perhaps? She considered this as she padded along, her hips swaying from side to side like the stern of a ship in stormy weather, and, before long, to her amazement, she found herself standing in front of Hotel New Deluxe.

The door was locked. She pressed her nose against the cold glass, peering inside, her fingers raised to her temples. Somewhere in a sea of darkness, at the far end of the vestibule, a little red light was glowing. What time do you think it is, Kati Bender? Not too late? Of course not! She needed to shit and pee—

As she fumbled with the door handle, the white smile of the black porter appeared in the darkness. Kati took a few steps back. The door opened slowly, without the slightest sound.

'Oops!' Kati cried, playfully, stumbling as she crossed the threshold and falling into the quick arms of the porter. The boy had muscles! Hard as steel yet soft at the same time, just like Daddy's were.

The porter's bright eyes stared at her strangely. What're you thinking, naughty boy? She noticed a strong smell of wood, a manly smell that was new to her. They moved arm in arm towards the stairs, and, as they passed the linen cupboard, its door ajar, which Maria had shown her two days earlier, Kati pulled the porter inside in a fit of drunken madness, completely surprising her victim with her sudden energy. They fell to the floor on a pile of unwashed sheets that Maria had left there after The Flesh Tones had left. The black man gave a brief, effeminate giggle in the murky, warm cupboard, and then took over.

He forced Kati's head downwards. Then, his body shaking and close to climax, he pushed her away, put his arms under her sweaty armpits, propped her up against the wall and plunged his manhood into her invisible flesh. With every thrust she felt an extra year of life being pumped inside her. She had to bite his neck to stop herself from screaming, which excited him all the more.

'Yes, sir!' Joey grunted.

Soon, Kati had drifted off into the idyllic valley of her dreams, cows grazing languidly with bells around their sagging necks, fish-ermen smoking their pipes by the grassy banks of a river. It was just like the village of her childhood, the only memory of contentment that she could still cherish, even though, in actual fact, she had never been happy there.

Part Three

The Festivities

61

'Dear bride and groom,' Jacob Bagman repeated to himself, as he stood at the washbasin at a quarter past six the following morning. 'We have gathered this evening—No! As father of the groom...'

A bluish sky vaulted the beach resort. Jacob's bedroom window was wide open, admitting the lively twitter of birdsong and the gentle rustle of the sea. Maria had gone downstairs in her apron to prepare tea and coffee for the early risers. Her festive outfit, a salmon-pink two-piece with mother-of-pearl buttons, was laid out on the bed alongside her husband's new navy-blue suit.

The hotel-keeper soaped his shaving brush, lathered his face with menthol-scented foam, his speech continuing in his head: As father of the groom, I would like to say a word or two on this joyous occasion. Dear bride and groom— perhaps it would be better to welcome the guests first and say something about the order of festivities? Ladies and gentlemen! Dear family, friends and all our guests! It is truly a pleasure for me as father of the groom, and brand-new father-in-law of our charming bride, to welcome you here... *The Flesh Tones*, our visiting brass band from Cologne, will shortly entertain us with a mini-concert of three waltzes inspired by the Oder, Donau and Rhine rivers. A recital by the flautist Max Serdijn will then be followed by our top attraction, the illusionist Mr Ivan Poestash, renowned for his celebrated matinées at the famous Tuschinski Theatre in Amsterdam. You'll hardly believe your eyes, I promise you! Then there will be some time to relax, for all except the waiters, that is – they remain at your disposal. And in the mean time... Lift those feet! Our musical combo, *The Swingers*, will entertain you until eleven o'clock, but no later – you know, the town council's policy... But the first dance, of course, is for...

The hotel-keeper hadn't slept a wink all night long. He removed his cut-throat razor with its discoloured ivory handle from a red leather sheath, angled his chin to the left, steadied himself, and readied the blade beneath what passed for sideburns on his right temple, like an ice-skater waiting for the starting shot. He went on to shave his right cheek with fastidious strokes.

Was 'Dear bride and groom' too formal? Why not German? '*Liebe Lisa, lieber Ludo*' was probably better... All those L's in a row. Perfect! Excellent idea... And he could drop the jibe about the local council. Why do everyone else's dirty work? That was Bastiaan Hermans's job, as chair of the association! A hundred guilders says he won't show up.

Despite his sleepless night, Jacob felt fit and full of beans. Blood coursed through his veins like waters down a mountain stream in spring, and even his digestion had been back to normal for a couple of weeks. Perhaps that gypsy woman in Amsterdam had been right after all. Amazing, those eyes of hers! His waterworks never gave him any trouble and he could run up the stairs without the slightest wheeze. He might have been pushing ninety kilos, but his body was still in excellent shape. Jacob could touch his toes whenever he chose, and, if his back itched, he scratched it! It was a miracle. How many mountains of food had he tucked away over the years? How many litres of milk, coffee, tea, water? Unbelievable when you think about it, his fifty-something frame still obliging him to this day!

He would be a grandfather soon too. He pictured himself in shorts, purple grazes on his knees, racing across a meadow somewhere north of Alkmaar. And now he was about to become a grandpa! Jacob was as old now as his former boss was when they took him away, Benno Lemberg who so longed for grandchildren, Uncle Benno who was dead, had been murdered, gassed. Benno had travelled through Belgium and France, but instead of Switzerland he had ended up in Zakopane in southern Poland, followed by Sobibor and Auschwitz. Could he have done more to help him? Was Uncle Simon's sack of gold coins just an easy way to escape further responsibility? Did

Benno Lemberg's son have a point after all, even if only a moral one?

His right cheek emerged from the shave, pink and reborn. In a haze of tears he suddenly saw his father in the mirror instead of himself, his dear father who had been a farmhand all his life, and who had collapsed one day in the middle of a field, shovel in hand, and died a week later.

The church had paid for a death notice in the paper underneath the caption 'God's little acre'. Jacob's mother followed three years later but was denied a death notice, as she had given up her membership of the Dutch Reformed Church directly after her husband's death. She had not collapsed on God's little acre. She was found cold and stiff in her chair one morning, her mouth open as if in final protest. Maria was pregnant with Ludo at the time. His parents would so have enjoyed this day, and his business success, the hotel, whether the bank owned the place or not.

It occurred to Jacob just how unfair life was. There were people of his age whose parents still enjoyed the best of health and who themselves had both children and the pleasure of grandchildren. Child, parent and grandparent united in the same person. The hotel-keeper moved his razor towards his left temple and was about to start on his left cheek when he was suddenly struck by a mild sense of panic. Both sides of his family had suffered from heart problems, and he was now nearly the same age as his parents were when they died. Was he about to meet his maker?

Death was a horrific chasm where people disappeared never to be seen again. What was the point of it all? The sons he and Maria had created and raised together with love? The business they had established? He didn't believe in the afterlife. The last traces of Jewishness in his family had died with his father.

Jacob pushed his chin to the right with one hand and started work on his left cheek with the other. The tightness and anxiety in his chest had disappeared as quickly as they had arisen. Ha! Nonsense. You're as fit as a fiddle, Bagman, you've never been seriously sick in your life. Perhaps good fortune was on his side after all. And hadn't his great-grandfather on his father's side lived to the ripe old age of ninety-three? That was a healthy generation if ever there was one. And to cap it all, he was an optimist; he believed in the future. Ludo and Liza would move into the fisherman's cottage, and before long their first child would have a little brother or sister to play with, at least that was the way things tended to happen. He envisaged substantial growth in short-stay tourism in the coming years. He would have all the bedrooms renovated, one after the other. And surely Bastiaan Hermans, with his three years of higher education, couldn't go on as chairman for ever? In due time, Ludo would take over the running of the hotel, and Felix would find his way. But as the hotel-keeper held his razor under the hot tap and started to shave his neck, he was overcome by a familiar yet still harrowing sense of powerlessness at the thought of Louis.

His second son would soon turn thirty, but the chances of him ever marrying were non-existent. Girls were simply not interested. Jacob had personally never believed in the breech-birth explanation. According to the doctors, Louis's brain had been deprived of oxygen during labour and had been irreparably damaged. Medical claptrap! Something must have gone wrong long before the birth. Although his mind worked perfectly in some matters – Louis could solve difficult equations at the drop of a hat on occasion, the answer dangling in the air before him, as if illuminated by a row of Chinese lanterns – Jacob had never really been able to understand what was going on in the poor boy's head.

Louis could be unruly at times, and there was no rhyme or reason to his epileptic fits. In the summer, he might suddenly refuse to help with the washing-up and start tossing the pots and plates around. Maria was the only one who could ever calm him down. Most of the time, though, he was a sweet boy, snuggling up to his mummy and daddy on the sofa like a little puppy.

But who was going to take care of him later on? Jacob had little confidence in Ludo in this regard, although there was always a chance that he might change his ways as he got older. Marriage and fatherhood had changed him completely and no mistake! 'Dear bride and groom...' No. 'Ladies and gentlemen' was much better. Why reinvent the wheel? 'Ladies and gentlemen—' Ouch!

Jacob had cut himself shaving. 'Strawberries and cream!' he muttered to himself in amusement.

He took a styptic pencil, rinsed it under the cold tap, and pressed it against the wound. To his eternal surprise, he enjoyed the searing, salty sting every time.

62

The bride and groom spent the night before the wedding experimenting with sex. Ludo had been horny as a toad all day, and Liza had been craving to submit to his powerful embrace at the earliest opportunity. She even sensed a little wetness early in the evening, and the last few drops of menstrual blood weren't its only cause.

Her period would be over the next day, she hoped, though it was always difficult to predict. Before making her way to Ludo's room, she removed the rust-stained towel from her knickers, flushed it down the toilet, and scrubbed the bowl with a brush to be safe. A touch of perfume here and there and she was ready for her darling.

Ludo was already lying naked on the bed when she entered the bedroom, looking like a young god who'd been washed up on a beach. He slipped one of the free condoms from the chemist over his seriously swollen member, and promptly asked Liza to get down on all fours. He wanted to take her from behind again, but not like before, by the back passage...

'What do you mean?' she asked innocently.

'Up your arse.'

'But that's—'

Ludo reassured her with his smooth, deep voice; everything went without a hitch. He began by caressing her back, kissing her neck and rhythmically massaging her buttocks with a mounting intensity until everything lay wet and wide open before him.

'Come, sweetheart, come to Daddy...' Ludo panted, lifting her luscious hips slightly and slowly thrusting his sheathed, dull-yellow sabre into the pale folds of her anus, enjoying the blissful snugness before suddenly breaking through into a space as wide as the universe. Did it hurt?

'No, no,' said Liza, glancing over her shoulder, a curtain of blonde hair hanging over her face.

Take it, slut, take all of it, he thought, slapping hard against her thighs, finally coming in a blistering eruption of pleasure. He removed his still throbbing member from his pregnant darling's body, carefully freed it from the condom – which he crumpled up in a tissue – and collapsed on his back at her side, exhausted.

He turned to look at her again shortly after, at the curve of her incredibly firm buttocks, and whispered a few sweet words that melted her, tenderly kissing her eyelids. Ludo suddenly noticed a birthmark on her neck for the first time and licked it with the tip of his tongue, a spontaneous gesture of love and still unsated passion.

He was to be married the following morning, but would never be content with just one woman. Men aren't made that way, not on your life, not him at least! He recalled Edo's Moscow stories, and was soon brooding over his plan to help old man Bender and his bitch wife to an early grave, or, better still, have someone do it for him. He had to avoid any personal risks. A staged car accident, perhaps, or injections with untraceable poison. Maybe there was a point to him knowing Edo after all...

Liza snuggled close to Ludo's chest. Fresh sweat, what a wonderful smell. She had learned something new and banished another of her fears. Her classmates in Karlsruhe had often whispered about what they had recently experienced, and she personally hadn't found the idea unpleasant. Liza knew that regular physical relief was as necessary for a man as food and drink, more so than for a woman, and was glad that she could satisfy her sweetheart in bed. She would be married tomorrow, and be rid of her fucking awful 'Bender' surname at last! 'Mrs Bagman,' she murmured, sucking her thumb, a habit she hadn't yet shed.

Her drowsy contentment was suddenly overcome by a shiver of anxiety. How would she tell Ludo after the wedding that she wasn't pregnant? She would have to make something up, a tragic miscarriage perhaps... Lord, it was terrible—it happened so quickly. Oh, Ludo, my darling—I was sitting on the toilet—I flushed everything away without thinking—I had no idea— She had read something about it once in a magazine famous for its American cartoons, love stories and knitting patterns. She didn't have to make anything up. It could all really happen like that.

The bride-to-be felt a sudden stabbing pain in her pelvis. The curse on her wedding day, the most beautiful day of her life!

'You seem a bit restless, my sweet,' Ludo grumbled, already consumed by gratifying post-coital drowsiness.

'It's nothing, dear, I'm fine,' whispered Liza, kissing his chest, before snuggling up to him once again and drifting off into dreams of the splendid life ahead of them both.

63

He could remember every single occasion that he had relaxed in a black limousine next to a beautiful blonde.

Under her pearl-studded veil, her mouth was like a shifting stain the colour of blood. The steering-wheel moved rapidly in her bony hands. They drove over winding roads coated in snow past the shadows of houses and farms. They were in Eastern Prussia, he was sure of that, and the linden trees, home to a multitude of storks' nests, had yet to turn green. They lined the sides of the road, looking like burnt broomsticks dipped in double cream.

Over his shoulder, he saw his brother on the back seat. He wore only rags, Hans Matti in his patent leather shoes and pinstripe trousers resembling Little Lord Fauntleroy, and holding a big bag of toffees in his hand. 'Eat up!' the woman commanded, the gold bands on her wrists jangling.

'But what about Otto?' whined Hans Matti, no longer daring to look back.

'Who?'

'Can I give some to my brother?'

'Yes, let's give him some!' the woman declared triumphantly. She slammed on the brakes, everything started to spin, and, after a couple of flashes of light, the next thing Hans Matti saw was Otto rolling down an embankment through the grey snow. 'Let's give him some more!'

'No, no,' echoed a voice from the depths.

The recurring nightmare always left him soaked in sweat. The sausage-maker turned over and groped for his watch on the bedside table: it was nearly six. He would shave, take a relaxing shower, and then squeeze into the tailcoat and silk shirt that Kati had insisted on having made to measure in Aachen. The once-in-a-lifetime outfit had cost a fortune, but Kati would not hear of hiring a suit. Hired clothes were for deckhands, whores and labourers.

Hans Matti had waited for his wife in the hotel restaurant the previous evening, but she still hadn't returned from her walk by the time everyone was heading off to bed.

The hotel-keeper and the sausage-maker had enjoyed a nightcap – a final glass of Friesian bitters – and had ended up musing about this and that. They might still be able to boast a glimmer of youth today, both of them, but it would soon be gone. As parents of married children they would belong to the older generation, and there was no looking back then, groaned Hans Matti in despair.

They may be a little longer in the tooth, he continued, but he was still bursting with energy and full of plans for the future. Plastic packaging had introduced countless new possibilities at work. The factory could prepack sausages in various shapes and sizes and offer them to the customer ready for consumption. It was more practical, simpler. He had plenty of new business ideas, for sure, and when it came to it – the sausage-maker shared a conspiratorial glance with his future in-law – well, man to man, he still had an eye for a pretty girl, if Jacob got his drift. Once *that* was gone, well, you might as well just hang yourself, didn't he think?

The two men suddenly developed a bond of complete trust. It was as if they had known each other for centuries. As they described their younger years, their voices lowered to whispers. They talked about the early days of married life, about earning enough to support their families. In spite of it all they were still men, and proud of it. Did Hans Matti fancy one last Friesian schnapps? The sausage-maker nodded, looking at his watch and wondering out loud what Kati was up to. Women were so fickle, so unpredictable!

Before they knew it, the men were trying to outdo one another in their confessional admissions. Jacob spoke of his trips across the length and breadth of the country in search of antiques, and the single ladies he had sometimes encountered on the way. You would never believe what some of them were prepared to do within ten minutes or so.

'Men and women are no different in that respect,' stated Hans Matti, having alluded to his mistress in Hamburg a couple of times without going into detail. Jacob countered with the story of his trip to Paris, taking care to be vague enough to keep the sausage-maker guessing.

When Kati hadn't arrived back at the hotel by ten-thirty, they decided to go up to bed. The black porter could let her in. He was asleep on a sofa in the cloakroom.

'*Gute Nacht!*'

'*Ja, Gute Nacht,*' yawned the father of the bride, almost asleep already.

Kati had collapsed beside him, breathing heavily and snoring like a soldier on a camp bed. There were pockmarks and wrinkles on her face that he'd never noticed before. She looked as if her neck had been bitten by a starfish. Or rather, the pinkish mark on her neck was shaped like a starfish. Insects were always drawn to her.

Half-asleep, Hans Matti had heard her stumble into the room. He had asked what time it was.

'Quarter past eleven,' she had replied, hoping for the best. She wasn't far off – it was only fifteen minutes later.

Her husband yawned and asked what she had been up to before promptly drifting off to the land of nod. In the meantime, Kati had slipped her dress off for the second time in ten minutes, grabbed a towel and hurried to the dreadful communal shower for an intimate rinse.

'Honey,' said Hans Matti in a quiet voice, giving her shoulder a gentle tug. It was time to get up. Breakfast would be served at seven-thirty, and she still had to visit the hairdresser.

'What hairdresser?' the sausage-maker's wife grunted, her head pounding like an anvil being hammered. Where was she? Why didn't he let her sleep, for Christ's sake?

'But it's almost seven,' Hans Matti insisted.

The fog slowly lifted and Kati regained consciousness little by little. The workshop of hammers and anvils became an entire factory. She experienced the sensation of a burning needle darting through her head from ear to ear a couple of times.

'Aspirin,' the sausage-maker's wife whined.

Hans Matti rummaged through their cases, her handbag, the drawer of the bedside table, but couldn't find anything. He then went downstairs in his camelhair dressing gown to where Maria, glowing in the early morning sunlight, was standing at the buffet table.

She looked at Hans Matti cheerfully. 'Coffee or tea?'

'Aspirin, if you have it!'

'What?' Maria responded, taken aback. Did he feel ill? Should they call the doctor?

'It's for dear Kati,' the sausage-maker explained. She felt wretched. All the excitement of the wedding – such an important day in a mother's life – was proving a little too much for her.

Maria nodded understandingly, groped around in a box full of playing cards, dominoes, thimbles, iodine, plasters, thread and other useful things the lady of the house would need to have at hand in a hotel, and gave Hans Matti a bottle of pills.

Kati should remember to take the tablets with plenty of water, otherwise it might upset her tummy. Hans Matti thanked Maria and nodded. Funnily enough, the aspirins were German.

64

He was used to jumping over ditches in Friesland, but here there wasn't a ditch in sight. The ducks that flew up from the reeds from time to time and over the rippling ponds in tender flocks behind his house in preparation for the big shoot – like the wooden chickens at the market in Harlingen painted orange to celebrate the queen's birthday every year – were nowhere to be seen. It was immensely different here from his Friesland birthplace, but it was still the Netherlands all the same.

The dunes that Louis had shown him the previous day had been a disappointment. Wierd needed more undergrowth to conceal himself and take aim undisturbed. After they had returned to the hotel, the northerner paid a quick visit to his room for appearances' sake, before heading off on his own to the dunes on the other side of town fifteen minutes later. He was surprised to find patches of pine forest and, sure enough, a young doe had leapt out of a sandpit not far from where he stood. A magnificent animal! A shame he didn't have his rifle.

Louis had discreetly asked him after dinner what time they would be setting off the following morning. Half-past four, Wierd had whispered, knowing full well that he would be gone by four. He had no use for his cousin whatsoever, but didn't want to rub him up the wrong way so close to the wedding. As if he was going hunting just for fun!

The Friesian had tiptoed past the sleeping porter in the hotel lobby in his stockings (the black man had opened an eye for a second but shut it again immediately), and, keeping close to the sleep-quietened houses of the resort, had hurried towards the western edge of the dunes, enjoying the sea air that he could still smell two kilometres away in the moonlit landscape. He discovered a hideaway behind a reasonably thick bramble and settled in. 'Come out, come out, wherever you are!'

Within a quarter of an hour, an entire colony of rabbits jumped from their holes one after the other, out into the pearl-pink light of dawn. Wierd took aim, fired and knocked down three in a row. He shuffled towards them, only to realise that one rabbit had only been grazed by the hail of lead. Quaking and trembling, the little runt was trying to escape, its hind leg lame, its bleeding eye seeming to plead for mercy.

'You ugly little rascal!' menaced Wierd, taking a firm hold of the creature by the front and hind legs and pulling until it gave a soft internal snap like a party cracker. It wasn't worth wasting a bullet to finish it off. If it had been a red deer perhaps, but not a rabbit. This was what hunting was all about!

In the hour and a half that followed, however, nothing stirred, no pheasant or deer, not even another rabbit. How did the bloody prince consort manage? According to the newspaper clippings, the place was supposed to be crawling with game. He suddenly heard a barking dog drawing ever closer, and a man's voice barely audible in the distance, 'Wouter, come here! Here, Wouter!'

Wierd froze, but the brute was standing beside him before he knew it, a steaming tongue hanging from its jowls. 'Bugger off!' he snarled hoarsely, terrified the beast might belong to one of groundsmen. The pitch-black Alsatian sniffed briefly at his crotch, licked the back of his right hand and then ran off. 'Wouter, heel! Here boy, heel!'

Once every sound had disappeared, Wierd clambered to his feet, dusted the sand off his dungarees, gathered his things, and started his return journey. Three rabbits! He would skin them with a sharp kitchen knife over the sink as soon as he got back to the hotel. He then saw something in the distance that he hadn't noticed before, a blue-green glow where the dunes merged with the town, with shades of red from the morning sun. Might be worth checking out, he thought, looking at his watch. There was still time – he just had to be back at the hotel for breakfast at half-past seven. He made his way along a broken path towards the trees. It was moist, fragrant and cool between the pines.

The scrawny Friesian heard the sound of German voices getting louder as he approached. He crept up to a grimy concrete wall and saw a partially cultivated area surrounded by tall pine trees. A group of men were busy flexing their knees and doing other gymnastic exercises. A wiry bloke in white long johns performed countless somersaults in the sand, clapping his hands after each one. He could have been a circus act!

More and more men with tired faces and towels over their shoulders emerged from whitewashed bunkers that popped up here and there between the reeds. A scrawny character with a pale white torso and prominent ribs was washing at a water pump, the handle grinding and squeaking rhythmically up and down.

A potbellied gentleman wobbled along a shingle path. He had a fluffy moustache and wore a white uniform with polished brass buttons that glistened in the silvery sunlight. He was followed by an unsightly creation wearing a blue jacket over a chef's uniform, a couple of pathetic hairs stuck to his oval bean of a head. The chef was slowly pushing a trolley with rubber wheels and a set of metal containers on top.

'Breakfast's arrived!' called the uniformed potbelly with the moustache, clapping his hands with enthusiasm.

Wierd was perfectly placed. It would have been like shooting pigs in a barrel. The Friesian deeply regretted that the war was over, otherwise he might have picked the Kraut bastards off one by one, and been a hero rather than a murderer. That was the crucial difference.

65

By the time Hans Matti had returned with the aspirin, his wife had already thrown up in the basin.

The sour smell of vomit permeated every corner of the room. The sausage-maker had to gulp back the swell of saliva in his throat to avoid being sick himself.

'It must have been that disgusting dinner,' growled Kati, slapping hot water from the tap on her cheeks as violently as she used to slap Liza when she was angry. She'd been forced to eat cheese schnitzels for the second day running, and she didn't want to see another one for as long as she lived!

Hans Matti climbed on to the bed and opened the fanlight, the bedsprings protesting loudly at his weight. Kati was still slumped over the washbasin, her breasts sagging, her face cadaverous, poking what remained of her vomit down the drain with her fingertips, utterly disgusted. Hans Matti mumbled something about the aspirin and that he was going for a shower.

'Shut up!' Kati groaned, a hand – like a sea cow's flipper – feebly rubbing her right hip. 'Don't say another fucking word...'

A great wave of nausea suddenly swept over her bare body. She grabbed her throat and vomited again. Hans Matti wanted to help, suppressing his own queasiness anew, but Kati told him to go to hell.

He scurried out into the corridor in his dressing gown, gratefully gulping great mouthfuls of fresh air.

Kati continued to retch as the last bilious flecks disappeared down the drain, and then cautiously sipped a glass of water until her breathing was normal and the sweating had ceased. Now she was on the mend. But when she could finally look at herself in the mirror, she was as startled as a child who sees a skeleton rattling about in a haunted house.

Her eyelids were puffy, her nose covered in strange blemishes, and her chin had never looked as full before. She had aged five years overnight. Jesus, what a nightmare! And they would shortly be expecting her downstairs in full regalia.

Kati looked at the door, pining abruptly for a hot shower and cursing her husband under her breath for being such a slowcoach. Then she saw her clothes draped over the chair, and was absolutely thunderstruck. Her golden violin brooch studded with nine miniature diamonds had vanished from the collar of her dress. Kati fell to her knees, her increasingly manic fingers roaming the area where she had undressed the night before. Nothing! She checked the bed, under the bed, the entire room. Nothing. No, no, no… this couldn't be happening! It was as if her heart had been dashed to the floor and shattered in a thousand pieces.

Kati had proudly worn the brooch when she was interviewed by General Von Oberhaussen, and also later when she was received by the Führer in Berlin along with a hundred other military personnel. There were no photos of the ceremonial event, a fact that had deeply disappointed her then just as much as it pleased her now. The brooch was the only heirloom of any value that she had from her family in Bavaria. But of course, it would be in the linen cupboard! She would check there later, she thought, immediately relieved. She couldn't have lost it… Impossible, simply impossible.

Hans Matti stumbled in, his hair still wet from the shower. 'Have you seen my brooch?' she asked him, just to be on the safe side.

'Brooch?' repeated the sausage-maker, still shocked by the sight of her ever-pastier face.

Sixteen years together and the idiot still didn't know what she was talking about. Kati threw on her yellow silk dressing gown and disappeared along the chilly corridor towards the shower. The humid haze of her husband's ablutions filled the white tiled room. She shivered in disgust until the warm relief of the shower took hold.

The German couple appeared in the central hall of Hotel New Deluxe arm in arm. Hans Matti was wearing his new made-to-measure suit, a frivolous pink cravat in his breast pocket lending it a festive air. Kati was wearing a black velvet dress with a fox-fur stole. The outfit didn't work without the luxurious neck ornament. When she bought it in Brussels the month before, she hadn't known it could get so hot in North Holland in mid-May. Perhaps she could get rid of the scarf later on, but for the city hall and the church it was staying where it was. She had applied acres of rouge to her cheeks and the pockmarks on her chin had been skilfully camouflaged with French face cream.

Kati completely ignored the black porter's immediate subtle look of recognition. Instead, she looked at her husband with a surprising degree of affection. For once he was dressed as a gentleman should be. She played the game with skill, although all sorts of anxieties continued to besiege her. Would the porter talk at some later date? Of course not! Her imagination was simply running away with her. And who would ever believe what one of those black people said anyway?

'Good morning, dear friends!' cried Maria, welcoming her future in-laws with enthusiasm.

'Morning, Maria!' The sausage-maker greeted her once again, this time in his wedding outfit, with an elegant bow.

Breakfast was ready, Maria announced. But perhaps Kati would first like to go to the hairdresser? He was working on Liza at the

moment, then it was her turn – Maria said she only needed a minute
– and then the rest of the ladies.

'Is he up to scratch?' Kati asked. She had had a shampoo and set
in Cologne and actually couldn't bear anyone other than her regular
coiffeur to come near her hair.

'He won a bronze hairpin at the gala in Ghent,' replied the hotel-
keeper's wife, who visited Amand Scapé's tasteful, well-appointed
salon once a month without fail. His prices were listed on a table
between the mirrors.

Kati agreed – a little tease and some hairspray could do no harm
– and then brought the conversation round to the topic of laundry
and linen. Maria was the happy owner of one of those modern roller
irons, no doubt, but could she remember the make?

'I have no idea,' replied Maria, who was still wearing her blue apron
with white flowers and was already halfway upstairs by this time. Why
didn't Kati take a quick peep in the linen cupboard? She knew where
to find it, didn't she? The wooden door next to the toilets. Maria then
hurried upstairs, free at last to get ready for the big day.

66

A radiant Liza Bender, at the height of her beauty and bursting with
youthful promise, gazed at her reflection in the mahogany dressing-
table mirror in her future mother-in-law's bedroom.

The wispy Mr Scapé ('Amand, *bitte*, and none of that Mr nonsense... I'm not *Mr* anything.') fluttered elegantly about her, brandishing combs, brushes and hairpins with flamboyant expertise, his
flitting gestures vaguely reminiscent of Mr Monjoux.

The proprietor of 'Coiffeur Scapé' preferred young men to young
women, although he regularly appeared in public in the company
of a thickset blonde whose fiery red lips ranged over a face of risen
dough. Everyone knew of her sense of humour and thunderous

253

peals of laughter. He always carried her shopping, for appearances'
sake.

But the entire village was well aware of his deviant inclinations
and often wondered what he got up to when they saw him heading
off to Amsterdam in his Citroën. Where did he end up, with those
wild brown curls and those narrow hips of his? They knew all about
the birds and the bees, but Mr Scapé was neither one nor the other.
He was quite simply unique.

The stylist had initially changed his surname only (from Schaap
to Scapé), but Hans Scapé didn't sound exotic enough so he changed
his first name too. Anyone addressing him as Hans Scapé and not
by his 'stage name' could expect a dirty look or to be snubbed altogether. Naturally, the people of this town were all vulgar and ill-man-
nered. It was rare for someone with more artistic inclinations – such
as himself – to be born in such a place. He ascribed his talent to a
distant French ancestor who, according to tradition, had served
under Napoleon and gone on to settle in the area. At the hairdressing
gala in Ghent – he had made use of Herman Nederleven's French
lessons with considerable flair – Amand had taken every opportunity to refer to his French ancestry, unaware that it did not endear
him especially to his Flemish hosts.

The rumours surrounding the Bagman family, which had been
doing the rounds over the past few days, had become the stylist's new
pet hate. He never read *The Boulevard* – an infantile rag; he heard
enough about it in his salon – although his advert ran without fail
every week at the bottom of page three: 'Coiffeur Scapé, styling and
accessories. No appointment necessary.'

To Amand Scapé, Maria Bagman was simply a treasure, Jacob as
cute as a teddy bear, and as for Ludo – who would be arriving shortly
to collect his bride – he had taken note of him from afar, often enough,
observing him in his swimming trunks on the beach, a tear in his otherwise avuncular eye. And now the young lad was getting married! The
hairdresser could barely comprehend that he was himself nearly forty-

five, though the boys in Amsterdam maintained that he didn't look a day over twenty-nine. Amand would dine out with his lovers in expensive restaurants, where he ordered the wine in French, sending it back with a grimace on the merest suspicion of its being corked.

'Not too hot, is it, *liebchen*?' enquired Mr Scapé. He always loved working with foreign clients as it enhanced his international appeal.

'*Alles gut*,' Liza assured him, entranced, enjoying the fingers teasing her hair.

Mr Scapé had washed her hair with camomile shampoo and settled her under the portable hood dryer, an aluminium contraption that one of the Friesian lads, none of whom were physically interesting, had lugged upstairs from the car after some gentle persuasion.

Once Mr Scapé had finished drying and brushing her hair, Liza was ready to put on her wedding dress, so the stylist summoned Maria and left the bedroom, demure. Ten minutes later, it was safe to come back in. 'We're ready!'

As a child, Mr Scapé had panicked at the sight of a bride. They unconsciously caused him to think of death, and he simply couldn't imagine how any hale and hearty young man could possibly be turned on by a girl tarted up to look like an Easter egg.

'So, what do you think?' appealed Maria, circling around her fairytale daughter-in-law like a sculptor appraising the perfect statue.

'Divine!' Mr Scapé squealed, feigning surprise and clapping his hands close to his chest. 'But it's time to get you back in front of the mirror, my darling – I'm not finished with you just yet.'

The dress was a sumptuous cascade of satin without the customary train. The lack of children on both sides of the family obliged them to forego the usual page or bridesmaid. After pinning up Liza's hair at the back in a sort of bun – in the blink of an eye and with obvious skill – and readying the rest of her golden curls, Mr Scapé carefully fitted the veil. They had made a good choice, he thought, not too small, not too big. Brides with oversized veils looked just like nuns from a distance.

255

'Well, *liebchen*, is it all all right?' Mr Scapé flicked the bride's partially exposed shoulder with his fingertip, as a chef might flick the edge of a plate before handing it over to be served, done.

Liza was simply speechless. Her eyes and eyelashes had never looked so spectacular – Mr Scapé always took care of the make-up for the annual operetta – and the lipstick he had recommended had only just arrived from Paris. It wasn't cheap, but her off-white wedding dress simply cried out for it. Mr Scapé had also palmed her off with some other glossy make-up accoutrements, proving himself a shrewd businessman into the bargain.

Ludo now hastened in in his slender suit tails to collect his bride. He held his grey top hat against his belly, a slightly dejected look about him. 'Well hello, my boy!' The hairdresser greeted him glowingly, his face like the rising sun.

'Morning, Mr Scapé,' said Ludo flatly. He was conscious of the power he had over gay men and liked nothing better than to toy with their interest from time to time, but this morning he was too nervous.

Maria, wondering what could possibly be preoccupying her eldest son, turned towards him and trilled, 'Well, Ludo, my dear, what do you think of your darling bride?' She carefully raised one of the folds in Liza's dress, a twinkle in her eye.

67

Breakfast that morning was even more extravagant than the previous day's. Jacob and Maria were both blessed with tireless constitutions and were unable to sit still – there was always something to keep them busy – and when Mr Zwaan saw that Maria was about to get up to clear some plates away, he intervened with the strict instruction that, for the rest of the day, she was a guest in her own hotel, and immediately turned to his boss to add, 'That counts for you too, Mr Bagman!'

Meanwhile, Uncle Bouke was starting to feel more at home with the German sausage-maker who was about to become one of the family. He was particularly curious about sausage manufacture as he had kept an amateur's appreciation of black pudding all his life.

The conversation turned to milking cows, and the old farmer tried his best to explain the process.

'It's very simple,' said Uncle Bouke, his red fingers pretending to knead invisible udders above his crumb-coated plate.

Hans Matti had mixed tens of thousands of udders into his smoked sausages in the course of his career (his secret was a measured combination of beech shavings, sawdust and plenty of seasoning) but had never actually touched a real udder before. Didn't the cows feel anything?

'Not if you know how to do it,' Uncle Bouke answered sagely, but it was just the same with the ladies. He grinned at his great-nephews, revealing a single, yellowing tooth. All three started to chuckle in unison, and before long they were roaring with laughter.

'*Die Weibe*,' the farmer explained, a glimmer in his eye. He could still remember a word or two from the occupation. Women.

'*Ach so!*' The sausage-maker grinned back.

Felix, who was expected on the eight-thirteen train from Leiden, was running late as usual. Hans Matti wondered in the meantime what was keeping his wife. What was taking her so long in that linen cupboard? She hadn't even folded a sock in ten years, and had now suddenly developed an overwhelming interest in roller irons.

Wierd calmly consumed one egg after another from the *Four-Minute Egg Warmer*. Fifteen minutes earlier, he had skinned the dune rabbits at the sink in his room with a razor-sharp knife, spattering blood over his face and neck in the process. He hadn't had a bath in four days, but settled for a quick rub down with a damp flannel. You couldn't get him under the shower for love or money. Cold water and soap were quite enough, the secret of a long and healthy life.

Louis caught sight of him when he went downstairs in his suit, gave a shriek, and made a beeline for the side kitchen. Maria asked her nephew what on earth was going on.

'I haven't a clue, Aunty,' lied Wierd, suddenly overcome with guilt.

Louis had crept downstairs that morning at ten to four and waited for Wierd in the hall. The Friesian hunter didn't appear at four, and there was still no sign of him at quarter past. The black porter, who had gone back to sleep again under his jacket on the sofa, finally woke up, realized immediately what had happened, and tried to explain in signs and gestures that Wierd had already left half an hour ago.

Louis started to tremble, his arms and legs jerking violently in shock. The black porter ran over to him, held the hotel-keeper's son in a tight embrace – just as he had done a couple of hours earlier with Kati, although this time it was different – and whispered a stream of strange words that sounded like a prayer to the unfortunate boy, and which appeared to have the desired effect.

Some minutes later, Louis returned to bed and lay there, flat on his back, gazing calmly for hours at the sky through the skylight window. His eyes reflected its shifting colours, just as the shadows cast by people and other things constantly changed shape and shade, though most people never even noticed.

'What's the matter, darling?' Maria asked him, having followed him into the side kitchen. Louis was sitting down, smoking a cigarette and staring at the black rubber mats beneath his feet, and their drainage grooves for water.

'Nothing, Mummy,' he replied, his face suddenly lighting up. 'Isn't it great that Ludo and Liza are getting married today?'

Maria looked at her son in silence for a moment.

'Have you seen Liza in her wedding dress?' She felt relieved. It must have been some trifling spat between the two cousins.

'No, not yet,' said Louis, jumping to his feet. 'Can I borrow the master key for a second?'

'But why?' asked Maria, who always carried the master key on her, as if she were guarding a treasure.

Wiebe had locked himself out of his room, and had asked Louis what he should do.

'Of course, sweetheart.' His mother smiled. 'Come with me. It's in my apron.'

When Louis entered the dining room ten minutes later in his best suit, the breakfasting guests welcomed him with exaggerated compliments, as insincere and infantile as the cloakroom lady's remarks about his party hat at the Rijksmuseum a couple of days earlier.

The hotel-keeper's son did not fly into a rage this time around, however. A radiant smile beamed on his chubby face, as if he were a soldier going off to fight, convinced that he would triumph come what may.

68

Felix Bagman woke up with an erection in his attic room near the Hooimarkt in the beautiful city of Leiden.

He kicked the threadbare blanket off the bed, rolled over, and immediately set about pleasuring himself, images of Liza Bender in various positions in his mind.

He used a paper serviette from the students' cafeteria to capture his sperm, having bought a couple of veal croquettes the night before to take home after a busy day of classes and experiments.

His neighbour had arrived home in a taxi around eight, back from a long haul. He had barely set foot in the place when a female guest had arrived, and, after the usual rituals, the rhythmic squeak of bedsprings climaxing in the customary primal scream, he had started to play the piano with an intense passion, each melody followed by gentle, feminine applause.

Love was a bizarre thing, he thought. Birds had courtship rituals and monkeys were known to beat themselves over the head with branches until they bled, all for the attention of a female. But the maladroit human comedy performed day in day out to coax someone into bed, wasn't that nothing short of a biological aberration? The bloke on the floor below even gave a concert *afterwards*! Where was the logic in that?

'The smell of chestnuts – unmistakeable,' Felix mumbled in observation, crumpling up the serviette containing his glistening seed, the swift massacre of thousands of his own spermatozoids consigned to a stainless-steel bin beneath his washbasin.

Fifteen minutes later, he went downstairs in his blue Monjoux suit, smelling of aftershave, his hair golden and curly. Werner Bokma was smoking a roll-up on the landing. He was a giant of a man, around thirty-five, with a wrinkled, permanent tan and white crow's feet.

'It wasn't too loud last night, was it?' asked the sailor, arching an eyebrow.

His girlfriend had just driven off to her villa in Assen. She was a blonde beauty who'd always had an interest in boys with both an athletic build and significant promise professionally. If they had no ambitions to be a doctor, then they were destined for local politics or a legal firm. His history teacher had once asked Werner what he planned to do in life.

'The murky deep, sir,' he had replied.

'What did you say, Bokma?'

'The murky deep.'

The whole class had laughed and sneered, including the platinum blonde who, true to form, had married a notary. But she couldn't slip on a new dress fast enough nowadays when her lover boy had shore leave.

Her notary husband's belly had expanded in direct proportion to his bank account in recent years, but his lust for life had faded, while Werner Bokma's had only intensified. Werner wanted to find out what lay hidden under the carpet of life, no matter how much garbage there was. Women were curious about that sort of thing. His lover had wanted to know what went on in the brothels of Montevideo in minute detail. It had made her as wet as a sponge, and Werner had to take her there and then, pretending she was the whore and he the client.

'You're a biology student, aren't you?'

'That's right.' Felix nodded, glancing at his watch. If he didn't want to miss the train, he would have to get a move on.

'I just got back from Trinidad,' Werner Bokma continued briskly, grabbing Felix's sleeve and pulling him into his apartment without any regard for the student's reluctance.

The living room was filled with decorated coconuts, ivory temples, chunks of ocean coral and other exotic souvenirs that Felix had previously examined and cherished, despite his profound envy, on the few occasions he had visited to play the piano. The sailor walked over to the table and opened a shoebox packed with colour photos of birds in various tropical landscapes. How did he know that Felix was so crazy about birds?

'We were stuck in port for a week,' Werner Bokma resumed, 'so I took off for a couple of days to the north of the island, for Arima Valley.' He rummaged through a pile of photos, 'Look, not a bad shot of a honeycreeper. The place is swarming with hummingbirds, oropendolas and the breathtaking motmot.' The east of the island was teeming with frigate birds, brown pelicans and parrots too, of course. Trinidad was a perfect paradise for parrots.

'Really?' said Felix, fascinated, barely able to comprehend that this man in his matted fisherman's sweater had already visited every corner of the globe.

Felix walked out on to the street a quarter of an hour later, the doves in the eaves cooing. He was too late for the eight-ten train, but had no need to hurry to catch the next one.

His neighbour had not only travelled everywhere, he enjoyed a rich and fulfilling intellectual and personal life. What lay under the carpet? A nice way of putting it!

Life was in evidence everywhere. Felix watched the students heading off to class, looking like they ruled the world. Technically he was one of them, but he felt different. Given half a chance he would set out on some voyage or other, following his heart as Bokma did, and leaving the rest to dream about their villas in the country and their careers. Didn't his father start out picking potatoes? He had to be patient.

Felix stopped in his tracks to watch a girl who was fiddling with her bicycle lock in front of a privet hedge. Her features were exceptionally delicate, and she had long dark hair. Jesus, who was she? He had seen hundreds of girls fiddling with their bicycle locks at all hours of the day, but had not given any of them a second thought, distracted by his love for Liza. But this time it was as if someone sacred was locking their bicycle, surrounded by a magical aura. An invisible lasso captured him and drew him towards her. He couldn't resist.

'Hi,' said the girl, unexpectedly turning towards him. 'I've seen you around. First-year biology, right?'

She had almond eyes with green-grey irises, and the force field surrounding her was magnetic. Her name was Violet, she was a second-year Russian student, but hated the Soviet regime. As long as *that* was clear! Was he was a member of the dreadful student union? 'A shower of mafiosi, if you ask me – the girls are all mafia whores.'

'You're right,' said Felix, and he mumbled something about being dressed up for his brother's wedding.

'Now I get it... hilarious!'

Felix was in a spin. Everything seemed to be shifting around inside him, like cargo on a container ship. He was suddenly head over heels in love with a girl he had only just met, a beautiful brunette who had meant nothing to him until a moment ago. His fantasy of the blonde, busty Liza Bender and her pearl-white teeth evaporated like morning mist.

'I'm different,' Violet confided, as if they had known each other for years. She had an overdeveloped sense of smell, and they were studying her in one of the university laboratories. Three people in every half a million had it. If she wasn't mistaken, he had just masturbated. She could even smell the strange chestnut odour of his sperm and the dried sweat beneath his aftershave. Why the long face?

'Give me your hand,' she said, and she scribbled her number on his wrist with a biro.

Felix had to run for the train after all. When he finally took a seat in one of the carriages, he felt his heart leap in his chest like a dolphin breaching the water. Jesus, he was in love! Apparently this sort of thing was supposed to happen when you turned twenty.

He laughed out loud as the fields of tulips whizzed past him in a haze.

All of a sudden, the wedding didn't seem so scary. In fact, he was looking forward to it.

69

Mr Zwaan had called his uniformed brigade to attention in the main hall, in military fashion. They formed a neat row in front of him, all seven of them. He peered through his old-fashioned spectacles at a list, which he had attached to a makeshift clipboard, and went through the day's events point by point.

Having detailed the ongoing supply of appetizers during the afternoon reception – crackers, peanuts, mini sausage rolls, chunks of cheese with pineapple and ginger, and slices of liverwurst with pickled gherkins – he moved on to address dinner.

'Who's serving the soup?'

'Me,' said a young waiter.

'And who's clearing the bowls away?'

'I am,' said another, raising his index finger.

'Main course?'

'Me and Jan,' said Guillaume, and he nodded his handsome head at a waiter with a skinny face, gaunt cheeks and a permanently surprised expression, for whom there was only one possible name, dreary, everyday Jan.

'Plates?'

'Willem and I will do it,' said the waiter also responsible for serving the soup.

When they had examined every aspect of the wedding dinner, Mr Zwaan turned to another page of notes, and launched into a speech about the evening's festivities as a whole. They were expecting 160 guests, but they should be prepared for any number from 130 to as many as 200.

Two men had been hired to replace Louis in the side kitchen, or rather a man and a woman, namely Johannes Wedekind and his wife Elsa. They had let Jacob know that they would prefer to earn an extra cent or two doing the washing-up than attend the wedding as functionless guests.

'What is of vital importance,' Mr Zwaan resumed, 'is that we clear the tables on time: plates, cutlery, glasses.' His tone was adamant as he looked each of his waiters in the eye. The supply of glasses was limited and they would have to be rinsed and returned continually. 'Who's on glasses?'

Guillaume raised a finger in a manner that betrayed an otherwise veiled loathing for his job, as if someone as good-looking as he should never have been obliged to earn a living by serving others.

'And another important point,' Mr Zwaan continued, flamboyantly ticking off each of the points on his list with a pencil. They were all aware what had happened last time, during the local music association's New Year reception. The bass player got so drunk on Jenever he could hardly stand up, and the pianist was all over the place. In principle, therefore, no strong drink should be served to the musicians. 'A beer at most, and only if they ask, and only later on in the evening. Absolutely no Jenever or liqueurs… Ah, Poteman, here you are at last!'

The waiters turned. The rotund Mr Poteman of Poteman & Co., Printers, beetled energetically through the arched doorway to the main hall, which was festooned with rustling streamers. The printer was holding a white cardboard box with a red lid in his hands.

Some unknown illness had left the man's face ashen grey, his left eyelid fluttering constantly, like the wing of a captive moth. He ran a small printing firm all by himself in a basement behind the Reformed Church, where the rattle of the presses could be heard virtually day and night.

'The vegetarian menu is on top,' Poteman advised the manager of Hotel New Deluxe.

'Leave it over here, Poteman,' said Mr Zwaan, amiably. The printer and the manager knew each other well. Poteman's son had rickets and they had spent many an hour together over the years in the Haarlem waiting room of the paediatric clinic.

'Promises to be a posh affair this evening, eh?' said Poteman, his sickly face marvelling at the decorations.

Once the printer had left and the staff had been dismissed to different parts of the hotel, Mr Zwaan opened the cardboard box, adjusted his spectacles, and began to read:

DINNER ON THE OCCASION OF THE MARRIAGE

OF LUDO BAGMAN AND LIZA BENDER

MAY 14, 1958

Dutch Chicken Consommé
Bouillon de Volaille Hollandaise

Traditional Duck Pâté
Pâté de Canard d'Amiens

Dutch Veal with Garden Peas and Duchesse Potatoes
Veau Hollandaise avec Petit Pois et Pommes Duchesse

Tutti Frutti Ice Cream Flambé
Glace Plombières Flambée

Coffee
Café simple

Wines
1955 Zeller Schwarze Katz
Médoc Guilhou Frère Aîné

A sumptuous and magnificent menu, thought Mr Zwaan with professional satisfaction. He then turned to the menu intended for Kati Bender.

Maria Bagman and chef Willem Jansen had concocted a Milk Soup (*Soupe au Lait*) from vegetable stock, since the chicken consommé necessarily contained meat extracts. As an alternative to the Traditional Pâté they had decided on a Gouda soufflé (*Soufflé au Gouda*), with the tofu dish after that. This course was also written in French on the menu but the spelling was incorrect. Poteman had only noticed the error after the menus had been boxed up and the letter block cleaned. Instead of *Tofou Coloniale aux Légumes*, the menu now read *Tofoe Coloniale aux Légumes*:

DINNER ON THE OCCASION OF THE MARRIAGE
OF LUDO BAGMAN AND LIZA BENDER
MAY 14, 1958

Dutch Milk Soup
Soupe au Lait Hollandaise

Gouda Soufflé
Soufflé au Gouda

Colonial-style Tofu with Roasted Vegetables
Tofoe Coloniale aux Légumes

Tutti Frutti Ice Cream Flambé
Glace Plombières Flambée

Coffee
Café simple

Wines
1955 Zeller Schwarze Katz
Médoc Guilhou Frère Aîné

'Good morning,' called a feeble voice from the back door. Mr Zwaan turned around. A giant of a man with a handlebar moustache and wild hair towered in the doorway. He wore a cape and was sweating profusely.

This was Mr Ivan Poestash, whose arrival was marred by his awful travel sickness. All he could think about was sleep, sleep, sleep. It sometimes took him up to six hours to recover. By sea, road or rail, it made little difference. It was the bane of his life and had cost him an international career. He was condemned to take whatever was on offer within the confines of the Netherlands. Even Belgium was too much for him.

The artist told his story with a brittle voice, and then asked if he might lie down for a few hours.

Mr Zwaan had heard that the man regularly performed at the Tuschinski theatre, and that he had even appeared at the Carré. He assured the artist that he would do all he could. There was always a room free somewhere in the hotel.

'Somewhere dark?' asked Mr Poestash, dizzy from a thumping migraine.

'As the grave,' replied Mr Zwaan, and he smiled graciously.

70

Parents whose children have done well for themselves, who enjoy good health, and whose eldest child gets married with plans to start a family, guaranteeing the family line, are among the luckiest people in the world.

Jacob and Maria Bagman felt wonderfully lucky. They had gone upstairs after breakfast and were sitting opposite each other in the quiet privacy of their living room, like actors waiting silently in the wings before the next scene.

They had to leave for the town hall in an hour – neither of them was particularly looking forward to the service in the Catholic church – and then there was a light lunch followed by the reception, the wedding banquet and the party in the main hall.

Jacob had every reason to be happy. After the turbulent years full of cares and problems, Ludo was finally about to settle down. A sweet girl, attractive, with an excellent financial background. They certainly wouldn't have to worry about the future, since Hans Matti's business affairs were all in perfect order. A dyed-in-the-wool entrepreneur and a good person too, you could see it in everything he did.

Maria stared at the antique wardrobe that had graced her great-grandmother's bedroom in Friesland a century ago, the sun playing on its polished wooden doors. It was such a tragedy that her mother and father had died so young. Smoke inhalation. The fire that had razed their farmhouse to the ground in under half an hour had taken them completely by surprise. They had died in each other's arms. Maria had been left with a terrible fear of fire, and every time she emptied an ashtray, at home or in the hotel, she would run it under the tap to ensure there were no smouldering cigarette butts.

She, too, was relieved that Ludo was settling down. Liza might still be a little flighty, but all that would change with the responsibilities of motherhood and the demands of running a home. Her thoughts drifted back to when her three sons were young. Her nose had been forever filled with the smell of poo, and she could picture the clothesline of flapping terry cloth nappies. She remembered staying up, often the entire night, because one or all of them were ill, or had aches and pains. She remembered dashing back and forth with hot-water bottles, glasses of warm milk and cups of tea. And now they were all grown up. No one had ever told her that the years would pass so quickly, but perhaps that was normal, and it had never occurred to her to talk to her sons about it.

She would give the new family all the space it needed, and in the meantime teach Liza in stages the skills required to run a good Dutch household, things like adding the milk to the roux on the back of a wooden spatula when making béchamel. Her own mother had taught her precious little in that department. Was Kati really sneering at her? Maria had noticed the way she would look her up and down from time to time, but they were simply miles apart. The hotel-keeper's wife had had to work for every penny, not so Madam from Cologne!

Oh, well, their relationship would probably improve after the birth of their grandchild. Surely they were both equally looking forward to becoming grandmothers? Liza appeared to be having a dream of a pregnancy. She was never nauseous and there wasn't even the slightest hint of a belly. The sight of her in her wedding dress! You would swear she had been on a diet for the past four months, not pregnant! But there was nothing so unusual about it. It was a blessing, really.

'Are you planning to say a few words at the dinner, Maria?' Jacob asked her, having gone over his own welcome speech in his head for the umpteenth time.

'I've written a poem for Liza and Ludo,' the hotel-keeper's wife coyly confessed. Jacob recalled a few recent occasions when he had found Maria sitting at her desk with a pen and paper and muttering to herself, before quickly stuffing what she had written into her apron pocket out of embarrassment.

It had taken time to find the right rhyme, but the final result was a poem of seven verses, each opening with the same refrain:

When a child leaves the nest to set up his own,
A mother at first might be tempted to mourn.

'You should read it between the starter and the main course,' Jacob advised his wife. 'No one will have had too much to drink by then, so you'll have their full attention. I'm so proud of you!'

'Let's wait and see,' said Maria, not yet sure if she would dare.

They were interrupted when Ludo burst in, looking even more dejected than he had half an hour earlier. The groom asked if he could have a word with his father.

'I'm right here, my boy, out with it!'

He glanced in awkward apology at his mother and asked if they might talk in private.

'I'll be getting on, then,' said Maria, getting up from her chair and straightening her skirt, before briefly adjusting her red coral necklace and leaving the room, feeling a bit like an intruder.

71

Ludo had looked everywhere to no avail. He had left them on the bedside table and now they were gone.

'But that's impossible!' Jacob wailed, when Ludo told him that the box containing the wedding rings had just disappeared all of a

270

sudden. Why hadn't he looked for them before now? He'd even spoken to Mr Zwaan about the rings just the day before...

'Jesus Christ! Fat lot of help you are!' What did he propose that Ludo do now? Borrow his parents' rings? Use curtain rings? This godforsaken dump didn't even have a jeweller's, and to get to Haarlem and back would take an hour at least—

'Monjoux!' Jacob cried, inspired, and the eternal optimist's eyes gave a twinkle. Monjoux had a display case of accessories in his shop, didn't he? He was sure he had rings! Why, only the other day, he had complained to Jacob that nobody ever showed any interest in his accessories. Whereas, in Limburg...

Ludo was off, leaving his top hat and cane with its silver pomegranate handle behind on the table. He raced out the back door of the hotel, grabbed the first bicycle he could, and sped towards The Boulevard like a man possessed.

Mr Monjoux was outside his shop, lowering its yellow awning that bore 'The Colours of Mozart' in bright red letters. He was dressed, as always, in the very latest fashion. He released the salt-seasoned ropes with care, making sure the canopy was level.

The appearance of the irate groom, his tails flapping in the wind, befuddled him even more than his attempts to second-guess the views of all his customers.

'Do you sell rings?!' Ludo yelled, standing up on his rickety bicycle and crashing into the curb.

'Rings?'

'The ones you put on your fingers!'

'Well, young man, let's take a look inside,' said the tailor.

Mr Monjoux stepped aside to let Ludo go first, then dashed behind the counter, opened a drawer, and scuttled towards the display case, key in hand.

Ludo looked around impatiently, grabbed three rolled-up pairs of socks from the basket beside the till, managed to juggle them, much to own his amazement, but quickly returned them to the basket.

'So, let's see what we have here.' Mr Monjoux acted innocent, but knew exactly what to take out from the cabinet and what to disregard. The young man before him was desperate. He could fob him off with any old rubbish and he would have to take it, whatever the cost. Better head straight for the most expensive stuff, the unisex rings, that's what they called them. They sold like hot cakes to young lovers abroad. They had been a blot on his accounts for almost a year and a half, however, expensive and unselling. Monjoux took a quick look at Ludo's hands. Did his darling bride have slender fingers or were they a little chubby?

'Slender, slender,' Ludo panted, desperately wondering what he would tell Liza. There was no way around it. The bloke at the registry office would be agog if they didn't fit! He wondered who might have stolen the rings – the black guy on the door? Probably. Jesus, what was his father thinking?

'What do you think?' Mr Monjoux opened a box to reveal two gold-plated rings with artificial diamonds in the middle on a bed of foam rubber, a near-identical pair, though one was a touch more slender than the other.

'Excellent!' Ludo exclaimed in haste, all set to grab the box from Monjoux's hand.

The shopkeeper raised his eyebrows. These unique specimens had to be imported especially from France and were sixty guilders apiece, including tax, he explained, and he made it a rule never to sell on credit. He ran his carefully manicured fingers over the display case.

'I don't have any cash on me,' Ludo confessed. What did he expect on his wedding day? And he knew the Bagmans, surely? And he had been invited to the party in the evening, hadn't he? He would pay him then, cross his heart and—

'Fine, fine,' relented Mr Monjoux, and handed over the box.

Seconds later, the tailor watched Ludo disappear, cycling like the devil. It reminded him of when he was young, pedalling across a steep valley on the way to school, dreaming of a career as a surgeon, as he might easily have been, had his life had not taken a different turn.

'Raymond,' called a voice from behind a curtain that divided the shop from the apartment at the back. His wife was standing on the stairs. Did he fancy a cup of tea?

'I'll be right there, *chérie*,' Mr Monjoux returned. He walked over to bolt the door, and flipped the sign in the window from 'Open' to 'Closed'.

Mr Monjoux loved his wife dearly, and although he had been intimate with her no less than twice that day already, he was amazed to feel the urge in his loins again.

And he didn't even need to worry about the day's turnover. It was already in the bag.

72

Edo Novak floated past the shops on Haarlem's main road on cloud nine. He hadn't worn his dress suit since the first year at university, but the quality of the fabric and the white silk shirt unbuttoned at the neck to expose a glimpse of his hirsute chest felt good to the touch.

The young Communist looked as if he had just walked out of a nineteenth-century bordello or a more recent high-society bash. Everyone stared at him, but he was quite oblivious.

The smell of rubber filled his nostrils, and his reflection in the shop window, streaked by the still visible lines of the window cleaner's chamois leather, was nothing short of spectacular.

He read a banner roped to the facade of a furniture showroom: 'This week only! 5% off Belgian and French lounge suites! Extra 5% discount for local newlyweds!'

Discount! An obsolete concept if ever there was one! Prices were fixed in the Soviet Union and everything centralised. Wasn't that much more efficient and equitable? The energy wasted exploiting

273

people, factories and raw materials, all in the blind pursuit of profit, not to mention the supposedly democratic gibberish spouted by the government, was simply disgusting. Who was actually running the country, anyway? A privileged clique! A few old families in full control of most of the nation's finances! A hypocritical sham!

The Netherlands lacked a spiritual elite, without which no state could survive. The ancient Greeks knew that, even Hitler had known that! And without the leadership of an advance guard, who naturally deserved the best the state could offer, the masses would never make any progress. The revolutionary flames were drawing closer by the day, the voices of integrity growing by the hour.

Drifting euphorically along, drinking in every detail of the world around him, he was reminded of the postcard he'd received the day before from Juan Antonio, a young Adonis from Buenos Aires. 'Caro Edo,' the Argentinian had written from Santiago de Cuba, 'make haste! Think of our time together in Moscow. You will be welcomed as one of us, as a true comrade. Success is our guiding light. We owe it to the world and to ourselves. And the girls here, Comrade, are truly fantastic!'

Edo's hand nervously felt his breast pocket: the extra gram of cocaine was hidden safe and sound in a wrap of paper. He walked on, and suddenly detected the smell of bread, the whiff of turpentine.

Thoughts darted around his head like silver balls in a pinball machine. The girls in Cuba were probably fantastic, he was willing to admit, but Cuba didn't have Kalmykian girls, the best lovers in the world.... Who had ever even heard of Kalmykia? Oh, look, a platoon of schoolchildren with their satchels. To the left... one, two... The flower of the nation, you could tell, even from here! On their way to academia and the future. But the future, my lovelies, might not turn out as you've been led to expect. She's pretty! Long blonde hair... nice! Cute guy beside her, too, on his racer... This was a world apart, no doubt about it. The whole country was rife with ghettoes! Rich married rich, and if some of the rich happened to be ugly, then

274

their children married into handsome rich families – easy enough if you had the money – making sure that the next generation would be good-looking. You only had to take a look at the grammar school in Bloemendaal and the technical school a couple of streets further along. A fine theme for a lecture: The Foundations of Human Aesthetics... Oh, very important, mustn't forget a flower for the bride, for our sweet German bride...

'Excuse me, sir.'

Edo felt a hand on his shoulder. Instantly, his eyes met those of a creature with a face as pale as death, wearing a dark blue cap. How much had he had to drink? Had he been on the go all night?

'To drink?'

Drunkenness in public places was prohibited, the overzealous officer announced, keen to give him a dressing down. It would be a scandal for the university! Would he consent to a breath-test?

'You want to smell my...?'

'I see. Sir is not only tipsy but stone-deaf as well!'

Edo surprised the young policeman with a blast of breath in his face, which obliged him to recoil. 'Shall we try again?'

Ha ha! Never heard of cocaine? mocked the young Communist, after the fuming officer was forced to let him go. Edo made his way along a narrow street towards the station.

A blind man in sunglasses was leaning against the wall, turning a hurdy-gurdy that hung down over his belly. The melody was not happy or sad, but inexplicably it made Edo feel sick, and he stormed up to confront the poor beggar.

'Here, take this!' he said, stuffing a five-guilder note into the man's hand. 'Go and play your organ at home, if you don't mind. Your music's not to everyone's taste!'

'Thank you kindly, sir,' said the handicapped busker. 'You're a good man, I can tell.' But Edo had already moved on towards a stall with a sea of flowers in front, all freshly watered and glistening in the morning sun.

73

The group were due to assemble in the main corridor by ten o'clock; departure for the town hall was at ten-fifteen sharp. Maria's face brightened when Felix finally arrived at nine forty-five, grinning from ear to ear. She stopped him in his tracks, inspected him from head to toe with a sparkle in her eyes, and kissed him on both cheeks. The family was finally complete.

'What's that guy doing on the door?' asked Felix. Like everyone else, he had been unable to avoid the African's greeting. Maria filled him in.

They could hear the trample of footsteps upstairs. The Friesian delegation – the men clean-shaven, the women styled and made over by Mr Scapé's expert hands – was now ready and waiting. The way Louis cheerfully interacted with Uncle Bouke and his nephews came as something of a relief to Felix. It looked as if he had finally put all the drama of the Rijksmuseum behind him.

'Well, look who we have here! Our young professor!' Aunt Femke treated Felix to three soggy smooches, the other aunts following suit. The student's cheeks were now covered with blotches of the Parisian lipstick that Mr Scapé had earlier applied and insisted had to be paid for in cash.

'Not quite,' Felix mumbled. He was still only in his first year. What if he failed his exams? Then Wiebe took him to one side for a moment to ask about the nightlife in Leiden. Was it as good as in Amsterdam?

Meanwhile, Mr Zwaan paced nervously back and forth amid the throng, repeatedly consulting his watch. Ludo had asked him a couple of weeks earlier if he would be a witness, and the head waiter had blushingly agreed. He only hoped that the groom wouldn't mind if he wore his usual work attire; he didn't own another suit. Ludo had no objection.

The thunderous drone of a diesel engine swept through the open doors of Hotel New Deluxe. The noxious smell of the exhaust fumes mingled with the fragrance of flowers wafting in the corridor. A moment later, and in marched The Flesh Tones in formation, carrying their drums, horns, clarinets, cymbals and other instruments.

Mr Zwaan, still under the impression that the council had refused to allow the German band to play in public, asked the conductor what was going on.

'We're about to escort the bride and groom to the town hall,' Ludwig Morgensenf explained, faithful to the instructions he had received from Kati Bender two weeks earlier. 'Places, please!' The clarinets shot to the front and the drummers to the back. Mr Zwaan tried to protest, but was lost for words. Perhaps things had changed but no one had told him? His long equine head looked right and left. Where was Mr Bagman? Even the bride and groom were late, damn it!

The linen-cupboard door suddenly swung open and Kati emerged, her face as red as a tomato. Mr Scapé had styled her hair perfectly an hour ago – and had even managed to flog her a pot of anti-wrinkle cream – but her hair had collapsed like a soufflé as a result of her recent endeavours.

She had searched the floor on her knees, like a common maid. She had then closely examined the stacks of towels, sheets, check tea-cloths and bathmats, all of which bore the embroidered logo 'J.B.' In the end, she had simply thrown the whole lot in the air, groping through the mounds of linen in chaotic desperation, as the women of Dresden had searched among the ruins.

But the brooch, which had accompanied Kati through life as a sort of lucky charm, and, in spite of everything, had brought her a measure of contentment, had vanished completely. She was sure it was gone for good, and once again wished she were dead.

'Where's your husband?' asked Mr Zwaan, who had hastened to address the sausage-maker's wife.

'How should I know?' Kati snarled, regretting at once her loss of composure. 'And it's Frau Bender to you!' Her sagging face caught sight of The Flesh Tones. 'Get a move on, Morgensenf! Play something, for Christ's sake!' She motioned vigorously with her arm, as if she were throwing something over her shoulder.

Ludwig Morgensenf produced a baton from his breast pocket, thrust it like a dagger at his band, and the ensemble started to play the opening notes of Strauss's *The Blue Danube*, the chubby German with the dented French horn and sleepy, innocent face taking the lead.

As if it had all been arranged in advance, Jacob descended the stairs at more or less the same moment, proud and dignified, with the bride on his left, Ludo and Hans Matti following behind directly.

Liza was radiant. A shaft of sunlight cast a honey coating over her white apparel. She looked back frequently at her beloved, her violet lips smiling sweetly. Ludo fidgeted awkwardly with his top hat. It was already too hot and it promised to get hotter.

74

Three quarters of an hour earlier, Hans Matti Bender had slipped out of the hotel unobserved, stationed himself by the advertising pillar with its map of the town, which the local tourist board had placed just next to the hotel the year before, opened up a copy of *The Boulevard*, and examined the masthead.

The editorial office – Hofmanshofje 3 – was easy to identify on the map. Within a minute or two he was standing in front of the former dairy, peering through the window. The place was deserted.

The sausage-maker read the card on the door – *Birth and death notices submitted before 12.00 on Tuesday will appear in the next edition (usual costs apply)* – but this was clearly not the information he sought.

Could the place really only open on Tuesdays? He'd already be long gone by then, back to Cologne, whilst Liza and Ludo would be parading along the banks of the Seine… Perhaps he should approach the journalist in private, though Jacob had strongly advised him against it.

'*Guten morgen*,' declared a vaguely familiar voice behind him.

Hans Matti turned to find before him the one-eared scarecrow who had accosted him on The Boulevard a day or two ago.

'They're closed today,' the Dutchman stated in perfect German. But surely it made no difference, as the article had already been published. Why had he felt the need to lie the other day? Just as he'd been on his way to Germany, Hans Matti had been dispatched to the Netherlands. Funny, that. They must have just missed each other en route!

'The man you refer to was my twin brother,' Hans Matti said, adding that this was the first time he had ever set foot in the Netherlands. He had wanted to ask the journalist what had happened to his brother. Perhaps he had additional information? He just wanted to know where—

'How much for it?' interrupted Arno Prins, testing yesterday's bruise on his cheek from Ludo Bagman's signet ring.

'What do you mean?' the sausage-maker enquired, his curiosity piqued.

Arno Prins informed Hans Matti that his father had left him a case full of documents, although this was only partly true. He had, in fact, dragged it out of their home one night along with a few other bits and pieces, long after his father had been arrested and the villa impounded. He was pretty sure, he said, that a copy of the photo on the front page of *The Boulevard* was among these papers. His father had been a big cheese in these parts during the war, everybody had respected him—

'When can I see it?' begged Hans Matti, his face trembling.

'This way,' said the former Waffen SS member, pointing to a run-down hovel across the street, a shingle path leading to its front door.

Moments later, the sausage-maker was staggering up an unpainted staircase behind Arno Prins to an attic room divided into narrow compartments with cardboard partitions. There were buckets of unpeeled shrimp everywhere, and the place stank like a latrine. A washing line hung from the rafters and zigzagged across the room covered in bone-dry clothing. The Dutchman knelt down in front of an old bedstead, scrabbled about underneath the low springs and eventually produced a black attaché case. He jumped up and asked again, 'How much for it?'

'That depends on what's inside,' the sausage-maker replied, barely able to conceal his disgust at the filth around him.

'No fucking chance, Heinz. It's all or nothing!' snarled Arno Prins, flipping the case half-open to tempt him. A pile of letters and documents, the glossy glint of photographs among them, were more than lure enough.

'Three hundred guilders,' Arno Prins demanded – four months' wages at the fish cart.

'I only have Deutsche Marks,' mumbled Hans Matti, rummaging in his wallet, greedily observed by Arno's glistening eyeballs in the gloom.

'Make that 400 Marks,' he urged, striking while the iron was hot.

But that was absurd! And what was the exchange rate? The difference in value was—

'Four hundred and it's yours!'

'The sausage-maker gracefully removed four notes from his wallet one after the other, as he was wont to do when leaving his mistress in Hamburg for a longer than usual absence.

Once outside he sat down on the bare pavement, flipped open the case, and poked around in the confusion of photos and papers. The snapshot of his brother in his impeccable uniform that had appeared on the front page of *The Boulevard* was indeed among them. At least he hadn't wasted his money!

But the remaining material presented something of a problem. Most of the documents were in Dutch, incomprehensible, and, besides, it was high time he returned to his darling daughter, who was to be married within the hour!

75

The Dutch flag hung listlessly from a shiny white flagpole in front of Bol's café. The German flag had been hoisted on a second pole a little further on, followed in turn by French and Italian flags, although no one had seen an Italian or Frenchman on the terrace of swaying umbrellas for quite some time. It was as if the proprietor wanted to divert attention away from the bizarre fact that the bulk of his turnover depended on the very same people who had occupied the place, killed many of its residents and destroyed many of its houses only fifteen years before.

As if in punishment, the Germans and the local sunbathers – sweltering on the sand or from the shade of their wicker basket chairs – were obliged to stare at a facade of cheap brick and concrete, the ugly and as yet unfinished restoration of The Boulevard.

Where a hotel with art nouveau features had once stood (waiters had swanned back and forth between potted palms to the sound of Balkan violins under a vaulted glass ceiling), cranes now dominated the landscape. After a year of heated debate, Councillor Nederleven had finally granted permission for the construction of a new hotel and, from the evidence of the construction drawings, the edifice's structure and choice of materials promised to be hideous beyond belief. According to one junior member of the council, the spirit of Eastern European architecture had already infiltrated the Dutch coastline. It was modern, Councillor Nederleven had retorted, and his party supported progress and modernity.

Elias Bol was looking for something behind the bar. His father sat at a table reading the morning paper and waiting for the first coffee drinkers of the day to arrive, which was normally around eleven.

Elias didn't give a damn about architectural form or beauty, unless it was of the female variety. True to form, he had picked up a fine example of feminine loveliness in Haarlem the night before.

'Where are you off to?' asked his father, without looking up from his paper. He had the head of an old tortoise nowadays, though he had once shared the same youthful good looks and agility as his son.

'Ludo Bagman's getting married today, or haven't you heard?' the blond Adonis replied. He was off to see what was happening at the town hall and had been invited to the big party in the evening.

'As long as you're back before the morning rush,' muttered his father, poring over another spy scandal, one of the core ingredients in his daily rag's diet of sensationalism and overstatement.

'And don't forget a couple of wedding favours for your old dad!' the café owner shouted. But his son was already making his way along The Boulevard, where sewage workers were emptying a septic tank with a hose, blending the smell of raw sewage with the fresh sea air.

A touch further inland, Fr Montfrans was sitting in his office under a stained-glass window that depicted a weeping Madonna, putting the finishing touches to his sermon. In addition to the regular blessings, which he had interwoven with his usual skill between the more personal passages, the priest had found it impossible not to make a biblical allusion to collaboration and treason in the course of his address, just to ease his conscience.

'Let those who have ears hear,' he muttered, reading it over once again, raising the cup of tea that his housekeeper had just brought him to his sensual lips.

If the scandal in *The Boulevard* had arisen earlier, he would have refused to conduct the wedding. The fact that the groom was neither Catholic nor baptised was reason enough. But Jacob Bagman's visit a couple of weeks earlier and the fairly substantial sum he had paid on behalf of the bride's mother for an especially splendid wedding ceremony made it difficult for him to back out of it now. The choir was already practising at the organ in the nave. He could hear their high-pitched voices through the walls.

The priest had no personal bone to pick with the socially engaged hotel-keeper, no matter what sins he may have committed in the past. The outings Jacob organised for local pensioners never discriminated between denominations: Catholics always got their fair share. He reminded himself that it was never too late for a change of heart, confession and remorse. God was love. And the children would be raised as Catholics, he had insisted on it to Jacob. The priest was aware that Liza was already expecting, but his heart was big enough to accommodate many millions of lost souls such as these.

'Can I have another cup of tea, Greta?' Montfrans called in the direction of the door, scribbling feverishly as if he were preparing for a seminary exam.

'They've just delivered the flowers,' the housekeeper announced, pouring a second cup and placing two cherry liqueurs in crackling red wrappers – his passion and his weakness – on the saucer. White chrysanthemums, for goodness sake! What could she do with chrysanthemums?

'Have Groenewoud put them in the vases by the altar,' Montfrans instructed good-heartedly, without looking up from the task at hand. The homily still needed some work.

Groenewoud was Greta's husband and the sacristan, but the priest always referred to him by his surname, even in his wife's presence. Groenewoud was around sixty, walked with a stoop, and had spent half his life at sea. The Virgin Mary had once appeared to him in the form of an emaciated whore on shore leave in Rotterdam. He had been about to close the door of her room when she suddenly became hysterical, staring at him through bulging eyes, her voice wailing like a siren, 'Begone, my child! Turn to God and the Church of Rome… Begone!'

As a sample of the paradise to come, she had given herself to him for free, and he had climaxed to the sound of angelic voices. Days later, he was baptised a Catholic at St Jan's cathedral in Den Bosch. A year after that he visited the seaside resort, met Greta quite by chance, and became a sacristan.

The Bagman affair meant nothing to him. He refused to read newspapers or magazines, and considered the radio to be little short of demonic. The sacristan lived with Greta in monogamous content in a couple of rooms next to the church, where he spent his evenings reading devotional books. Before they went to bed, they knelt together in prayer at a makeshift altar, but never made known out loud what they most desired: a trip to Lourdes.

Three years earlier, Groenewoud had encountered unexpected spinal problems. It made him think about his past, and filled him with remorse, but he refused to visit a doctor. He now found it a growing hardship to move between the pews on Sunday with the collection bag, which resembled the folds of black bulldog's neck. His back was as crooked as a question mark, like Jesus carrying the cross to Golgotha.

'You should take care of the flowers!' his wife instructed, sticking her insect face round the door of the upstairs room where her husband was pottering.

'All right, OK, I'll see to it,' the sacristan mumbled. Dreadful chrysanthemums! The very idea! And white ones at that!

A few hundred metres to the north-west, pigeons cooed in pleasant boredom under the railway station's vaulted, cast-iron roof. An enamelled warning sign nailed to a pillar read: 'Danger! Do not touch the overhead cables!'

A bald gentleman in a sleeveless jacket sat beside his gangly wife on an otherwise empty platform, enjoying a ray of sunshine that filtered through a crack in the roof and ran down the middle of his face.

The express train from Maastricht thundered in, and the sight of an Indonesian-looking man in dress suit and tails stepping elegantly out of First Class wearing smart English shoes attracted some attention. He was carrying a bouquet of red roses with long stems, their black-rimmed petals curling downwards. The gangly woman couldn't take her eyes off him and was frozen to the spot until her husband pulled at her arm peevishly.

Edo had been unable to restrain himself and had snorted the remaining cocaine in the toilet as the train had been passing Overveen. He climbed the cold stone steps to the exit as if floating. Three schoolgirls huddled head to head, their hands held up to their giggling teenage mouths, followed their prince charming's every move. Finally, the kind of man they had dreamt about. Handsome, but a gentleman, it was written all over him!

The pigeons, disturbed by the din of the train, were now fluttering over the centre of town, where an unusual scene was slowly unfolding.

A horse-drawn carriage, with a blood-red varnished cabin and glass doors, juddered its way along the gently sloping streets. A wiry gentleman held the reins, balancing between two brass lanterns, their glass rattling. The man wore a long brown coat and had the bearing of someone desperate for the toilet but unable to relieve himself. His golden cravat was decorated with a tiepin from Gouda, the place of his birth.

The carriage was followed by a hansom cab and a couple of calash carriages, all driven by coachmen with the same formal attire and constipated bearing. They crossed the Hogeweg in the direction of The Boulevard, the clatter of hooves echoing off the passing facades, sometimes several times over. The horses, all of them black, their coats splendid, issued forth steaming piles of dung every few metres, which immediately attracted the pigeons above.

When the procession passed a school, the children in the classroom dashed to the window, the sill of which was full of shrivelled plants and bits and bobs made out of toilet-roll tubes and coloured card, ignoring the teacher's admonishing yelps and the tap, tap, tap of her ruler on the lectern.

Some had pressed their somewhat snail-like noses up against the window, just as Liza Bender had done when she had seen her surrogate father for the first time through the window of the Nazi limousine, the very same Liza Bender whose wedding had prompted this extraordinary spectacle.

76

In addition to private coach hire, De Vlieger Ltd also leased out wedding cars and historical coaches, but the fact that Jacob had employed the services of the local transport magnate for the wedding was a surprise that he had managed to keep even from his wife until the very last minute.

After playing the famous Strauss waltz, The Flesh Tones had launched into a musical tribute to the Rhineland, the oompahs and clashing cymbals loud enough that the wedding guests were initially unable to hear the thunder of approaching hooves. As the echo of the final flourish faded, the guests in the vestibule of Hotel New Deluxe turned towards the street, where a coach drawn by Friesian horses in traditional Friesian harnesses had come to a halt in the radiant sunlight.

'Jacob! You rascal!' an overjoyed Maria admonished her husband. The hotel-keeper beamed with pride, declared that nothing was too good for his children and that, aside from his own wedding day, this was the most beautiful day of his life. His wife rewarded his last remark with a kiss.

'Oh, Ludo!' Liza squealed delightedly, nuzzling up to her husband-to-be, who made a grimace that feigned gratitude to his father. I'll look a right monkey in there, he thought, and quickly lit a cigarette.

'Friesian horses and harnesses, the real McCoy,' Uncle Bouke mumbled. He watched as one of the mares licked the pale yellow palm of the porter's hand. Good Friesian stock, sturdy legs, noted the elderly farmer. He knew as much about horses as his nephews did about motorbikes, which they rode every day to work.

The three aunts sported the same hairdo and looked more alike than ever. On Mr Scapé's advice, Jetske had left her special hat behind. The eminent coiffeur had said that such a hat was no longer the fashion here.

The hotel-keeper stepped forward to announce that it was high time they made a move.

'Indeed, ladies and gentleman, time to set off!' Mr Zwaan agreed, peering at the list of carriage allocations that he had just received from his boss.

Jacob walked the bride in her trainless dress to the door with all due charm and solemnity. Liza held her bridal bouquet of red roses, seasonal flowers and fire lilies, which was wrapped in tulle with pink and blue ribbons, against her imperceptibly pregnant belly. The driver of the first carriage, his whip sticking out of his seat like a car aerial, opened the glass door with its transparent handle, and bowed slightly, resting his white-gloved hand on his buttoned coat.

'Thank you, De Vlieger,' said Jacob. The man at the reins was the head of the transport firm himself.

'Congratulations, Bagman,' he whispered back.

Daniel De Vleiger had, in fact, handed over the business to his son on his fiftieth birthday and now spent most of his time on the golf course. Although he had retired, there were two things he wouldn't give up for love or money: driving the bridal coach and leading the funeral coach (a reconstructed landau, the horses adorned in stylish black blankets) to the cemetery.

When Ludo was seated, De Vlieger closed the glass door, clambered up to the coachbox, took hold of the whip, and had the horses move forward a couple of metres.

'Mr and Mrs Bagman, and Mr and Mrs Bender,' Mr Zwaan announced, reading from his list like a palace attendant.

The ebony hansom cab had now moved up to take the place of the bridal coach. The vehicle had a black leather folding hood that could be raised in the event of cold or rain, but the fine weather made it redundant.

Kati came first and the attendant groom immediately offered her his hand. The sausage-maker's wife, the fox-fur stole draped around her shoulders, almost knocked his arm away. She wasn't one of Bagman's pensioners, for God's sake! She climbed the wobbly step up into the hansom in her stilettos, and settled gracefully into the sea-green leather of the seat.

Once all four of them had been seated, Kati suddenly realised she would be moving backwards, a problem on account of her delicate constitution. A game of musical chairs ensued, the coach groaning, its iron springs wavering. In the process, Hans Matti lost his corsage, a white carnation with a sprig of green, which Mr Zwaan had pinned to his lapel after breakfast.

The sausage-maker shuffled and peered helplessly at the floor. Maria recovered the flower, and swiftly returned it to his lapel. Kati had categorically refused a flower herself, fearing the pin would damage her black velvet dress. She also had a childhood hatred of carnations.

'So, now we can get going,' Maria sighed contentedly, squeezing the handbag on her lap. She reassured Kati that she preferred to travel backwards, even on the train, since it afforded her a longer view of the passing scenery.

The sausage-maker's wife replied that in her case the opposite was true, probably because she preferred to look to the future. As with the bridal coach, the carriage suddenly jolted forward to make room for the first calash. This was intended for Uncle Bouke and the three Friesian sisters, who felt like princesses and acted accordingly.

The German brass band had been informed that they were only expected back in the evening and had headed off for the first refreshing beer of the day.

'Felix and Louis Bagman!' summoned the manager of Hotel New Deluxe. He peered down at the list once more, and pronounced the names Wiebe, Wubbe and Wierd Lubbersma with a drawl.

The five cousins were one too many and somewhat cramped in the four-seater calash. But it wasn't as if they were headed for the Pyrenees, and they set off just as cheerfully as the other guests. Wierd called jovially up to the coachman to ask if he could join him on the box, but the driver, his back wrapped in a brown blanket, squeezed the reins and didn't react.

'Hey, chief!' Wierd shouted again, but the driver kept mum, enduring the hideous Friesian accent in silence, his shoulders hunched, recalling his schoolboy misery, and Siderius, the Friesian headmaster, who would lash out violently with a sadistic grin on his face at the least provocation. The desire to learn had been beaten out of the coachman for good, a cause of real, lasting regret.

'Are you OK, Louis?' asked Felix, concerned that his elder brother might be uncomfortable squashed between the smart but substantial figures of Wiebe and Wubbe.

'I'm fine, Felix,' Louis responded quietly, feeling around in his pocket as if he were looking for something.

The coachman came to life, gently lashed the horse with the whip and the carriage set off. The boys enjoyed the same innocent excitement that affects the outset of a school trip.

The blood-red cabin of the first carriage was about to turn the corner, its rear end like that of a corpulent old dame, when a loud roar caught the attention of the guests. They had forgotten the baskets of wedding favours, yelled Mr Zwaan.

'The wedding favours!' Felix shouted to the carriage in front.

'The wedding favours!' Jacob bellowed in turn at the bridal coach, his hands cupped around his mouth, but for some reason or other De Vlieger didn't react.

Two waiters now came running after them, each holding a wicker basket containing the same seasonal flowers as Liza's bouquet. They raced after the procession, and finally managed to pass the baskets to the cousins in the last carriage.

Louis grabbed a handful of sugared almonds, removed their blue and yellow wrappers – the resort's official colours – and passed them out to his brother and cousins to suck on the way.

77

The water had never seemed as calm, blue, and magnificent as it did today to Liza, although she had in fact only laid eyes on the North Sea for the first time a year ago.

De Vlieger had given the reins the slightest tug to the right at the new water tower, turning the carriage towards the southern part of The Boulevard instead of left towards the leafy town centre. Jacob had explicitly asked him to do so. Having hired the coaches, he wanted the two families to enjoy them as much as possible. They would arrive at the town hall ten minutes later than originally intended, but what was ten minutes compared with an eternity of marital bliss?

The carriages turned back towards the centre via a loop road between the dunes and a recent development of modest villas with the occasional low-rise apartment block. The regular clip-clop of the hoofs on the cobblestones made Liza think of castanets. It was swelteringly hot and stuffy in the coach, and the bride had started to perspire in her satin dress, which itched and tingled against her skin. Even her sanitary towel suddenly felt uncomfortable. There had been no wetness when she woke that morning, but her period had still to pass, and a leak simply didn't bear thinking about!

'Look! They're waving!' Liza pointed excitedly with a rustle of her bouquet at three young girls standing by the side of the road and signalling like mad.

'Mmm,' was the extent of Ludo's response, as he sat with the black cane between his legs, his top hat dangling over its silver handle.

I used to be as young and innocent as those sweet little girls, Liza mused, and not that long ago either. But now she was on her way to a ceremony that would change her life for ever. She would soon be rid of her two-faced mother and her clown of a father for good, although something had happened a little earlier that had unsettled her.

When Hans Matti had hugged and squeezed his daughter in the hotel lobby, Liza had suddenly been overwhelmed by a warm feeling of love for him. He may not have been her biological father, but he had always been her *Vati*. It dawned on her for the first time that he had always been good to her. Her happiness was suddenly tempered by doubt and anxiety. Did Ludo love her enough? Did she love him? And what was love, anyway? A tear formed in the corner of her left eye. She blinked and wiped it dry with the sleeve of her dress. Dour Ludo stared into space and didn't notice.

However hard he tried, he kept coming back to the same thought. He took a couple of deep breaths, but it didn't help. He told his bride that their wedding rings had disappeared.

'What are you talking about?' asked Liza, convinced that her darling must be playing one of his famous jokes.

'I've looked everywhere,' the groom confessed.

'What are you talking about?' Liza repeated, tensing visibly.

Ludo rummaged in his trouser pocket, and produced the hideously kitsch rings.

'*Nein!*' she wailed, slapping the box away. She threw herself back in her seat with a dull thud, her arms and legs kicking out in anger, the carriage juddering.

'Is everything all right?' De Vlieger enquired, his hawk-like nose peering down at them like a buzzard might from a branch above.

'Never better!' the groom shouted back through the glass door, picking up the rings.

For at least a minute, the bride and groom listened in painful silence to the dull clatter of the horses and the plaintive groans of the carriage wheels. Hotel Berkhout, B&B Levenslust, Hotel Zon en Zee and other hotels and boarding houses drifted past at a leisurely pace, 'Rooms available' signs on every door.

'Try it on, for pity's sake,' Ludo pleaded, extracting a still slightly defiant finger from under the wrap and ribbons of the bridal bouquet. The ring was either too small or her finger too big – either way, it didn't fit.

Liza readied herself for another tantrum, but Ludo leaned over her affectionately and whispered that the rings were really meaningless. Just a bourgeois farce! Why didn't she wear it on her little finger?

'This one?' the sausage-maker's daughter sniffled.

'Why not?' Ludo took his bride's left hand as tenderly as he could and slipped the ring over her little finger. Not a bad fit, actually. 'Till death do us part,' he added with a smile. 'I love you,' he went on to whisper, his voice husky.

'And I love you, idiot!' Liza whimpered, and slapped him gently on the face with her bouquet. 'I love you too!'

Two old ladies had seen it all from their park bench seats in the sun. They looked at each other in silence, their national-health dentures agitating back and forth.

Maria was enjoying the vista from her open carriage. She squinted and nodded every now and then, as people do in anticipation of something important, when they suddenly sense their participation in a grander scheme of things, where past differences and frustrations seem to vanish for ever.

Behind her rhinestone-studded sunglasses, Kati reflected on her fling with the handsome black man from last night, but it wasn't long before this cheering image was tarnished by murkier thoughts: she must have lost her brooch on the street. Why was life always such a punishment? She glanced furtively at Maria. She wouldn't be seen dead in such a ridiculous get-up. And yet she was happiness itself; it was completely maddening. But what if she'd had my past? Kati mused, surveying the battlefield of her life for the umpteenth time. It was like looking at 10,000 photographs in a row, all now framed in gold but all of a battlefield nonetheless.

Her daughter Liza looked like a goddamned princess in that bloody carriage. At her age, Kati was pouring tankards of beer and serving omelettes all day long, putting up with the filthy pigs pinching her buttocks – and much more besides – just to keep from starving. Oh, yes, Maria Bagman, you'd've been in for a surprise! she thought. But that had been reality during Germany's 'crisis years'. Had they ever had as grave a crisis in the Netherlands, she wondered.

'It's all about quality sausage meat.' Her husband's voice interrupted her musings.

'It must be a marvellous line of work, Hans Matti. I'd love to visit the factory one day!' the hotel-keeper replied, his voice full of admiration.

The Friesian contingent in the carriage behind them started to sing, as if they had already been drinking.

'Yoo-hoo!' whooped Maria to her family, followed by something incomprehensible in dialect.

The words fired past Kati's cheeks like bullets. She stared straight ahead and tried her utmost to think of nothing at all.

78

Yet another bumblebee had flown in through Hotel New Deluxe's open front door, looping around the black porter's frizzy head – he swiped at it but missed – and then heading enterprisingly towards the bar, where the waiters had gathered around one of the tables, their unfastened black bow ties slumped over their shoulders like dead songbirds.

They all drank coffee and dug into a cake that Willem Jansen had quickly put together from the cider-drenched leftovers from the wedding cake, some whipped cream and preserved fruit. It was going to be a long day for everyone.

Mr Zwaan had run a clothes brush over his team of waiters in the corridor, the cherry-wood handle rattling their buttons. He had then headed off to the town hall where he was due to act as one of the marriage witnesses. Once their supervisor had left, the waiters began to chat straight away, like a class of schoolchildren when the teacher leaves the room.

The German with the square moustache was the first topic of conversation. They were all convinced that Hans Matti was the man in the photo in the paper. His twin brother indeed! Fucking Krauts haven't changed a bit.

The conversation then turned to the bride and her vital statistics. One waiter praised her buttocks, another preferred her breasts, and a third maintained that every part of her body was a different instrument and that you needed a whole orchestra to play a symphony. The men agreed wholeheartedly. Ludo Bagman had landed the tastiest bit of skirt any man could want.

Guillaume listened in silence and, after a while, perked up and turned the discussion to the 'darky' at the door. The men chuckled expectantly, knowing their colleague's funny-man reputation. Guillaume informed them, straight-faced, that lions in Africa spent hours licking their arses after they'd eaten a 'nigger'.

'You don't say,' muttered Jan, walking right into it. 'Why's that?'

'To get rid of the taste!'

There was a loud report of laughter. The porter stuck his ebony face round the corner out of curiosity. This simply added fuel to the fire, producing a second explosion of laughter, and the waiters roared until they were out of breath, pointing at each other like a load of drunks. By now, the racket had grown loud enough to be heard on the street.

'Ha-ha! To get rid of the taste! To get rid of the taste!' Jan repeated the punch line. 'Funny!'

Inspired by the relaxed, easy atmosphere, one of the other waiters interrupted the giggles with a new observation: 'If you ask me, that fat German cow has her eye on Guillaume.'

'What on earth gives you that idea?' the handsome waiter exclaimed in disgust.

'She can't take her eyes off you!'

Guillaume frowned and poked desultorily at the cake with a fork, but a cynical grin suddenly spread over his face as he declared that he would rather – and here he took an unsuccessful swipe at the bee that had landed on the pineapple on his fork – that he would rather screw... a fucking bumblebee than that German heifer.

Another explosion of laughter followed, but this time the curious porter did not show.

The door between the bar and the kitchen had blown open and the bumblebee glided through with graceful ease, attracted by the various aromas that were streaming everywhere. The atmosphere in the kitchen was also relaxed. The chefs leaned back against their worktops, smoking cigarettes and listening to Willem Jansen tell a story about his time as a galley boy in the merchant navy, a good ten years ago at least.

Pay had been low and the work could be dangerous. Fortunately, there had always been the chance to earn an extra bob or two on the side. He had smuggled luxury razor blades and expensive cameras from Buenos Aires to Hamburg for a while. Could anyone guess how?

The lads shook their heads in unison.

Inside frozen cows! He would wrap the contraband in greaseproof paper and hide it in the freshly slaughtered carcasses that were brought to the freezer units after loading. By the time they had arrived in Hamburg, the meat was frozen solid and the customs men couldn't penetrate beyond the surface. An onshore buyer was part of the schemes.

'Brilliant!' exclaimed the pastry chef, who hungered for adventure, and had been thinking for a while about a life on the open waves.

A cook with a puffy face and a gourmet's belly suddenly came to life, grabbed a broom, and tried to crush the bumblebee that had just buzzed its way into the kitchen. But the bee managed to escape and soared into the main hall, where Mr Poestash had elected to take up residence on stage in advance of his performance later the same day.

The magician had now completely recovered from his earlier bout of travel sickness. He had left the room assigned to him by Mr Zwaan after a mere fifteen minutes, although it usually took hours before he felt better. It was miraculous!

He had installed all the bits and pieces he needed for his performance at leisure, adjusting the mechanism of the circular saw with a pair of pliers, to make its rotations sound all the more harrowing. When he was done, and had tested everything a couple of times, he twisted the corners of his moustache and looked out over the hall from the stage.

'Ladies and gentlemen!' he bellowed, testing the acoustics. There was no real need to do so; his performance was accompanied throughout by taped music recorded in Hilversum.

The illusionist, who had only been in the business for three years and had previously sold stink bombs and fake vomit at a novelty shop in Hoorn, wondered what he might do for the rest of the day. Did his quick recovery owe anything to the sea air?

The two girls he needed for his circular-saw trick – the public only ever got to see one of them and smuggling them both onto the premises was always a bit of a bother – were due around six. Just as he was thinking how nice it might be to take a walk along the promenade on such a beautiful day, he heard a buzzing sound above his head and started to beat the air frantically around him. In spite of his imposing figure, he was terrified of insects, especially beetles and spiders.

The bee zoomed back to the central corridor and veered off into the side kitchen, which was always humid and smelt of rotting food, although everything, including the floor, was cleaned on a daily basis. This was Louis's domain, and he kept the key to the room hidden in a secret place.

The insect headed for the enamel sink, the cavities in the white glaze filled with all sorts of invisible morsels left over in spite of Louis's thorough daily scrub. He took more care over the sink than he did with his own teeth.

One drop after another fell from a tap that had been needing a new washer for centuries. Louis had listened to the sound countless times when there was a brief hiatus in the supply of dirty dishes, and he had the chance to smoke a cigarette on his stool, the feeling that he was just in the way never far from his mind. He had also used the place a lot recently to play with himself in secret, panting over his drawings of Allah's virgins, his breath like a warm desert wind.

The bumblebee buzzed around the sink and crashed into a droplet of water. Surprised, the creature flailed around in the air for a moment and then continued its flight, heading upstairs now, where the beds were still unmade because Maria hadn't had time to make them.

Anne van Bennekom, who usually helped her clean the rooms, had suddenly disappeared without a trace. Rumour had it that she was having an affair with one of Sam Stikker's brothers, who had survived the war and was now big in sweets in Amsterdam. He was a good thirty years older than she was, but if everything went well, she'd never have to make a bed or scrub a toilet again.

79

The procession arrived in the square in front of the town hall and made an extra turn around a large flowerbed full of tulips and hyacinths. One of the horses pulling the bridal coach missed a step and whinnied, flicking its glossy mane. Jacob had the chance to observe to his great relief that his colleague Bastiaan Hermans was among the assembled crowd.

The number of onlookers was overwhelming. Jacob's anxiety about numbers for the evening's festivities disappeared in an instant. At least a hundred people were in front of the town hall, all crowding around the fountain, its three brass herrings spewing a torrent of water from their gaping mouths. The local press had made such a fuss about the wedding that everyone wanted to see it with their own eyes.

The hotel-keeper spotted Joris Pakhoed, half-hidden behind a beech tree, a notebook and pen in hand. He nodded cordially, but the journalist pretended not to notice and quickly turned his head, overcome once again by a feeling of pure disgust. The shamelessness with which the wedding rode roughshod over people's sensitivities, and the fact that the German's crime had gone unpunished, was simply astonishing!

Engel Holboom watched the spectacle in silence from a nearby tram stop, the clock above his head reading thirteen minutes to eleven. His brother Klaas hopped from one foot to the other, sucking on a peppermint that rolled over his teeth every now and then with a hollow clack.

Holboom & Sons had a sideline in car hire for both weddings and funerals. Engel had imported an old-fashioned Opel from Düsseldorf for weddings, and had it sprayed a soft pink. But Bagman had chosen that crook De Vlieger instead, and that said it all.

'Maybe the coaches were the bride and groom's idea,' Klaas Holboom ventured.

Engel sneered at the bridal coach and the creaking procession that followed: 'Look at that hideous old bag in the fur. In this weather!'

Luigi Lamborghini, his instinct for good business as astute as ever, had strategically stationed his ice-cream cart in the middle of the throng. Yellow, pink and green scoops of vanilla, strawberry and pistachio (off-season, his range was less extensive) were soon scattered like confetti through the crowd. Every time the Italian lifted the silver cloche, billows of frosty air caressed his cherubic fifty-year-old face.

Meanwhile, Mr Zwaan and Mr Poteman (in a dirty green jacket) bundled a girl in a wheelchair up the steps to the right of the town hall and inside. The hotel manager's daughter was now twenty, but her growth had been impaired by her illness and she had the body of a child. She had been unable to sleep all night, excited by the big event to which she had been invited. Her mother was bedridden yet again, but had been able to run up a party dress from a Simplicity pattern: an upturned fuchsia with white dots. Annabel dreamt that today was her own wedding day, something she had thought about a lot in recent years. After two decades of rattling around in her wheelchair, no one would ever have suspected that her brain and body were intimately connected, that she had desires.

It was only in early puberty, when Annabel had developed the inclination to consult her reflection in the mirror, that her dreadful destiny finally dawned on her. She had wailed for nights on end, screamed about how much she wanted to die. But one day her peace of mind had returned and she had greeted the world as she always had, expectantly and with a grateful smile.

Louis Bagman had smiled at her in a special way once or twice in her dreams, just as he had on the day they had first met. The girl had an irrepressible desire to take care of Louis and even kept a photograph of him under her bed. When she looked at him, she didn't see the dimwitted boy that others did, but rather someone wonderful and mysterious, as an intellectual might see something completely different in a scratch on a canvas from what an ordinary person sees, snorting with contempt that a monkey could have painted it, and probably better than this charlatan artist.

She fell asleep each night with a clear picture of Louis in her mind. The boy loved her too, she was sure of it. But how was she to befriend him? How did you go about such a thing? Perhaps he would invite

299

her to dance at the party tonight, and hold her in his arms like a doll...? Perhaps they could slip off together and...

The bridal coach came to a standstill in front of the town hall, casting an impressive shadow in the morning sunlight. The horses, the coachman's pointed nose and the taut, wafer-thin reins looked as if they had been cut from black card by a découpage artist.

A gentleman in some kind of conductor's uniform, who had been keeping a lookout from the town hall steps, now disappeared into the hall and pressed a button on a Bakelite switchboard. A set of state-of-the-art bells then began to carillon, 'O Christmas tree, O Christmas tree, How lovely are thy branches' from the town hall tower instead of the selected Mendelssohn perennial. The carillon had just been installed and the clerk had no idea how to change the music.

The wedding guests hummed along to the familiar Christmas carol, unaware that something was amiss. Few of them registered the inappropriate melody, caught up as they were in the excitement of the moment.

De Vlieger descended and opened the coach's glass door. The bride and groom stepped out carefully, and ascended the red carpet to the town hall's open door. Cries of admiration could be heard from the crowd, most of them in response to the attractive choice of wedding dress.

Ludo was aware of the hundreds of eyes staring at him, his arm as gentle as it could be around Liza's waist. When they were halfway up the stairs, Ludo's drinking buddies, a rowdy all-male bunch from the local bar, made its presence felt: 'Time to get hitched, mate! Cor, she's a bit of all right... Congratulations! Just don't expect her to stay the same forever... you'll see... Give me the bachelor's life any day... A couple of minutes, and your freedom will be gone for ever!' The groom turned, grinned, and waved hesitantly, like a film star on the steps of a plane about to head back to Hollywood.

A gallant Jacob helped Maria down from their coach. He beamed happily in the company of his family, glinting like a newly minted coin, which further inclined some of the crowd – who had only come to catch a glimpse of the hotel-keeper with the dubious recent past – to believe in his guilt.

And that Kraut with the glasses had a bloody nerve! Cracking the whip for years during the occupation, and now look at him! As if butter wouldn't melt...

Sweating like a pig, Kati cursed her fur stole and heavy outfit under her breath. Just as the bride and groom's parents stepped onto the red carpet in their smart, shining shoes, a small group of locals hazarded a low jeer. Joris Pakhoed's eager pen sprang to life.

Hans Matti and Jacob were both unsettled, and turned to look at the protesters, but the noise quickly gave way to stunned silence. Everyone's attention was drawn to a young woman with a strikingly dark complexion, and even a hint of a moustache, who had appeared from behind a pillar and pushed her way to the front of the crowd. She squeezed between two coaches, dashed towards the sausage-maker, and stuffed a white envelope in his hands.

'Please read it!' she implored, staring intently at the father of the bride, her thick eyebrows questioning, her eyes beseeching.

'*Danke schön!*' the sausage-maker blurted politely, completely at a loss as to the identity of the person standing in front of him or what to do with the letter.

'What does Priskedotchka want with Hans Matti?' Jacob asked his wife as they carried on up the steps, Liza's dress sparkling from both the sunlight and the town hall chandeliers.

Maria had no idea.

80

Edo, together with various other friends and acquaintances of the Bagmans, had already been waiting for at least a quarter of an hour for the arrival of the bride and groom when a horse-faced man pushing a girl in a wheelchair came in, followed by an odd-looking fellow whose left eye blinked with a nervous twitch.

'I'm sorry, excuse me,' the horse-faced man muttered, just managing to avoid Edo's toes.

'Excuse me,' repeated the squinting man, who apparently wanted to sit on the same row as Edo, obliging him to get up.

The wheelchair was parked in the corner, Mr Zwaan applying the brake. The girl glanced around, her sickly eyes full of curiosity and, for a moment, meeting Edo's. The Communist had always found the sight of invalids difficult. He examined his nails for a time, and then looked around the room for the umpteenth time, pretending to be interested.

The tall, bottle-green windows (which admitted a great deal of light) were a work of art designed by the Belgian architect Luc de Vlaminck, whose career was almost as sinister as the circumstances in which he had first obtained the commission for the town hall windows 'for the sum of one thousand, seven hundred and ninety guilders'. The Van Tateses, with their excellent taste and international contacts, may have had a hand in it.

As far as Edo was concerned, buildings like this were proof of the likely imminent collapse of the present regime. The self-assured, stiff-jawed portraits decorating the walls differed little from the political clique running the country. His contempt for the philistines who aspired to join this gallery of the late and the 'great' was absolute. The so-called socialists were the worst of all. They wanted it both ways, and coddled the upper classes as much as they clashed with them. Real revolution scared them shitless.

Edo's thoughts drifted once again to the letter from Santiago de Cuba. He would need at least two thousand guilders to get there, preferably in dollars. Such was the way of the world, but not for long. It was about time Ludo withdrew a little cash from that fat Kraut's piggy bank!

Through his haze of cocaine, he stared at an attractive blonde on his right. She was sitting next to a hale old gentleman some had called 'Doctor'. Betsy Prins had accompanied her new sweetheart to the wedding against her will.

Bodisco was there first and foremost to show his support for the Bagmans, given the rot that had been broadcast of late. He was also well aware of his fiancée's family history, although he would never have imagined that she had stripped and shown her naked pubescent body to Ludo as an eleven-year-old, and later, shortly before her world had fallen apart, had even gone to bed with him a couple of times. The hotel-keeper's son still had a soft spot for her, and she for him.

Betsy Prins had left her two children in the far north of the country in her ex-husband's care, and never wanted to see them again. She had done an admirable job in satisfying the desires of the near sexagenarian doctor. She would let him bind her to the bed by the wrists and ankles, much to their mutual delight.

The doctor looked around the room too, mumbling to himself, and when his gaze returned to Betsy's delicate profile, he thought for a second that it was perhaps time they got married. They could still have a child – something he had never envisaged so late in life, even in his wildest dreams – and the family heirlooms, art and the hundreds of letters he had written throughout his life could be passed on to the next generation, and not end up in an auction or, worse, on the local rubbish dump. He would be remembered by somebody, even after he'd become a boring urn of ashes. A clause in his last will and testament stipulated that he had to be cremated.

'Ladies and gentlemen, the bride and groom!' The town hall clerk now made a dash for the ceremonial table, which was flanked by tall, elegant chairs intended for the bride and groom's families and the witnesses.

Ludo Bagman and Liza Bender crossed the Italian marble floor followed by a procession of family members ordered by degree of kinship. The customary solemn silence filled the room momentarily, only to be broken by a squeal of approval and a ripple of applause.

Ludo nodded at Edo, who smiled back with a cynical twinkle, and then caught sight of Betsy Prins. He hadn't seen her for more than eight years. She looked prettier and sexier than ever. Ludo felt a terrible pain in his heart, suddenly realising that he was in the process of making a terrible mistake. Fine, Liza was good for his bank balance, but how incredible it would be to spend his life with Betsy, and—

'This way, please,' ushered the town clerk.

Once everyone was seated, a door opened in the wood panelling and a man dressed in purple robes and with greying hair shaped rather like a Roman helmet calmly entered the room, a leather portfolio in his hands.

'In my capacity as Official Registrar,' Julius Rozengal began in a stately voice, after an affable nod or two at the bride and groom and the assembled guests. 'In my capacity as Official Registrar...'

81

Kati had rejected Jacob's offer to engage a local girl to translate the wedding speech simultaneously for her, though Hans Matti liked the idea. She could manage on her own, she had snapped. But now she was here, she didn't understand a word.

The man in the absurd purple outfit spoke such a gurgling, guttural language that it might as well have been Russian. Even after four days in Holland, she was still completely unaware that '*mooi*' meant '*schön*', '*liefde*', '*liebe*' and that '*ik heb*' was the Dutch equivalent of '*ich habe*'. When in God's name was he going to shut up, she wondered. He'd been harping on for fifteen minutes at least.

Much to her irritation, her husband – who sat next to her in one of the ornate high-backed chairs – was fiddling incessantly with the inside pocket of his jacket. Jacob sat on their left, his chest rising with each shallow breath. The hotel-keeper stared at his son and future daughter-in-law, sitting side by side like royalty, unable to look away. He listened intently, trying not to miss a single word of the service. Some said the registrar was a poet. They were right! What a speech! Maria glanced affectionately at their faithful manager whose imminent responsibilities as a witness had made him almost shaky from nerves.

Felix and the Friesian delegation sat opposite. Just before the ceremony had begun, Louis had slipped from his seat and stolen out of sight, to the very back of the stage. He wasn't used to such attention, Jacob thought. Perhaps it was for the best.

Kati's fox-fur stole induced a veritable torrent of perspiration. She peered repeatedly out of the corner of her eye to ogle the outrageously handsome man with dishevelled blue-black hair in the front row. The collar button of his white silk shirt was undone, exposing the hair on his chest. His eyes roamed around restlessly, revealing his doubtlessly reckless and romantic soul.

She ignored the prolix registrar. Her thoughts instead drifted back to the black porter, this time with disgust. Blacks were nothing more than animals when you thought about it, ready to take advantage of a poor woman whenever the opportunity presented itself. I'd rather have that handsome creature there any time! She crossed her legs in her own distinctive way, adjusted her hair, and looked up once again, the words 'Look at me! Look at me, goddammit!' repeating over and over in her head.

But the message didn't reach its target, and the dark-haired hunk didn't hear or answer her plea.

'Married life is like being on board a ship far out at sea,' the registrar continued, 'sailing life's temperamental waves, where calm can turn to storm in the blink of an eye.'

Hans Matti understood Dutch better than his wife, and tried to listen as best he could, but curiosity finally got the better of him, and he surreptitiously took out the envelope, discreetly spread the letter (written in excellent German) on his knees, and read as follows:

Dear Sir,

I'm sure you're wondering why you have received this letter from a complete stranger. I saw your picture yesterday on the front page of The Boulevard.

I write to inform you that I am the daughter of one of the Georgian soldiers stationed here during the war. My mother is dead and I am desperate. She always refused to tell me who my father was. I know he was a handsome man, born in the town of Borjomi, but his name remains a complete mystery. A former neighbour, who has since passed away, told me his surname ended in 'adze' or something like that. Please help me, sir. You must have known him, the man responsible for my birth, and I would do anything to find out what has happened to him. I have some savings and would even risk going to the USSR and possible imprisonment to find him.

I am not married, and work at Van der Werff (the bakers), where you can always reach me.

Yours sincerely,

Truus de Boer

P.S. My mother's maiden name was Priske, and everyone here calls me Priskedotchka. My address is Beatrixstraat 12, named after our princess.

Hans Matti sniffed and then gave a sneeze, as if someone had just dusted his moustache with pepper.

'What's that?' his wife whispered hoarsely, nodding at the letter.

'Nothing, dear,' Hans Matti responded, gazing proudly at his stunning daughter, whose mascaraed lashes trembled behind her veil.

After his maritime simile, the registrar became still more poetic. Marriage was also a house full of mirrors where husband and wife lived in full and constant view of each other. The mirrors, over time, become cracked and scratched, what they reflected sometimes monstrously disfigured. Even then, their love for one another, as husband and wife, should remain undiminished. Marriage is...

Jacob had been listening carefully until now, like a choirboy attending to the word of God, but the house of mirrors was too much for him. He turned his attention away from the stage, his eyes narrowing to look properly for the first time at those around him. The handsome fellow in the dress suit was Ludo's Communist friend. His son's flirtation with the far left secretly filled him with pride. It was proof that his heart was in the right place, however blunt and unfeeling he could be on occasion. It was just a phase.

Dr Bodisco beamed with satisfaction beside his new flame. Hadn't the old bugger landed a beauty! She could easily have passed for his daughter! Jacob then studied the faces of Herman Nederleven, Bastiaan Hermans and Baron Van Tates, his presence in particular proving quite a surprise. The aristocrat winked back roguishly. The chair beside Johannes Wedekind's, where Louis had been sitting, was now empty.

'Before I call upon you to declare your wedding vows, I would like to read a short poem I've written,' Julius Rozengal, registrar and poet, held forth:

> *When you said: 'Come with me, my love,*
> *I'll show you the world in all its colours',*
> *I replied, 'Why, come with me, my love,*
> *I'll show you the world—'*

A loud dry bang from the hallway outside penetrated the council chamber, as if one of the wooden chairs had fallen on the marble floor all of a sudden. The room gave a shudder, petrified, as one.

Julius Rozengal turned and looked in astonishment at the clerk, who had been standing in the corner, his hands clasped devoutly. The clerk in his funny uniform, desperate to escape notice, dashed out and along the corridor.

'—*the world in all its colours*', the registrar had resumed, clearing his throat awkwardly, only to have to break off for a second time.

The crowd of guests collectively turned their heads like a colony of dumb penguins, the nearly married couple included. The clerk stood in the doorway, trembling and as white as a sheet, gibbering what sounded like 'Terrible, terrible!'

'We need a doctor!' he cried. 'Dr Bodisco, come quickly! Someone has just tried to kill himself!'

Everyone was frozen in time, captured exactly as they were when they first heard the shot, like the poor wretches in Pompeii, their movements and screams drowned out when the flow of boiling lava preserved them for all eternity.

82

The vast pool of blood on the immaculate white marble floor initially led Dr Bodisco to presume that Louis Bagman was dead.

But the boy was still alive. The handgun he had let slip as he had fallen lay beside the leg of a table on which was an old, dusty bouquet of dried flowers. Louis had shot himself in the stomach, and was breathing but with some difficulty, gurgling and groaning. Dr Bodisco felt his own blood drain from his temples, and mimicked the boy's struggle for air for a few seconds. He knew Louis well, but had never seen such a horrific thing in all his thirty-four years in practice.

He quickly pulled himself together, tugged open the tie around his neck, and sank to his knees.

'Louis, can you hear me?' Bodisco turned his head to the right, and peeled open the boy's blood-drenched shirt to assess the seriousness of the injury. 'Louis, dear boy, keep breathing... That's it... slowly in and out! You'll be fine! Good boy... Excellent!'

A trembling mass of arms, eyes, mouths and partly obscured faces filled the doorway. Those at the back clamoured for a better view, both men and women gaping and screaming.

'An ambulance! Someone please call an ambulance! I need a couple of strong men! Let's get the boy off the floor! Warm water and towels... For God's sake, is there a bench anywhere?'

Herman Nederleven and Felix Bagman anxiously wormed their way through the crowd and approached the wounded boy, while Edo hastily squeezed past the drab figure of Johannes Wedekind to go outside, the glaring sunlight making everything seem red and black before his unfocused eyes. He accidentally knocked over the basket full of wedding favours that had been left by the door in advance, and raced down the steps, heading for the tram stop on the other side of the square. Jesus, he thought, what a load of nutters! He had to get out of this madhouse on the double.

On the street, people had also heard the shot, and tried to stop Edo to ask what had happened.

'What's going on?' Joris Pakhoed entreated, waving his notebook in the air.

'Nothing... absolutely nothing...' Edo growled, barging through the crowd, his arms flailing. He wasn't involved in the wedding. He was on his way to a completely different event... And he struggled over to the blue tram, which was already standing there, as if by prior arrangement.

Joris Pakhoed raced up the town hall steps just in time to see Louis be carried along a side corridor, a trail of blood on the marble floor. Dr Bodisco was supporting his head and issuing instructions.

'What's going on?' the journalist repeated, cursing his bad luck for not bringing a photographer. Murder? Suicide?

But his questions evaporated. A protective membrane screened the wedding guests from the world outside, and they stared at each other like characters in a silent film. Hearts pounded in throats like food that the guests had been force-fed, and that now had to be swallowed or choked on. Then came the sudden, bloodcurdling scream of someone on the point of death from over by the wheelchair next to the panelled wall.

Baron Van Tates had followed the registrar to the mayor's office. The mayor himself had left for Israel the day before as part of a European delegation involved in peace talks. Van Tates had lifted the receiver and dialled the number of the hospital director in Haarlem, a personal friend of his, but could only reach his secretary. If they didn't get an ambulance here sharpish, he would wring her neck, goddammit!

He bit his lip and thought about his wife, trapped behind the wheel of her car for forty-five minutes in the hills around Grasse, left to die when her life might easily have been saved.

Once Liza had recovered from the initial shock of the shot, she decided that she could only have imagined the whole thing. She wandered around aimlessly in her wedding dress, cursing Ludo for having abandoned her yet again. Where *was* he?

She was suddenly overcome by a maddening desire to curl up next to the body that had borne her, just as she had done years ago, when her mother would play with her from time to time or read her fairy tales, before the hostilities began. Kati was rooted to the spot, her eyes glassy and motionless.

Liza limped, rustling and distraught, over to the door and watched with the well-dressed crowd as Louis was lifted up, a pool of blood on the floor. The bride burst into hysterical tears, felt her father's moustache brush her face, and pressed herself into his arms with all

310

her might. The bubble in which she had been living for months had suddenly burst. How many times had she and Ludo joked about her parents' murder, as she licked the hair on his chest or gently squeezed his throbbing member? But death wasn't something abstract to laugh at. It was real and terrible. Where was Ludo? Jesus Christ, where *was* he?

Liza looked up at her father for a second, black lines of mascara running down her red cheeks, and buried her face in his chest once again. She was overwhelmed with a nostalgia for the days before she had met Ludo. Although her life had been awful back then, it was a safe and happy dream compared with this nightmare.

Everything now appeared to her in a completely different light. How could she have been so stupid? Her love for Ludo had blinded her, and she had chosen to ignore her mother's warnings. The disappearance of the rings had surely been a sign. Hadn't the idea of helping her parents into the hereafter been Ludo's? He was a monster, pure and simple. As dim as his poor younger brother.

Liza felt a tearing pain as menstrual fluid filled her sanitary towel. She began to groan.

Ludo was by her side, all of a sudden.

'Sweetheart, I'm here. Louis's alive! I've just seen him. They've put him on a bench. The doctor says he's going to make it!' But just as he was about to comfort her with a hug, she unexpectedly pushed him away, as if he were some drunk trying to grab hold of her in a bar.

'Clear off!' she snapped, in a voice that was more like her mother's than she would ever have imagined.

83

The white banner featuring a red rose held by a blackened worker's hand had once been draped above the entrance to a well-known

Amsterdam conference centre and had later decorated the stage at Hotel New Deluxe during a meeting about what constituted 'Europe'. Councillor Nederleven had then accommodated it in his office, above the antique divan, where he tried to relax after lunch.

It was here that Louis, writhing in pain and sweating feverishly, now lay beneath a motto reading 'Together as One!', feebly flicking away an unseen fly from his cheek. The leather seat underneath the boy's body was cracked and dry. His face appeared healthier than ever at one point, but it was now growing paler by the second.

Dr Bodisco had stripped the clothes off his torso with a pair of scissors, and treated the wound with a dressing from the first-aid box that Herman Nederleven had produced. Louis's belly had been ripped open. The wound was irritated and the bullet still lodged in his chest, but they had managed miraculously to stem the flow of blood. The local doctor calmly asked Nederleven if the ambulance was on its way, doing his best not to upset the patient.

The councillor nodded and brushed past Ludo in the doorway on his way out. Ludo hadn't dared join Felix at Louis's side until now. The groom stared at his younger brother, his eyes brimming over with bewildered tears, feeling helpless and ashamed, and whispered 'How serious is it?'

Felix shrugged his shoulders. The student's face had turned an ashen grey. Dark blue shadows had formed under his eyes; he had the look of someone severely depressed, on the verge of a new low.

Ludo walked over to the wall, gulped in horror at the sight of the bloodsoaked rags, leaned carefully over his prone brother and asked, 'Louis, can you hear me? Louis, it's Ludo... Why did you do this? Louis—'

Ludo recoiled in shock as his brother started to groan and flail around, as if a plague of flies had landed on his wounded body. Dr Bodisco explained, his voice remaining inexplicably calm, that Louis had a fever and was probably delirious.

312

The doctor passed a key to Felix, and asked him to fetch his bag. His car was parked just to the right of the fountain. He needed a stethoscope and fresh dressings right away.

At that moment, Jacob and Maria came in, humbly, clutching each other, fragile. Their eyes moved from the doctor to Felix as they asked how seriously Louis was injured.

'His pulse is excellent,' Dr Bodisco lied, upbeat.

Felix threw his arms round his parents, gave them a supportive squeeze, and disappeared down the corridor, where the crowd had gathered at a respectful distance beside a plaster pillar.

The door was shut. Maria's gaze roamed around the room, which was split into strips of light and dark by the venetian blinds. Unable to hold back, she bolted over to her son, fell to her knees by his side, took hold of his hands, and tenderly kissed him.

Jacob wanted to say something, but he couldn't.

Louis had now turned a deathly pale, although his breathing was still calm and regular. His eyes suddenly opened, their glistening vitality filling Jacob and Maria with surprise and hope. They even imagined a faint smile around his lips, as if he had been playing a prank on everyone. When he was a toddler, he would sometimes collapse and lie on the ground, motionless, for a few seconds, only to jump to his feet in triumph and shout, 'You all thought I was dead, didn't you?'

Louis stared helplessly at his parents. A tear welled up in his left eye, and then he looked away with a whimper.

Jacob turned to his wife in tears. The past now pricked Maria's conscience: the man was dark and strong and was standing there all of a sudden; it was possible that Ludo was his child. A terrible feeling of guilt overwhelmed her. Was she being punished for her sins? Was there a God, after all, seeking revenge? Jacob was similarly reproaching himself. He saw his life as a game of cards, felt lame with remorse, and realised the full extent to which he had failed his poor son.

At the window, Dr Bodisco made a gap in the blinds with his thumb and index finger. He peered down at the sun-drenched square – there was still a crowd of people, as there always was for the dawn parade on the Queen's birthday – and turned away worriedly. What was keeping the ambulance? Ludo, stilted, skulked in a corner, next to the chair on which his brother's bloodstained jacket lay, and gave a shrug of his shoulders.

Louis opened his eyes again and gazed at length at his parents. It was as if they were no longer distinct, as if their individual spirits had liquefied and slowly merged together, three spotlights converging on a central point, until they became one. A blissful tranquillity filled the room and seemed to last for ever. But then Louis started to shake and gurgle, a stream of blood trickling out of his mouth and running down his chin. Dr Bodisco rushed over and took hold of the boy's now cold wrist. The pulse was barely perceptible. He quickly gave him an injection, cursing the absent ambulance.

Louis had drifted off in the meantime and could now feel the heavenly caresses of the virgins from his favourite book all over his body. In reality, these were his mother's kisses. The caresses soothed during the descent of a perfect crystal mountain on crystal skis. He thundered downwards and even further down and then up again, everything around him violet with shafts of golden light, and, for a moment, the most incredible view he had ever seen came into sight, beyond that of his wildest dreams. Then he fell into a hole in the ground, struggled up to the surface again with the primitive energy of a drowning swimmer, and skied a little further over the mountains, the light all around him dazzling. But another chasm loomed, deeper and darker than the first, pulling him downwards into its churning gullet. A black ink slowly filled his throat... He felt cheated – like billions before him – and suddenly wanted to cry out, resist, but he couldn't.

On a whim, Ludo had checked Louis's jacket and found a piece of paper in a pocket, a page from one of the Heineken notepads from

314

behind the bar. Louis had scribbled one line in spidery letters, a sentence that detonated as soon as Ludo had read it: *Ludo, now it's your turn to suffer.*

The groom stifled a groan. His parents and the doctor turned to him in alarm. Even Louis appeared to move, as if he wanted to say something.

Ludo crumpled the paper in his fist, marched along the corridor, made his way through the crowd, fanning them aside like clouds of cigarette smoke, to the gents. His tear-strewn face as wet as the toilet bowl beneath him, he tore up the note, tossed the pieces into the shallow, yellowish water and flushed, realising as he did so that the rest of his life had been flushed down the toilet with it.

When he got back to Councillor Nederleven's office, Felix was leaning over the couch with a medical bag at his feet, his father and mother next to him. Dr Bodisco had closed the venetian blinds completely.

Louis was dead.

84

The ambulance finally arrived half an hour later, a whirling milky-blue light but no siren, and a couple of ambulance men glided the stretcher into the back, the lifeless body of Louis Bagman draped in black.

They had done this sort of thing so often that they conveyed the impression they were handling nothing more important than a cargo of unripe cheese. Dr Bodisco handed them a death report, and the hotel-keeper's son was whisked off to the funeral home next to the Dutch Reformed Church.

One wedding leads to another, they say, but no one would have imagined that the marriage of a German sausage-maker's daughter to a Dutch hotel-keeper's son would lead to a funeral.

The fine spring weather continued, regardless. The North Sea waves broke on the shore, rustling the shells with hypnotic monotony. Whistling day-trippers set their umbrellas up on the beach. Elias Bol did the same on the terrace but in silence. He had lingered at the town hall, his mouth drooping like an upturned horseshoe. Anyone fortunate enough to have time off to take the blue tram to the beach for a day of pleasure would never have guessed that the splendid town hall – designed by a Belgian architect – would be home to someone who had just died, casting an entire family into a bottomless pit of despair, without the slightest glimmer of sky.

Jacob, Maria, Ludo and Felix were all in a state of shock. Their movements were suddenly different now. Their own voices surprised them when they had to speak, and they felt as if they were sinning, as if it was inappropriate to speak or even to breathe, as if they too would be better off dead, out of love for their dead son and brother.

They were convinced at the same time that they only had to blink and the horror would disappear. Louis simply couldn't be dead. It was totally absurd, impossible. But it was true. So they went round in agonising circles, exhausting and maddening, aware of the familiar sights and sounds of everyday life that carried on in spite of Louis's demise.

The family blinked, and blinked again, but to no avail. Louis was dead and had already been taken to the funeral home on Poststraat, which some locals called 'heaven's gate' in accordance with their unwavering faith in God, His good works and the paradise that awaited them, while others avoided it like the plague, hopelessly unbelieving.

Mr Zwaan and his daughter were going through their own hell. The child had suffered a hysterical seizure in the council chambers, exhausting every ounce of her energy in revolt against what had taken place. It seemed for a moment that, in her anger and anguish, she

316

had mustered enough strength to get up from her wheelchair, crippled limbs and all, and seize God by the throat.

Instead, Dr Bodisco promptly gave her an injection, and her father had wheeled her home through the warm streets, Annabel lolling in a daze on her chair in her fuchsia party dress. When Mr Zwaan told his wife what had happened, she quickly crossed herself in the Orthodox style, her grandmother having been Serbian, and he then quickly returned to Hotel New Deluxe, where Jacob was in dire need of help.

The hotel-keeper begged him to make all the necessary arrangements, and then took refuge with his family upstairs. From being a witness at a wedding, the manager had been reassigned to organize a funeral. He assembled the hotel staff and told them the official version of events. They all shared the same shock, dumbfounded and anxious, separately wondering what the tragedy might mean for them personally. They could all forget about the bonuses they'd been looking forward to. How would the family survive, with high season just around the corner?

Mr Zwaan then advised the magician Ivan Poestash that the groom's brother had shot himself and died, interrupting the service before the couple had taken their vows. The variety performer, who had just returned from a stroll down The Boulevard and along the beach, shook his head in dismay, unable to believe his ears.

'As for the fee—'

'Fee? Surely you don't think I'm that heartless?' the illusionist exclaimed, astonished, recalling his own grief for the dear father he had buried less than six months ago in Alkmaar. He expressed his sincere condolences, and said he would pack up and leave within an hour.

Mr Zwaan then made his way to Jacob's office to make a series of phone calls. His boss's grubby Rolodex fortunately had all the numbers he needed. First up was The Swingers' frontman, who reacted with a hungover yawn. The call had clearly woken him up.

Max Serdijn, a close friend of Jacob's from Amsterdam and an eager amateur flautist, was, by contrast, deeply moved, and wanted to come over immediately to comfort the hotel-keeper and his family. The manager thanked him on behalf of the family for his kind words, but suggested it might be better to wait a little. The deceased had not yet been readied for burial, and the family was still in a state of profound shock and utter despair.

'OK. I'll light a candle for Louis on Kalvestraat this afternoon,' a clearly choked Serdijn decided, signing off and hanging up with a gentle click.

The wedding guests had made their way back to Hotel New Deluxe in small groups, only to encounter a uneasy silence there, which was only broken a few hours later when Uncle Bouke and his three nephews slunk downstairs.

Their grief and consternation was overwhelming, but their hard-working routines and the sudden tension had started to play on their stomachs. They were keen for a hot lunch and surreptitiously gobbled handfuls of peanuts and crackers that had been laid out earlier in glass bowls ready for the midday reception.

Mr Zwaan caught sight of them and realised immediately what was going on. He approached Uncle Bouke, a pair of scissors, a tube of glue and a fountain pen in his hands, and asked if they would like to have lunch.

'What do you mean?' asked the old Friesian farmer, unwilling to admit to the needs of his cast-iron constitution.

'I'm sure you must be hungry,' said Mr Zwaan.

Uncle Bouke mumbled something to the effect that the boys… could probably use a warm meal, and that he would probably join them, although, under the tragic circumstances…

'I'll have a table made up for you,' said Mr Zwaan, and headed off to the kitchen, where Willem Jansen was slumped dismally beside an old knife rack, staring at the speckles on the granite floor, in which he had discerned different patterns and even movement.

The chef had put the finishing touches to the wedding cake just a couple of hours earlier. When the news reached him of what had happened, he had wanted to pour the whole pot of chicken soup down the drain, simply to relieve the tension he felt, but instead took a swig from a bottle of Madeira that he kept for culinary purposes only.

'Willem, could you put something together for the Friesians? They've been asking…'

'But what?' Willem Jansen stared back at Mr Zwaan as if his own son had died.

'The wedding dinner, I suppose.'

The manager then went to the hotel café, sat down at a table near the fireplace with his scissors, glue and fountain pen, produced a piece of white card from his inside pocket, and wrote in a sombre double line script, 'a death in the family', colouring in the letters with blue ink. He then wrote 'for an indefinite period' on a separate piece of card and coloured it in in the same way.

When he was finished, he headed for the vestibule, carefully removed the notice that had been displayed in the window for a couple of days, brought it back to the table next to the fireplace, and glued the new card over the old text.

Shortly afterwards, a new notice appeared on the door of Hotel New Deluxe:

Owing to a death in the family,
Hotel New Deluxe will be closed
for an indefinite period.

The Management

85

Hans Matti had accompanied his daughter along the sunny streets back to the hotel. Nothing could persuade her to travel back in the bridal coach, which had been waiting outside for the happy couple, a nervous Daniel De Vlieger at the reins.

After tripping on the cobbles at least three times, Liza had abruptly stopped and kicked off her wedding shoes beneath a rosehip bush at the side of the road. 'That shit, that dirty little shit,' she repeated incessantly. She would never forgive him for abandoning her in the town hall.

The sausage-maker mumbled that his actions were understandable: her darling husband had simply wanted to be with his dying brother. Kati followed the pair of them, enduring her own private calvary of desperation and sweat. She had taken the fur stole off and held it in her right hand like some kind of barbarian returning from the hunt. The fox's snout and glacial beady eyes monitored the pavement.

'Let's just get out of here!' she gasped, puffing and panting. 'Out of here... bloody madhouse!'

How could she say such a thing? Hans Matti looked back at her in shock. Someone had just died. How could she?

'You've just answered your own question!'

Back in Liza's hotel room, the sausage-maker's wife promptly started to undress her daughter, ordering her husband to go and pack their bags.

'Kati, my dear,' he objected yet again. 'We can't just—'

'Get out!' Kati screeched.

Hans Matti headed next door, where he fell on the bed, before resting his elbow on his knee like Rodin's *Thinker*. He had never felt as incredulous as he did now. He too was convinced that he only had to blink and the film could be remade, allowing for the wedding scene to be shot according to the original script.

Kati had unzipped her daughter's dress down to the waist in one go. As Liza stepped out of the snowy mass of tulle and tugged the veil from her hair – Mr Scapé's artistry vanished in an instant – she could hear her mother roaring at her.

'What the hell is that?' Kati pointed at Liza, who stood almost naked before her.

The bride looked sheepishly down at a bloodstain the size of a Deutschmark that had leaked through her sanitary towel and onto her knickers. She stammered something incomprehensible.

Kati had reached the apex of her perplexed fury: her godawful daughter had been messing with her all along! She wasn't even fucking pregnant! This descent into Dutch hell had been entirely unnecessary! She wanted to strike out at absolutely everything but anger seemed to sharpen her mind. This was fantastic news! Yes, this was...

'Jesus Christ!' the sausage-maker's wife shouted all the same, determined to wring out the very last drop of her daughter's resistance.

Liza threw herself on the bed, her arms and legs thrashing about, and confessed whiningly that she had invented the pregnancy because she had always been so unhappy. She wanted to be free, to travel. God in heaven, she had never even seen a hippo in the wild. And the whole world was heading off to America these days...

'Liza!' Kati snapped. This was simply perfect. They had to go back to Germany without any delay, and leave this horrendous swamp behind forever.

The bride realised that all was now lost. She even considered telling her mother about the murder plot that she had hatched with Ludo. But she assessed the situation in the blink of an eye and decided there would be nothing to gain from such an admission.

'*Mutti*?' Liza looked over her shoulder at her mother, a devious idea in mind. Kati growled back. She simply couldn't bring herself to be civil to her daughter. '*Mutti*,' repeated Liza. 'Does this mean I'm properly married or not?'

'What do you mean?'

'Is the marriage valid or not? Or do we have to hold the wedding ceremony again?'

What? Again? Was she out of her mind? This whole country was a mental institution, and all the people here were lunatics! It was in their blood! Had she taken a close look at the Friesians?

'But I want to get married to Ludo,' Liza persisted.

'You'll make life a complete misery for all of us.'

'Six hundred a month,' Liza retorted, rising from the bed, and cunningly narrowed her eyes. It was as if she were sixteen again, bargaining for a new dress or a trip to the cinema.

'Four hundred,' retaliated Kati, matter-of-factly.

'Five hundred. And a new passport!'

'OK, all right,' she agreed, feigning reluctance even as she watched her grin of victory unfurl in the mirror above the sink.

There was a knock at the door. Hans Matti had been unable to maintain his *Thinker* posture any longer. Despite the Bagmans' tragedy, he had felt a sudden surge of pain in his heart in remembering his brother Otto.

'My dears,' he snivelled behind the door. 'Perhaps it would be better if we...?'

86

The effort to comprehend Louis's suicide not only consumed his family but also provided sustenance for all the local gossips, who had more to talk about than ever.

While some saw it as further evidence of Jacob Bagman's unsavoury wartime history – the shame had simply become too much for his son – others were convinced that Louis had lost his mind. And others reported that they had seen the hotel-keeper's son staring at toddlers with his unmoving fish-like eyes, and that the government would be better off locking up people like that as far away as possible. Evidently, the town had narrowly avoided disaster.

Each sombre tick of the Friesian grandfather clock in the Bagmans' living room revealed that another arduous second had passed. Jacob had begun a litany of self-reproach, detailing not only his failings with regard to Louis but also towards his parents, Benno Lemberg and even Uncle Simon. Maria finally interrupted, only to confess that it was she and not her husband who had failed Louis, and that she was ultimately responsible for his death. This went on for half an hour or more.

Suddenly the door opened and the black porter entered in silence. He had changed his wedding outfit for smart trousers, a white shirt and a black tie. Ludo stifled his rage – what kind of impertinence was this? – and recognised the man's unusual vitality. The room suddenly accommodated an unfamiliar energy that imbued the family with a dreamlike tranquillity. His face radiant with compassion, Joey walked over to Maria and took her in his arms. She started to sob uninhibitedly for the first time. Jacob got up to comfort her, but the porter signalled with his deep brown eyes that he should leave her be for a little while. Once Maria had calmed down, it was Jacob's turn to surrender to his embrace. Even Felix and Ludo – almost choking on his grief – yielded to his mysterious power, restraint and shame finally set aside.

Through his tears, Felix couldn't help thinking about the girl he had met that very morning in Leiden; he was in mourning and head over heels in love at the same time, which left him with unfamiliar feelings of guilt and disloyalty; Ludo only wished his friend was there. Where had Edo disappeared to?

'Ludo, shouldn't you see how Liza is doing?' Maria prompted, after the black porter had left in the same quiet and unassuming way that he'd entered.

'I'm going, I'm going...' he muttered, only too well aware that the game was over, and that he had lost.

Louis passed away at twelve minutes past twelve. At precisely thirteen minutes past three, Maarten Hartenaas, whose prudence was shared by all in his profession, parked his brand-new French hearse outside Hotel New Deluxe.

He got out of the car, breathed in the sea air with a smile of contentment but immediately rendered sombre his clean-shaven face. He saved Saturdays for his dear children, and Sundays were for God, and because the folks at the funeral home had called him an hour before to inform him that a service on Monday would be ideal – as smoothly and swiftly as possible was their rule of thumb – one or two matters had to be settled straight away.

Mr Zwaan had ignored Hartenaas's first call, but when he tried again less than half a minute later, the manager lost his usual patience and slammed down the phone. The undertaker had called back within a minute, kind but resolute, and had initiated a series of virtuoso expressions of condolence followed by some philosophical reflections. Death was a part of life, and the family trying to cope with this tragedy was not the first and would certainly not be the last. He had retrieved the body of a young girl earlier that week. The poor child was just eight years old. 'Such is life, or as they say in France, *c'est la vie.*' He loved to visit France. The French always seemed to have the correct expression for everything.

Hartenaas finally came to the point and asked if he might meet with the family at around three to discuss their choice of remembrance card, obituary notice and coffin design, and their preferences for the service, and other such important matters.

'But the body hasn't even been laid out yet,' resisted Mr Zwaan, with a sigh.

'My colleagues at the funeral home are, I'm sure, hard at work preparing the body at this very moment,' came the almost exuberant reply.

'Fine, so be it,' conceded the hotel manager. He then went upstairs, reluctant, beads of sweat on his brow, to let Jacob know.

The funeral director met the deceased's father in the vestibule, emitting a profusion of condolences as soon as they were introduced, his bird-like face assuming the most grief-stricken air.

Ludo had gone in search of Liza, and Maria simply wasn't up to the meeting. Mr Zwaan discreetly withdrew, and Felix had gone to the toilet with a sudden bout of diarrhoea.

'What a delightful hotel you have,' the undertaker said softly, as he followed Jacob along a wide corridor, his black leather attaché case under his arm, glancing into the festive, decorated rooms, the paper streamers now coated by an invisible veil of sadness.

'My son was going to get married today,' Jacob explained, directing him to the table reserved for regulars by the fireplace in the café.

'Oh, I'm so sorry,' replied Maarten Hartenaas, who had picked up something about a suicide. He had heard all sorts of things in his line of business, but this genuinely surprised him.

'The coffins,' he began, once Felix had joined them, opening a folder of black-and-white photos. 'I know that this must be difficult for you, dear friends. But I have a variety of options available and I would kindly ask that you make your choice…'

87

Anyone would have been forgiven for thinking that the Flood had begun all over again on the day of the funeral. The rain gurgled in the gutters and washed the remains of dead leaves and litter into little sodden clumps, while some of the town's lower-lying streets were knee-deep in water. The town's sewage system had been dysfunctional for years, and this was now an annual event. Lack of funds and obstructions at district level meant the necessary overhaul of the system was still out of the question.

The opportunity to condole the family of the boy who had taken his own life attracted reasonable numbers. Everyone had suddenly become conciliatory, even those for whom *The Boulevard*'s allegations were completely convincing. So, Bagman had been in the wrong. But what of it? Even the royal family were corrupt.

The mourners brought vast amounts of flowers with them, the size of each wreath depending on the nature of their relationship with the hotel-keeper's family in the past, and the estimated personal and commercial gain they attached to it in the future.

Fr Montfrans had been one of the first to hear the dreadful news – by telephone from the town hall. He had immediately sent the ladies' choir home, torn up his sermon, fallen to his knees in the side chapel, and prayed for some hours at the foot of a wooden statue of the Virgin Mary. This was the work of the Devil. The following day, he instructed Groenewoud to collect all of the white chrysanthemums that had been set out in vases around the altar, and bring them to the funeral home. Although the deceased had committed the terrible sin of suicide and wasn't even a Catholic, the flowers had been paid for by his father all the same. Bagman was a good man, and his life at that moment was surely a living hell.

Baron Van Tates had his gardener drive the four kilometres into town with a bouquet of wild flowers. The aristocrat had selected the flowers from his own garden, arranged them by colour, and included a letter of condolence to his former porcelain supplier and his family: '*I know how it feels, dear friend, when someone dear is suddenly and cruelly taken. May God be with you, your wife and your children at this difficult time. With affection, Xavier Van Tates.*'

Bouquets of carnations, chrysanthemums, lilies and roses had been sent by Johannes Wedekind, Hendrik Edelweiss, Mr Monjoux, the Holboom brothers, representatives of the town council, the Italian proprietor of the ice-cream parlour Pico Bello, Willem de Rover (who was in Antwerp, buying a second-hand car, but who had immediately heard about the tragedy), and dozens of other friends, business associates and close and not so close acquaintances of the bereaved in and around the resort. A wreath of white roses the size of a wagon wheel had been sent by the board and members of the local trade association. It was draped with a black sash reading 'Rest in Peace', followed by the name of Bastiaan Hermans, in his capacity as presiding chairman.

Those who were unable to find an excuse not to pay their respects in person filed, impassive and reluctant, along the hallway of the funeral home. After signing the condolence book, they milled about the main parlour, where grief and the scent of burning candles engulfed them like a cloak.

Jacob and Maria and their two sons displayed incredible fortitude, greeting well-wishers with what passed for smiles, thanking them for their kind words and helping to serve them coffee, milk and sugar. Despair occasionally overwhelmed them, and the masks fell from their faces as they collapsed into each other's arms, declaring their failure to fathom the dreadful tragedy, or words to that effect. Until they pulled themselves together again, directing everyone to 'pay your respects to Louis by the coffin. He looks so smart. And so serene. No, no... There's nothing to be afraid of'.

The mourners were more or less compelled to view the body, mostly with Maria, although most would have preferred to avoid the tiny room with its flickering candles and aromatic sea of flowers, where each of them would, in time, also be laid out.

'So?' Maria would ask, as if seeking some last compliment for her unfortunate son.

'He looks so serene, just as you said.'

'I agree. Nothing troubling about it at all.'

Louis did indeed appear to be more at peace with himself than ever before, the frozen suggestion of a smile on his boyish face. His waxen mask hinted at a new wisdom and a vague, reproachful superiority towards the world he had departed, as if he hadn't fallen for eternity into a deep and dark chasm but was still skiing over the crystal mountain landscape instead.

'I'm so sorry, Mrs Bagman,' well-wishers volunteered, 'it must be so hard, but please don't lose heart!' And then they were free, thank God, to return to the coffee and the world of the living, where the Friesians had all assembled, shuffling awkwardly back and forth and gorging on one slice of cake after another to calm their nerves, although the funeral itself wasn't until Monday.

Some among them had started to reminisce about the deceased. The occasional unabashedly upbeat story with Louis as its hero set bellies shuddering, teaspoons clinking amid stifled laughter. It relieved the tension briefly, until another diffident well-wisher was escorted to the tiny room with the mahogany coffin – Maarten Hartenaas had made a fair profit – to visit the corpse, and whole procedure started anew. It was horrible, but there was no escaping it. And the very idea that time would ultimately heal such gaping wounds was beyond reason.

An anonymous red rose wrapped in shiny cellophane had been delivered to the funeral home early on Saturday morning. Maria had placed the ruby flower on the coffin, its stem unfortunately broken in the middle. Jacob suspected it had been sent by Herman Nederleven, but Ludo knew better. It was a final farewell from his friend and comrade Edo Novak. He had tried to call him at least a dozen times since the death of his brother, but Edo had unplugged the receiver and clearly wanted nothing more to do with the unfortunate waiter. Better safe than sorry was his motto.

Perhaps it wasn't so strange, though, in view of his impending mission to save humanity. There might even have been some justification for it.

88

It was Monday morning and the Bagman family was making its way to the edge of the dunes, this time to the town cemetery rather than the town hall.

Instead of traditional Friesian horse-drawn coaches, four black limousines had been supplied by the Holboom brothers as transport. The funeral home had hired them through the undertaker in Haarlem, and the brothers received their usual commission.

De Vlieger had offered the free use of his best carriage to carry Louis to his final resting place. Jacob had thanked him profusely but declined, weakly explaining that the horses reminded him too much of the wedding, of the days when everything was...

'I understand,' De Vleiger responded, adding a few choice words of consolation.

A period of bewilderment, grief and unbearable tension was now at its zenith for the family. Everyone had dreaded every minute between Louis's death and the funeral, but the weekend had passed by, nevertheless.

The funeral cortège set off at eleven-thirty from Hotel New Deluxe, headlights beaming through the pouring rain. The Benders were noticeably absent.

On Friday afternoon, a distraught Ludo had knocked, then banged on the door and rattled the doorknob of the hotel room to which Liza and her parents had retreated.

Hans Matti was at a complete loss. His radiant, blonde-haired princess, who had set off to be married that very morning, her darling Ludo at her side, was now a pitiful mess, hunched up in bed in a white cotton dress. Her one wish was to get back to Cologne as soon as possible, to go home and banish the whole affair from her mind – Ludo, the suicide, this hotel, this miserable resort, the entire country.

'But Liza, darling... Liza...'

'Never mind "Liza, Liza!". Just pack the bags!' Kati snapped triumphantly.

'But they couldn't,' entreated Hans Matti. 'Jacob, Maria, and the boys... In their time of grief...'

'Get packing!' Kati snarled, afraid that, if they dallied, her daughter might let her father talk her into staying.

Mother and daughter had finally given in to the drumming on the door and Hans Matti's protests. When Ludo walked in, sweat pouring down his face, Liza and Kati turned away in unison, as if the groom, who was still wearing his dress suit, was truly a monster.

'Come here, dear Ludo,' Hans Matti mumbled, leading the hotel-keeper's son out into the corridor and closing the door behind him. He promised that everything would soon resolve itself. It was just the shock of it all, the shock and the stress. How were his parents and Felix bearing up?

The sausage-maker shuttled tirelessly in the hours that followed between Kati, Liza and Ludo, the latter desperate to talk to his bride in private.

'Come on, my darlings, be reasonable! Where's your compassion? What has Ludo done to deserve this?'

Mother and daughter had closed ranks, however, and refused to relent. They had packed, and were threatening to call a taxi if Hans Matti didn't get a move on.

'I don't know what to do,' Hans Matti confided in a moment of despair. 'Liza and her mother are possessed all of a sudden!'

The sausage-maker finally threw in the towel at eight-thirty that evening. With Ludo at his side, he walked into the living room where Jacob and Maria were sitting hand in hand on the settee, the distant murmur of the sea wafting comforting music through the open balcony doors.

This was the first opportunity Hans Matti had had to offer his condolences. He embraced them all, murmuring how tragic it all was. If only he could do something to turn back time, but it was beyond him. He spoke for his wife and daughter too, aware that Ludo was standing next to him and that he knew his words were lies.

'We feel we should be on our way,' Hans Matti then heard himself say, hesitation in his voice. Liza and Kati were simply unable to cope with the situation. It wasn't his personal choice, as he hoped they understood. And they would be back before long. After the funeral. Can I count on your understanding, dear friends?

The hotel-keeper and his wife nodded, exhausted from grief, barely able to make out his question.

Hans Matti promptly turned round, the faces of the people he had almost seen as family suspended in his mind for an instant in a scattered strip of light.

'Get a move on!' he yelled on returning to their room, his mouth so far open his tonsils were visible beyond his tongue. 'Let's get out of here now! *Schnell, schnell!*'

Ten minutes later, they had fled the resort in their wine-coloured Mercedes, the sun setting swiftly in the muddy orange sky. Hans Matti clutched the wheel, his entire body stiff with rage, racing up to every bend in the road as if thieves were in hot pursuit.

Before long they saw the first sign for Amsterdam. The rest of the journey was child's play.

Ludo could only muster up the courage to go upstairs to his brother's attic room later that night. The words that Louis had written on the note block were large, clear and hammering at his head: *Ludo, now it's your turn to suffer.*

The idea that Louis might have written something about the time they had left Felix outside the town hall added panic to his desperation. Ludo entered the shady attic room, his heart pounding. Louis's bed was as it always was, as if he had just got up. Clouds drifted by outside, bearing the faces of the Greek gods who had governed the world until others had assumed their colossal task.

Ludo made a methodical search of the whole room, anxiously startled by his own every move. The wardrobe was almost empty, there was nothing under the mattress, he twice looked in the drawer of the bedside cabinet just to be sure – there was nothing – and he even investigated an empty flowerpot. No sign of any letter or note, nothing, thank God.

He finally started to flick through the books that were stacked at the side of the bed. But the almanac with its bewildering mathematical formulas, in which Louis had scribbled here and there in pencil, contained nothing incriminating, neither did *Our Countryside Friends*, the colouring book with its pictures of hares, robins, young foxes, carp and other such creatures. The last book Ludo looked at was a sturdy volume bound in red leather about the Muslim world, and full of racy prints that he examined in detail.

He suddenly heard a noise behind him. Felix had been watching his brother in silence from the door.

'Those Muslims can look forward to a good time in heaven, apparently,' said Ludo, holding up a print of a naked girl taking it in the mouth from a potbellied Arab.

'Mum and Dad are going crazy,' Felix replied. 'I put sleeping tablets in their tea.'

The two brothers said nothing more.

89

Ariaan Pruis Cannegieter, alias Aadje Pruis, had had a run-in with his boss just before the wedding, and was fired on the spot. De Vlieger's eldest son, who ran the business very differently from his father, had slammed the desk with his fist, the dismissal delivered as if a sentence pronounced on Aadje Pruis in a court of law.

In spite of his impressive surname and the suggestion that one of his ancestors had defeated the Russians off the coast of Arkhangelsk, Aadje Pruis had always lived from hand to mouth. His savings amounted to the princely sum of nineteen guilders, and, with three children to support, it was essential that he find another job immediately.

The elder of the Holboom brothers had heard of his situation within an hour, and had offered the professional chauffeur occasional work driving one of the black Opels that were rented out to local undertakers. There was a real dearth of funeral vehicles. Did he have a respectable black suit? Aadje Pruis eagerly said yes, not realising what he was committing himself to exactly. The next day Louis Bagman had died, and Aadje was called to work at his funeral.

Working with mourners required a certain level of experience (it was not a skill learned in a day), but Aadje had been asked to drive the hearse rather than one of the four funeral cars.

'I can't,' was his first reaction, hoping to get out of it. He had known the deceased personally for over twenty-five years. But Holboom insisted that they had an agreement, and that this was the ideal baptism by fire.

Aadje had reluctantly agreed, thinking only of his family. But now he deeply regretted his decision. He simply couldn't understand that the same ebullient boy he had taken to the Bollenstreek and Amsterdam under a week ago, the party hat on his head, now lay dead in the coffin behind him, beneath a mountain of flowers, asleep for all eternity.

'Lousy weather! We'll be up to our knees in a minute!' A man from the funeral home had said this as they were carrying the mahogany colossus outside, the downpour unrelenting. 'Careful! Keep it straight, Aadje... That's better... Good. We don't want to lose the wreath! Gently does it, glide it in... Come on, put your back into it.'

Before the lid was placed on the coffin, Aadje Pruis had taken one last look at the body. He just couldn't believe that, one day, he too would be lying there like a wax dummy. Death was all right for other people, but not for him! A sickly smell surrounded the bier, and Aadje had the impression it was trying to infiltrate his still-living pores.

'This is a mistake, Aadje! A big mistake!' he muttered to himself, as he peered out at the rain-drenched road through the swishing windscreen wipers, the black flags on the wing mirrors like grit in his eyes. He would never drive a hearse again. It was back to the buses for him, hire coaches ideally but public transport if need be. No, the funeral sector was not his cup of tea.

All at once, he thought he heard a thumping sound from the coffin. Fear beetled up his spine.

'No way, Louis, I'm not falling for that one! You're dead, pure and simple, dead as a dodo! I'm not falling for it!'

The cortège crept through the streets of the seaside resort at a snail's pace, allowing the locals to stop and doff their hats, but the heavy rain kept most indoors. Those who had chosen to attend the funeral had already been waiting in the auditorium for some time, silent and rather soaked.

Julius Rozengal, the registrar, was going to read a couple of his poems, followed by organ music by Bach. Bastiaan Hermans had agreed to address the mourners on behalf of the local trade associ- ation, and one of the family would also make the long journey up to the lectern, although which of them it would be had not yet been decided. None of them appeared to be up to it. Collective shock had taken hold of them again, and such was the tension that they were all at breaking point, and felt dizzy.

'Such foul weather!' Maria broke the silence all of a sudden, their car limping over the tracks at a level crossing, the rain still falling heavily.

She then decided that she would speak for the family at the lectern. Women had more courage when it came down to it.

The atmosphere in the limousine that transported the Friesian del- egation was also one of great sadness, but their grief was altogether different. They had already grown used to the idea that Louis was dead, to a certain extent. The four men had played dominoes the evening before, and had even argued – true to form – because Uncle Bouke – also true to form – had been accused of cheating. None of them had really known Louis that well. He may have been a blood relative, but no one had been close to him.

Femke had done her utmost to support Maria, her sister, while Jetske and Tijtske had thrown themselves into bedmaking and the like, which helped pass the time. Now, though, they hankered after the normality they had left behind in Friesland.

On Saturday morning, the boys had gone for a walk along the beach, Uncle Bouke leading the way. When they got back Mr Zwaan raced out to advise them that the police had called. Wierd had been summoned to bring his revolver to the police station immediately. No one doubted that it was suicide, but they still had to be follow procedures. And did he have a valid license for the weapon?

'Jesus Christ! Didn't I tell you not to go hunting?' Uncle Bouke thundered, fearing the worst.

Wierd, the young shipbuilder, was received with the utmost consideration, however, and even offered a cup of coffee. The investigating officer's wife had given birth to their first child the night before, a baby girl weighing seven pounds, and, according to Dutch tradition, the coffee was accompanied by rusks decorated with icing and sugar drops.

Wierd elaborated a confusing tale: his poor dead cousin had convinced him a week before to bring his rifle and revolver with him from Friesland, so that they could go hunting together in the dunes. Pangs of conscience made him change his mind at the last minute, and he called off the hunt. His shotgun licence was only valid in Friesland. Louis must have stolen the revolver from his room and used it—

'Fine, I've heard enough,' the police officer declared, putting an end to the interrogation. The chief of police had already made it clear that he should settle the matter as quickly and obligingly as possible.

Herman Nederleven had sent a telegram to Tel Aviv half an hour after the suicide, and the mayor had called immediately. He wanted to know every detail of what had taken place, and urged the councillor to accommodate the poor Bagmans. If they wanted a German brass band to play at the funeral, the council should authorise it.

'The band has left already,' Nederleven replied.

Jacob and Maria and their two remaining sons couldn't eat a thing in the days after the tragedy. The Friesians, by contrast, made full use of the free hand they had been granted in the kitchen in the circumstances. Grief appeared only to increase their appetites. They feasted on veal scallops, great dollops of mash, garden peas, and other such delicacies left over from the wedding banquet, free to eat to their heart's content. Ice-cream cake covered in warm fruit purée and whipped cream was on the menu every day.

When Wubbe revealed to Mr Zwaan that he had once eaten Indian food in Leeuwarden with his mates from the shipyard, and had picked up a taste for spicy food, the tofu dish prepared for Kati Bender was dished up forthwith. Willem Jansen's culinary creation was tasty, crunchy and spicy, and enjoyed by one and all.

All of the hotel's staff, even the black porter, had been packed into the fourth and fifth limousines, except for Mr Zwaan. His wife was too ill to push their daughter to the cemetery in the driving rain, and the task had fallen to him. The girl was protected from the elements, staring out vacantly from behind a clear plastic window that formed part of the hood covering her wheelchair.

There was nothing to be seen from her rickety refuge, however, nothing apart from the tin-grey rain. Her mouth fell open every now and then, like a skylight window with a broken latch.

Epilogue

On a scorching August day in 2005, a well-preserved Dutch gentleman wearing a simple, loose-fitting suit of Chinese linen with shiny white buttons made his way back to his apartment near the Puerto del Sol, Madrid, having spent the afternoon sitting on a bench in Retiro Park.

A paperback edition of Turgenev, which he had been reading until he'd almost dozed off, weighed down the inside right-hand pocket of his jacket. He passed an African man under a sycamore tree, a monkey on his left shoulder, both of them dancing to the electronic blare of a boom box. The gentleman initially had the urge to make a complaint about this animal cruelty, but changed his mind and instead tossed a euro into an empty McDonald's coffee cup on the ground by the dancer's feet, walking on with a gracious nod. Only a gifted or seasoned observer, a writer or a doctor, perhaps, would have noticed that the youthful pensioner was dragging his left leg slightly.

Madrid's traffic droned on in the dry heat of summer, punctuated by occasional toots and blasts, just as vehicles all over the world droned on, tooting and blasting, in sizzling Cairo, in the narrow streets overlooking the Bosporus, in Buenos Aires, in Moscow, in Rome, and despite the eternal promise of Paris, where he had tried and failed to settle down no less than twice, somehow unable to get used to the place.

The gentleman in question was none other than Felix Bagman, once a reluctant businessman and now a familiar presence on the shelves of bookshops everywhere due to his scholarly yet popular success, *Parrots*.

The love he had felt once upon a time for Liza Bender, the sausage-maker's daughter from Cologne, had turned out to be a youthful whim, of course, an aberration, a hormonal mistake. Two generations had grown up since then, old walls had fallen, and new ones had arisen. His parents had been dead for over thirty years now, and buried beneath the same black marble stone, its gold lettering sullied by the sea air, their second son Louis beside them.

His other brother, Ludo, had died a couple of weeks earlier, at an age no one would ever have thought he'd reach, least of all himself. The former catering industry boss had since been cremated, and his ashes scattered in the North Sea, the same sea he had stared at from his bench on The Boulevard every day during the last years of his life, his hair pitch black and unruly, and the corners of his mouth twisted and bitter. He had refused to be buried, preferring the heat of the fire to the cold of the earth. He had put off the decision to the last minute, until he had had no choice.

The sea rustled just as it had when Felix was a little boy, when he had caught his first butterflies in the dunes with a shrimp net, carefully fixing them to a red velvet pincushion from an old jewellery box of his mother's. 'Do you like it, Mummy?' Mummy liked it very much.

This was Felix's first visit to the Netherlands in almost thirteen years. He took a taxi from the airport to the centre of Amsterdam, checked into his hotel, and then ordered a couple of meat croquettes on Leidsestraat, but could only manage to eat half of the first one. He then wandered about for an hour over the city's oppressive canals and bridges before returning to his room in Hotel de l'Europe, where he had once spent the happiest night of his life. It could have been three centuries ago, perhaps even four. It was anyone's guess and nobody cared.

'Quidado, señor!' A girl leading a child by the hand called out to Felix, as he was about to cross the busy street directly outside the park. He hadn't even noticed the Volkswagen Beetle with its open sunroof, its driver's sunglasses glinting.

'Muchas gracias!' Felix replied, doffing an imaginary hat – had he been wearing a hat, he would certainly have doffed it – to her, this young mother or au pair, conjuring up a smile on her charming face.

He had had hundreds of women over the years. He had stopped counting at 214, on the occasion that had followed a three-minute standing ovation at an ornithology conference in beautiful, elegant Krakow.

There had only been one Liza, Liza de la Mortange, the chubby daughter of a banker from somewhere near Geneva. She had been more attracted to Felix's narrow lips and sleepy leonine eyes than to his status as a celebrated author.

He had never met another Violet. A man only ever gets one opportunity to fall head over heels in love; if you miss the train or jump off too soon, the chances are it's gone for ever.

Brushing aside the sands of time, Felix recalled how, when Louis's funeral was over, and the bedraggled mourners were back in the parlour drinking coffee and gobbling slices of cake as if there were no tomorrow, he had experienced the life-affirming impact of death for the first time. An unfamiliar desire to jump up and down, kick lampposts, kick in front doors and make love had possessed him.

Louis was dead, but he was still alive and well. His concealed but sheer relief at this seemed like the purest form of betrayal. The young student was unaware at the time that most of those present felt exactly the same way, although they all determinedly kept straight faces.

Maria had prepared a speech after all. She turned first to her son in the coffin, the corners of her mouth trembling, and read a story from one of his old school books entitled 'The Dune Rabbit'. The heart-rending tale told of a poor crippled creature almost blind from myxomatosis, who was still the butt of the other rabbits' constant jokes. Everyone now understood the story to be a parable of Louis's own tragic existence, the boy who had taken his own life with a single bullet, the poor boy who was now waiting to be interred for eternity.

After the Bagmans' four shovelfuls of muddy dune sand had landed with four dull thuds on top of the coffin, Mr Zwaan's daughter had wheeled to the front of the crowd with all the energy she could

341

muster and cast a hand-made crêpe-paper rose into the grave, its red dye running all over her hands. Her father arched over her unsteadily, like the leaning tower of Pisa, protecting her from the rain with an enormous umbrella.

'Farewell dear Louis!' she had whispered. Only three years later, her heart finally submitted to the muscular paralysis that had raged though her fragile body like a relentless forest fire, and she was brought back to the eastern part of the country to be laid to rest in the Zwaan family plot.

The Friesian relations left for home that same afternoon by train, all of them equally determined never to go back. Ludo drank himself into oblivion at a bar in Overveen and staggered home in the small hours. Felix headed back to Leiden that night with his parents' blessing – they needed to be on their own – and immediately called the girl he had encountered just a couple of hours before Louis's suicide.

'What took you so long?' was her faintly catty response. Felix could picture her enchanting face to the last detail.

When Felix told her what had happened the girl wailed hysterically, as if she had lost a loved one of her own. Sobbing and snivelling, she had begged him to come over. They lay in bed in her attic room for two whole days, side by side, listening to the rain drumming on the roof, trembling with delight, although Violet had not yet surrendered to him. She had forced him to scrub himself in the shower for half an hour with fresh soap when he first arrived, claiming she could smell the funeral. The student of Russian could actually *smell* death, she said. Felix had never believed her until the police had enlisted her help one day in the search for a missing girl, and she had located the child's lifeless body buried far below ground, sniffing like a dog beside a rose bush. The case had shocked the entire nation at the time, and many still remember it to this day.

On the third day she had said, 'You can sleep with me for real today, but only if it's somewhere we'll never forget.'

Felix whipped open a drawer with a flourish, stuffed a one

hundred guilder note that his parents had given him on his eigh-teenth birthday into his pocket, dragged Violet outside, and the pair had giggled their way to the train station. Three quarters of an hour later, they were walking past the Victoria Hotel in Amsterdam, Felix immediately reminded of that dreadful day with the Benders, but by the time they had reached the Mint Tower they couldn't contain themselves any longer, and had marched into Hotel de l'Europe and booked a room.

'Do you have any bags, sir?'

'Not right now!' Felix said quickly, at which the man in epaulettes at the reception desk smiled rather thinly.

'That'll be thirty guilders, sir.'

The room had a balcony overlooking Rokin Street and the water-buses that were moored along the quay. They kissed in full view of the city, bathed in a silvery sunlight, then went inside and had each other for the first time (it was not Felix taking Violet or vice versa, they had each other), on a wonderfully bouncy bed that was, in fact, two beds put together.

The junior suite with the balcony still existed: four hundred and eighty euros, excluding breakfast. Felix would have been happy to pay a further thousand euros to sleep there once again, but a foreign couple – a balding forty year old man and a girl almost half his age – had booked the room for three days. Felix had pressed the wrong button in the elevator and happened to see them down the corridor. They were loudly cursing the years that separated them, but were secretly sure that the future would bring them ever closer.

Felix listened to their gasps and groans from his room on the floor below, his face pressing into the eiderdown, and, from the depths of his despair, he reflected on his life with the woman he had loved most, every hair on her head recollected perfectly – or so he thought – although he hadn't seen her in fifteen years. She had children of her own now, even grandchildren, all of them doubtless as dark and lovely as Violet herself.

Felix was going to take a taxi to the seaside resort of his youth, perhaps for the last time, the following day. He had reached the age when everything was done perhaps for the last time: eating a croissant with ham and cheese; emptying his bladder; hearing his heart beat...

The new future had dawned, of course, much faster than some had expected, and with much more pomp and circumstance. One New Year morning, a tyrant fled his tropical and thoroughly corrupt paradise only to be replaced by another equally corrupt dictator.

Edo finally reached Cuba three months later, after a long roundabout journey by boat and plane via Canada, America and Mexico. Two comrades from Moscow and a harem of mulatto girls gave him a royal welcome in a hotel with a colonial palm garden in Santiago de Cuba. He spent a week with them, cooled by revolving ceiling fans, singing hymns from the Spanish Civil War and songs from Mother Russia. The former history student had found where earthly paradise and social and political evolution were conjoined. He couldn't imagine a better place to live, certainly not in the Netherlands. Five months later, the revolutionary had sent Ludo a postcard from Havana. Life was wonderful, he said. The defeat of the 'capitalist octopuses' – he now quoted Che Guevara with the same enthusiasm that he had once quoted Sartre and Marx – had been celebrated on a seabed of rum, the most succulent fruit imaginable, and unqualified physical bliss. And this was only the beginning! The world's old structures were already teetering on the brink, doomed to collapse. He thanked Ludo for his contributions in the past, although he had, in fact, financed his trip with a gift from an industrialist's son living in a wealthy Amsterdam suburb, who received a lengthy letter in epic prose once a week.

The red rose with the broken stem on Louis's coffin had not been Edo's final farewell after all. Ludo read the postcard as if he were reading the numbers on a winning lottery ticket that was too old to be still valid, assuming the same expression that would contort his lips in years to come as he looked out over the sea, old and bitter.

All this had occurred before the second summer following Louis's death, when the Bagman family had already been back in business for some time, surprised at their own resilience, which none would have thought possible at first.

Life went on, and the number of German tourists steadily increased year on year, reaching a deluge. Jacob negotiated additional loans from the bank, allowing him to refurbish the rooms at Hotel New Deluxe one by one and install showers and WCs en suite, in line with modern expectations. The bridal suite even had a bath. The tramline to the capital was discontinued and replaced by juddering diesel buses – a stupid and irreversible decision – as part of a series of measures to demolish and then hideously rebuild the homeland.

Felix breezed through university, working every summer from June to September in the hotel. He would disentangle himself from his beloved Violet early in the morning and make his way home, feeling faint. She had become his addiction. His parents only knew of her by name at first. It took a year and a half before the student dared to bring her home to the place of his birth, as if there was a curse on love that hung over Hotel New Deluxe. He lugged plates of Dutch beefsteak, fried liver and Wiener schnitzels from kitchen to table, helped guests to check in at Reception, ordered supplies, and took over as much of the bookkeeping as his father would allow.

Without fail, Ludo would disappear off to a local bar, where his affair with the German bride-to-be had given him an increasingly mythical status, especially among certain women excited by the story. He was always drunk by the time he got home in the early hours and usually confronted the following day with a hangover. Customers frequently complained about his lack of good manners.

Jacob occasionally alluded to 'selling the whole kit and caboodle' in conversation with his wife, but the new loans meant there wouldn't be much money left, and they would not only be robbing themselves of their only source of income but Ludo too. What kind of future would he have without the hotel? So they just kept going. What else was there to do? For most people, changing one's life is only ever a theoretical question.

Felix graduated *cum laude*, was offered a research post at the university, and concentrated his doctoral studies on the social and sexual behaviour of the parrot. His supervisor died a year later from stomach cancer, and was replaced by a new professor of ethology, a young fellow with a head of grey curls, a permanent smile and impeccable papers. Felix mocked him from the outset, sensing there was something not quite right about him. The hotel-keeper's son said goodbye to the university within a month, took a job with a grain broker, a German emigrant with a French surname, whose fortune was reportedly 'immense'. He also turned out to be an avid birdwatcher.

Nine years passed in the blink of an eye, in a universe replete with physical pleasures and growing prosperity. Felix and Violet moved into a flat in Amsterdam where she invited exiled Russian poets for drinks, men with dark eyes like Rasputin's. Violet not only translated their poetry, she also got drunk with them or explored the foggy world of drugs with them, then lured them into bed, preferring Felix to stand by and watch. 'Do you love me, Felix? Do you fucking love me?' she would shout, during bouts of Slavic passion involving every imaginable position.

He felt physical pain, he felt heartsick, he died a thousand deaths. But his love for Violet was as boundless as his fear of losing her. It was all in the spirit of the times, and he silently endured it, as if it were a new form of fascism, in which sham tolerance had taken the place of real tolerance, and the sexual revolution meant little more than the construction of a new prison with new prison guards.

But he went along with it in spite of his feelings. One day, during some kind of 'happening' with 'like-minded' individuals in a revamped barn in Friesland, he caught sight of a vaguely familiar face tirelessly humping both sexes at the same time whilst surrounded by an earthly hell of similarly copulating bodies. The women were lying on thin mattresses waiting their turns like nymphomaniac whores. The handsome man with East Indian features was none other than Edo Novak, renowned intellectual and talented self-publicist, who had breathed the same air as Castro and Brezhnev. After a year and a half in Cuba, the island apparently became too confined for his tastes. The heartbeat of the new age was also pounding on other continents, and he shuttled back and forth across the seas – business class – as a sort of diagnostic specialist (and, here and there, as a political gravedigger).

The wealth Felix derived from grain slowly took on astronomical proportions. Bonuses and his colossal commission on deals rained down on him every six months. It was child's play: buy from location A, where there was a surplus, and sell to location B, where there was a shortage, and then skim the profit. He made frequent trips abroad for the company, which satisfied his hunger for freedom to a certain extent. But it wasn't enough.

His visits home became less and less frequent as Ludo grew jealous of the vast sums of money his brother now earned. It seemed so god-damned easy and didn't require the least physical effort! When he was forty, Ludo bought a second-hand sports car – as red as a traffic light – which he raced along The Boulevard in the summer in a billowing white shirt, picking up women and girls with his surly actor's looks, while his father and mother poured beer and served meals. The burden gradually took its toll as they resigned themselves to the fact that their son's profligate lifestyle was slowly but surely devouring their business.

The idea that Hotel New Deluxe had once boasted a staff of seven waiters and four chefs seemed to hail from a bygone era: Jacob was barely able to meet the ever-increasing Social Security costs. Employing staff during the summer months had become a virtual guarantee of commercial suicide, but he did it all the same, unable to make Mr Zwaan and his other loyal workers temporarily redundant.

They were human beings, after all, and human beings had to be treated like human beings.

Jacob and Maria had by this time been introduced to Violet, whom they hoped would become Felix's fiancée. They even had a couple of dinners together, and, for a while, everything seemed just as it had been when Ludo was about to get married and the future still seemed shiny and unblemished.

Jacob suffered his first stroke around the time that Violet had started to talk about children. He died eighteen months later at the age of sixty-four, after a short but miserable illness akin to the one that took his father. His death finally drove Ludo onto double whiskies and his first DTs, turned Maria into a complete nonentity, and plunged Felix into a second hell. He had known for several months that he was infertile, which for Violet – the fire of her promiscuity now magically extinguished, the smoulder of her maternal instinct remaining – had become the most important thing in the world.

'Perhaps we should think about adoption?' Felix had ventured one day, a few months after his father had been laid to rest.

'Never! I want a child of my own.'

It is said that success breeds success, although the same might be said of poverty, illness and death. Whatever the case, it remains a fact of life, perhaps stupid but true all the same, that where the grim reaper has paid a visit, new victims inevitably fall before he disappears again, not to return for years on end.

By the time Maria succumbed to a heart attack eighteen months later – she was wandering about the house with a watering can and suddenly collapsed in a heap on the floor, soon to follow her dear husband and son Louis to the grave and the black marble tombstone – Felix had been living alone in his flat on the Leidsegracht for two years already. Violet had left him one morning after three independent medical tests, one of them in Belgium, confirmed that he was indeed sterile.

'I love you, dear Felix. Jesus Christ, I'll always love you… But please try to understand. I have to follow the call of my soul and of my blood. I'll always be there for you, no matter what. My heart and my body are yours whenever you need me.'

Felix read the note that Violet had left, the birds outside twittering as cheerfully as they had on the day they had met.

She moved in with an actor renowned for his distinctive Shylock. Twenty years her elder, the man had got her pregnant within a month, and she later gave birth to twins, a boy and a girl, both of them famous TV soap stars now, and plagued by the inevitable desire to earn millions. Violet's daughter now had two children of her own.

After Violet's departure, Felix made a tally of their savings, enough for ten years of complete freedom if he was careful, perhaps even longer. He thought back to the autumn morning at the ruins of Leiden castle, to the moment when he had contemplated suicide, but was saved by the sight of a parrot flying out to sea. He resigned a few days later and, before the month was out, the focal points of the book he would go on to write had been set out on paper. His book, *Parrots*, opened with the following sentence: *'The parrot is much admired for its ability to imitate human speech, but a parrot is wiser than a human being, for it is an animal.'*

Felix travelled the world for three years, collecting material for his book in both rainforests and libraries. He put the finishing touches to his work one New Year's day, surrounded by flowering acacias on the island of La Gomera. The book went on to be translated into thirty-nine languages, and was once described in a *New York Times* supplement as reading 'like a novel'. The predicate certainly didn't hurt sales.

He subsequently received invitations to give lectures across the globe and settled in monogamous isolation in a series of different locations, including Buenos Aires, New York, Istanbul and Paris, the last eight years having been spent in Madrid. Felix felt his existence was a mistake without being an absolute failure. The same might be said of most lives, but his was a mistake nonetheless.

He enjoyed life's pleasures without really living. He had never completely understood why his brother had committed suicide. Was it for the same reason he himself might still be inclined to put an end to it all, in protest at the chronic indifference and cruelty everywhere, more abundant still than water and air? He wondered where his parents had found the energy to keep going for all those years, to remain human in spite of everything, to be selfless, put others first. It sobered him to think of them, but when it came down to it, he knew he was unlike them, selfish.

The women and the girls comforted him, for an hour, or a week, sometimes for a month. He even had what might be called a romance now and then. But sooner or later the women would leave, driven away by his refusal to make a commitment unreservedly. He also knew that he would never even have looked at other women if Violet had not left him. He understood her, too: he couldn't expect her to spend her life with a man whose existence served no biological purpose. This awareness stayed with him always, like a scar on his soul.

It could have happened anywhere. In Jakarta, in London or in Tbilisi, where the Georgian translation of *Parrots* had been presented to the public in the city's Botanical Gardens, which look out over the Caucasus mountains, the call of a mosque blending in sonorous harmony with the bells of an assortment of Orthodox churches beside a silent synagogue in the valley below.

It could indeed have happened anywhere, and it finally did happen on a winter's night three years earlier in Tallinn, the medieval cobblestones glistening in the moonlight of an ice-cold frosty night, Felix returning to his hotel with hired company. He politely made his way over to the mini-bar, heard a sort of grating sound in his right ear, stumbled towards the bathroom soaked in sweat, yanked the magnifying side of the retractable shaving mirror towards him with trembling hands (everything looked even worse that he feared), and saw that his mouth and the left side of his face had slumped, his left eyelid drooping like that of a drowsy dog.

'Please help me,' he groaned at the girl, who was frozen to the spot.

Half an hour later, he was in the emergency room of a private clinic, where a Finnish doctor swiped his American Express through a machine, apologising for the inconvenience. Sadly enough, his face was still out of kilter a week later, although he had been assured of a complete recovery, a promise reiterated by his doctors in Madrid, where Felix did indeed begin to live a more or less normal life again after a year of rehabilitation.

The attack left him with a slight drag in his left leg and the numb sensation of a rubber limb in his left arm and fingertips.

The road through the dunes was as magnificent as ever, uncharacteristically Dutch in all its meandering randomness. By chance, the driver of the taxi he had ordered at the reception of Hotel de l'Europe turned out to be a resident of the resort, despite his bronzed skin and large, soft camel's eyes. He had even grown up there, and started on about its nightlife and all it had to offer. An Amsterdam drawl mixed with a good dose of Arabic had driven out the last traces of a coastal accent. Felix peered at the twenty-four-year old from the corner of his eye, an apple-shaped air freshener dangling from the rear-view mirror and smelling of apricots, and suddenly felt incredibly old.

'You're on a tourist visit?'

'Yes, that's right,' affirmed Felix blandly as they drove into a leafy street, flanked by houses with conservatories that still had something of Hollywood about them.

He left his bags in his room at Hotel Sissi, which he'd chosen on the internet because of its name, and made his way through the streets of his home town, full of sweating tourists in cheap sunglasses, the smell of chip fat undiminished, to the funeral home on Poststraat.

It was jarringly empty. Besides the woman who worked there, who kindly directed him to the condolence book in the vestibule, only one other woman was hovering around. Felix had difficulty recognising her from a distance.

'Betsy!'

The National Socialist chairman's daughter was now plump, her hair an exaggerated grey. After the death of Dr Bodisco in 1989, she had openly continued her affair with Ludo, which had begun in secret a month after Louis's suicide. She was his only love and their affection for one another was mutual. But they had given each other complete freedom.

'He looks at peace, don't you think?' said Betsy Prins, arranging a bunch of roses that she herself had placed on the coffin earlier.

His brother's face was a waxy yellow, like that of every other corpse, but his features lacked the customary restfulness, in truth. Felix had never really known what had gone on in his brother's head, behind his now perpetually closed eyes. People know so little about one another in the end.

He thought back to the last time he had seen his brother. He remembered how surprised he had been that he'd aged so little. The alcohol, which was his downfall, had done a good job in preserving his tissue. The hotel had been sold ten years earlier, when the market was at its lowest, when the bank had demanded repayment of its loans.

Complete panic now took hold of Felix, not because of his brother's death or his own diminishing life, the first assault on which had already been successful, but because he felt nothing at all, as if his whole body had turned to rubber in sympathy with his left arm.

'The cremation will be half an hour earlier than it says on the card,' said Betsy Prins, passing him a funeral invitation in the empty hall. 'Poteman's son has never printed anything without some kind of mistake on it. Just like his father! Perhaps you will join us later... join me rather, at home? Ludo and I lived together for the last couple of years. There's heaps of personal stuff: papers, letters and the like... Hofmanshofje, number 28. Around five?'

Once outside, Felix Bagman stood still for half a minute, looking as lost as a bewildered day-tripper. He then shuffled off towards The Boulevard, careful to avoid the road that would have led him past the former Hotel New Deluxe.

After the hotel had been demolished, an idiosyncratic construction took its place, a concrete colossus in the shape of a circus tent. The hysterical clatter of slot machines and other electronic amusements could be heard through the sliding doors. Near where their living room used to be, there was now a cinema, the floor of which was inevitably littered with chewing-gum wrappers and popcorn after every film.

The last time he had visited the amusement arcade, Felix had noticed a plastic negro with crimson lips holding a sign by the door that read 'Welcome!'

According to the bald man with earrings who sold tokens from a cash register, the plastic negro was modelled on a legendary black man who had once worked at Hotel New Deluxe, although he had never met him personally. Legendary?

'They say he fucked half the town back then,' the cashier elaborated with a salacious grin. Apparently, the African's real name was Fréderique Immanuel Didier. He had gone on to study economics and law in Amsterdam and was now a high-ranking official at the United Nations in New York.

The pages of his pocket edition of Turgenev rustled inside his linen jacket as if the book were a living creature that had just woken up. A refreshing breeze caressed his clammy skin, lessening the Madrid heat and twisting the street dust into little whirlwinds here and there.

'*Tenemos refrescos, dos euro!*'

Calle Ave Maria, full of car horns blaring, had nothing in common with Kerkstraat, but all Felix had to do was shut his eyes for a moment and he was immediately catapulted back home to the place of his birth, which he'd only just left a week before.

'*Tenemos refrescos, dos euro!*' a woman with a round, Arabic face bawled once again from behind a stall full of magazines, sweets and tourist tat.

Betsy Prins served Felix coffee and chocolate éclairs, as if it were an old-fashioned birthday party rather than a meeting to settle his brother's affairs.

'Ludo told me to dump the lot,' said Betsy, depositing a box of papers on the floor. 'But I know how important stuff like this can be. My brother sold my father's archives. I could wring his neck.'

Felix asked out of politeness how her brother Arno had fared since emigrating to Australia.

'He's in an old people's home in Sydney,' she replied. He hadn't a brass farthing to his name out there among the kangaroos. She sent him a hundred euros now and then. Anyway, was there anything that Felix thought he might like to keep?

Felix rummaged through the papers as if he were organising his way back in time. He found piles of old bills (reminders, final demands, reminders of final demands, bank statements documenting Ludo's spiralling debts), but also three love letters to Liza, which he had kept for some unknown reason. He also found a sepia photo of his father and mother on their wedding day that he'd not seen before, a postcard from Edo Novak ('Long live the Cuban revolution, long live Fidel!') and a small bundle of letters that had been typed on his father's old Remington portable. They turned out to be copies of the missives his father had sent to Gabriel Lemberg in which he graciously explained that the question of the missing antiques was not what he thought. There were three of them, the second and third both beginning identically: '*Dear Gabriel, I have not yet heard from you in response to my previous letter. I have no doubt the postal services are to blame – California is not exactly next door, but...*'

Felix tore up the three letters as if they had been junk mail.

'And I have no idea what this is!' said Betsy, holding up a golden brooch studded with tiny diamonds. 'I'm not a great wearer of jewellery, myself. Was it your mother's, perhaps? Then you should take it...'

'Bloody hell!' Felix was catapulted forty years back in time to when Kati Bender was rambling around the hotel in a frantic state, repeatedly asking all and sundry, 'My brooch, you haven't seen my brooch, have you?'

Two days after the cremation service in Driehuis-Westerveld, Felix switched on the TV in his room in Hotel Sissi. It was the middle of a chat show with Edo Novak, seventy-five at least, as tanned as ever, barely changed at all.

'If it's Islam we're talking about,' Ludo's erstwhile friend held forth, 'if it's Islam we're talking about, then it's about time we in the Netherlands settled our differences once and...'

Felix switched off after ten minutes, bored.

'*Buenos tardes, señor!*' A mousy face greeted Felix at the entrance to the building on Calle Ave Maria, which he had reached on foot after all. He could always find his way home, and there was still plenty of time before his first beer.

The lift with its wrought-iron cage appeared to be out of service. Felix calmly ascended the three flights of stairs, as he had done many times before, but he was sweating profusely this time, and sensed his heart was working overtime. He pushed the bell on the red-panelled door and was treated to the chirps of electronic canaries. A middle-aged woman in purple slippers opened the door and greeted him with informal kindness as Señor Felix. She led him to a small room with a bright yellow sofa, the air-conditioning humming pleasantly.

'Do sit down, Señor Felix. Would you like something to drink?'

'Is Felicia here?' replied Felix in more or less impeccable Spanish.

'She's in the kitchen,' said the woman. 'But all the rooms are occupied for the moment. You ought to telephone in advance. You can use this room if you like. It wouldn't be the first—'

355

'*Muchas gracias, Isabella!*' Felix deposited the usual fee on the coffee table – euros still confused him.

Two minutes later, a fragile girl in a white cotton skirt and a top the same bright yellow as the sofa pranced into the room. Her belly button was pierced, and her toenails, which were red, stuck boldly out of her plastic shoes.

'It's breezy outside, isn't it?' she gabbled as her skirt fell to the floor, and she climbed on to the well-preserved and perhaps Scandinavian gentleman's lap in her G-string. 'There must be a storm on the way from the Sahara.'

She looked like Violet. They always had to look like Violet, even if he had to search for days on end, even along the darkest alleyways of Africa.

Felix wrapped his arm around her, saw her dazzling white incisors appear for an instant above her raspberry-red lower lip and imagined the pulse of her young body mingling with the blood streaming through his decayed arteries. He placed his left hand on her left thigh and moved it slowly up over her silky skin. He began to feel a quiver of delight, but then his body suddenly short-circuited and he started to convulse.

'Please don't cry, señor. Shall I do one of my tricks for you? Come on then, close your eyes.' She covered his eyes with her hand, like a child playing peekaboo with her granddad. 'Come on now, eyes closed... No cheating! That's right... OK, you can move now. Why aren't you moving? Don't tell me you're—'

And what did fate have in store for the Benders?

After returning to Cologne, the sausage-maker did everything he could to heal the rift, but his daughter and wife were adamant: they wanted nothing more to do with Ludo Bagman and his family.

Liza took the express train to Cannes that summer and strolled all by herself under the swaying palm trees, wearing a new outfit every day. She went swimming in the sea and played tennis all afternoon with another German girl.

One evening, as she watched the sun disappear like a ball of fire into the violet sea from her hotel room balcony, she was suddenly overcome by an overwhelming desire for Ludo. She almost collapsed from the distress it induced. Had it all been as awful as her mother had said, and she herself had thought? Now she was free, and had her very own cheque-book, but where did it leave her? She thought back to Heinrich, the handsome PE teacher who had introduced her to the art of lovemaking, and wondered what had become of him. The world was crawling with eligible men, and, as the daughter of a millionaire, she was sought after, a catch. She had all the time in the world.

She returned alone to the French Riviera the following year, but the year after she accompanied her mother and Gabi for a holiday in Rimini, Monaco and Nice, all the places that Kati Bender had once claimed to detest. No more was ever heard of her dream home in the Bavarian Alps.

Hans Matti never escorted the ladies, claiming on every occasion to have urgent business to attend to in Hamburg. He had made his mistress pregnant, and she gave birth to a baby girl. The financial side of the matter was all settled with easy elegance. He was a father for the first time in his life, and unexpectedly so, although he held his little daughter on his lap in the manner of a grandfather. His existence was graced with an unexpected completeness.

In the years following the wedding, the sausage-maker returned to Holland twice. He visited the island of Texel, and he scoured the cemeteries around Amersfoort (where hundreds of Russians lay, wretched and nameless, underground, as did hundreds of nightmares), but there was no trace of his missing brother. He had had Arno Prins's texts translated without delay, but they contained nothing of use in his search. One day, he removed the photo of himself and Otto from his wallet, placed it underneath a hefty cash ledger at the bottom of a drawer, and never looked at it again.

Liza also experienced life as a downhill slope for a time. She was thirty all of a sudden and exhibiting the chubby contours of her

357

mother. The word spread at the sausage factory that she had been so drunk at Mardi Gras that she had allowed absolutely anyone to screw her, even in the toilets. Her mother, eyebrows raised, would examine the occasional man that Liza dared to bring home – the last one when she had just turned thirty-six – and invariably reject them. When Liza complained that, at this rate, she would never find a husband, and that she would soon be too old to have children, Kati simply snorted, 'Rubbish! Stop talking such rubbish!'

Kati and Hans Matti were spared any illnesses and enjoyed a long life. Around her seventieth birthday, Kati began to experience a particularly strange physiological sensation: she developed a sudden and irresistible craving for meat.

Standing in the kitchen of their expansive villa one morning, watching her husband devour three fried sausages for breakfast, she suddenly demanded that he let her try one.

'What?' asked Hans Matti, incredulous.

'Give me one of those sausages, goddammit! Are you deaf?'

From that moment on, the Bender household was always well stocked with meat. The sausage-maker's wife started her day with white bread and black pudding, lightly fried in good butter. In the evening her silver cutlery cut into quarter-pound steaks, preferably as rare as possible. She became addicted to well-seasoned pork chops, sautéed liver with bacon and ravioli stuffed with minced beef.

After the fall of the Berlin Wall, Hans Matti took a bus trip to East Prussia with a group of his elderly compatriots. Kati asked him to bring back a side of pork from the region, having heard that pigs raised on Prussian soil were the best of all. Hans Matti nodded in agreement.

Gabi died the day after Kati's eightieth birthday and was replaced by her niece – also called Gabi – who took care of the Benders as they lived to a ripe old age. Liza was also quite old by this time. Hans Matti was well into his nineties, but his hearing, pulse, blood pressure and bowels were all in excellent shape. Kati's desire for meat remained insatiable, although she had become as deaf as a post. On the rare occasion all three were seen together in public, Kati was invariably taken to be Liza's sister, which always brought a cracked pink smile to her painted lips.

Liza collected the post from the mailbox at the front of the garden everyday, determined to stay active. One cloudy summer morning that was so cold that Kati had asked Gabi to kindle a fire, she was astonished to find a letter from Holland. She read the envelope with her nose almost pressed against it. The letter was addressed to her mother and not to her.

'*Mutti*, there's a letter here from Holland.'

'What?'

'A letter!' Liza repeated.

'Who's it from?'

Liza pressed her nose against the plump envelope and barely had the time to say 'Felix Bagman, Poste Restante, Hotel Sissi' before her mother snatched it from her hand.

'Rubbish!' barked Kati. 'What a load of rubbish!' She tossed the letter into the open hearth, where the fire flared up for a second and then settled down.

Gabi would dump the ashes from the fire on a building site behind the villa, where work had started on the foundations for an apartment block some time before. A sign reading 'Résidence Blondi' had already been positioned at the outer edge of the property with the estate agent's name and telephone number in giant letters underneath. The housekeeper had quickly sifted the ashes that summer afternoon and dusted the fireplace with a brush, but she hadn't heard the sound of a golden brooch studded with tiny diamonds grating gently against the side of the copper tray.

The apartment block would be completed in eighteen months, but it was bound to disappear one day just as everything else did. And someone would find the brooch, even if it took a thousand years. The finder would wipe the dirt off with his fingers, and look up in delight,

359

entirely unaware of the secret nocturnal gratification of a German sausage-maker's wife in a Dutch linen cupboard, which had ultimately brought about the return of the jewel to German soil. The linen cupboard, the Benders, the Bagmans and the laughter and the tears of their already long-forgotten lives would mean nothing to him.

This is why God allowed for the possibility of His existence in creation; it comforts people, and protects them from madness.

Author's Declaration

The characters, locations, and situations in the novel *The German Wedding* are entirely fictional. The words of the characters are their own. The book is a work of fiction. Any resemblance to reality is purely coincidental.

Pieter Waterdrinker
Moscow, Summer 2005